SCHOOLS AND CULTURAL CITIZENSHIP

'Why study the arts at school?' This book offers a fresh perspective on this question. Informed by rigorous research, the book argues that the arts help young people to develop key skills, knowledge and practices that support them to become both critical appreciative audiences and socially engaged cultural producers. Drawing on a three-year study in partnership with the Royal Shakespeare Company and Tate art museum, *Schools and Cultural Citizenship* sets out an ecological model for cultural citizenship that goes beyond the classroom to include families, the media and popular culture.

The authors introduce new, interrelated concepts to challenge how we consider arts education. Chapters provide fresh insights, guidance and practical recommendations for educators, including:

- Key insights from the Tracking Arts Learning and Engagement research
- Detailed case studies featuring arts-rich schools and arts-broker teachers
- Analysis of the importance of immersive professional development for teachers and the benefits of partnerships with arts organisations
- An ecological model for cultural citizenship

Focusing on the ways in which cultural citizenship can be taught and learnt, this is an essential read for arts educators, education staff in arts organisations, researchers, postgraduate students, arts education activists and policy makers.

Pat Thomson is Professor of Education at the University of Nottingham, UK and Convenor of the Centre for Research in Arts, Creativity and Literacy (CRACL). She was previously a school principal in disadvantaged schools in Australia.

Christine Hall is Emeritus Professor and former Head of the School of Education at the University of Nottingham, UK.

Their collaborative work on the signature pedagogies of artists working in schools is widely cited and informs the work of Creativity Culture and Education in Europe, Australia, Wales, Scotland and Northern Ireland.

SCHOOLS AND CULTURAL CITIZENSHIP

Arts Education for Life

Pat Thomson and Christine Hall

Routledge
Taylor & Francis Group

LONDON AND NEW YORK

Designed cover image: Photo by Sara Beaumont ©RSC

First published 2023
by Routledge
4 Park Square, Milton Park, Abingdon, Oxon OX14 4RN

and by Routledge
605 Third Avenue, New York, NY 10158

Routledge is an imprint of the Taylor & Francis Group, an informa business

British Library Cataloguing-in-Publication Data
A catalogue record for this book is available from the British Library

ISBN: 978-0-367-55338-8 (hbk)
ISBN: 978-0-367-55339-5 (pbk)
ISBN: 978-1-003-09308-4 (ebk)

DOI: 10.4324/9781003093084

Typeset in Bembo
by Taylor & Francis Books

CONTENTS

ILLUSTRATIONS

Figures

Images

Table

ACKNOWLEDGEMENTS

The research in this book was funded by Arts Council England's major research fund. Our partners in this research were the Royal Shakespeare Company and Tate. We are grateful to Jacqui O'Hanlon and Dr Emily Pringle for their continued support, engagement and conversations throughout the project and beyond. We couldn't have asked for more committed and knowledgeable research companions.

We are hugely grateful to the 30 secondary schools, 60 teachers and 6000 students who willingly engaged with the research. We hope that you recognise yourselves in these pages and that you feel we have kept our promise to tell your stories. We hope, as you did when you agreed to participate in the research, that this book contributes to efforts to make the arts strong in every school.

Special thanks to Lexi Earl and Corinna Geppert whose work as researchers on the Tracking Arts Learning and Engagement (TALE) research project informed this book. We wish we could have employed you for longer. It has taken us quite some time to do the further analysis that appears in this book.

Some of the book's content has already appeared in various forms. We have used writing as a means of developing our ideas, but we have worked further on them here.

- Our website researchtale.net contains project records and a blog which reported visits to the schools.
- An early paper, Thomson, Pat, Hall, Christine, Earl, Lexi and Geppert, Corinna (2019) Subject Choice as Everyday Accommodation/Resistance: Why Students in England (Still) Choose the Arts *Critical Studies in Education*, 61(5), 545–560, analyses why students chose arts subjects over others, and it provides important background to the TALE research project.

- We developed our ideas about cultural citizenship by writing two book chapters: Thomson, Pat, Hall, Christine, Earl, Lexi and Geppert, Corinna (2019) Towards an Arts Education for Cultural Citizenship. In Riddle, Stewart and Apple, Michael, eds, *Reimagining Education for Democracy*, Routledge; and Thomson, Pat and Hall, Christine (2020) Beyond Civics: Art and Design Education and the Making of Active/Activist Citizens. In Burgess, Lesley and Addison, Nick, eds, *Debates in Art & Design Education*, Routledge. Chapter 9 draws on both chapters.
- We wrote about partnerships in Hall, Christine and Thomson, Pat (2021) Making the Most of Arts Education Partnerships in Schools, *Curriculum Perspectives*, 41(1), 101–106 and drew on this analysis in Chapter 3.
- We first wrote about atmosphere and signature pedagogies in art rooms in Thomson, Pat and Hall. Christine (2021) "You just feel more relaxed": An Investigation of Art Room Atmosphere, *International Journal of Art and Design Education*, 40(3), 599–614. We have substantially added to this initial analysis by including drama rooms – see Chapter 5.
- Our paper on cultural capital, Thomson, Pat and Hall, Christine (2022) Cultural Capitals Matter, Differentially: A Bourdieusian Reading of Perspectives from Senior Secondary Students in England, *British Journal of Sociology of Education*, doi: 10.1080/01425692.2022.2083582, forms the basis for Chapter 8.

1

INTRODUCING THE TRACKING ARTS LEARNING AND ENGAGEMENT RESEARCH

IMAGE 1.1 Walking in

DOI: 10.4324/9781003093084-1

The path from the station to the school was busy. I was surrounded by groups of teenagers wearing the school's distinctive turquoise and black uniform. I was somewhat distracted by the person in front of me; she was carrying a bag laden with what looked like art materials. I wondered whether she was a visiting artist. Teachers probably wouldn't need to bring so much with them, I reasoned, their materials would already be at school. I didn't know whether there would be an artist in the school on the day I visited, but I knew it was possible as the school employed a lot of visiting artists. Indeed, the consistent engagement with artists and arts organisations was one of the reasons we had chosen the school for the TALE research.

As I entered the school grounds I lost sight of the bag.

IMAGE 1.2 Starting the day

I thought again about what we already knew about the school. It had been part of a national creativity programme which we were involved with and was one of the 54 national exemplar schools. It had been part of our research on artist signature pedagogies, and even though neither of us had personally done the field work in the school we had read and watched the data. And I had met the arts lead in the school at Tate teacher professional development programmes and had enjoyed chatting with him about the school, his take on arts education and his own photographic practice. I'd followed him on Instagram where he posted his own photographic work, on Flickr where he created school albums and I'd looked at his website, where he had developed resources for teaching threshold concepts in photography. We had also followed the development of the school's creativity wheel and habits of mind, both of which bore evidence of his influence.

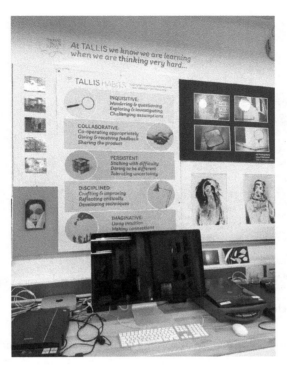

IMAGE 1.3 Habits of mind display

We already had a strong sense of what the school might be and do. So it was really no surprise when I was told a few minutes later that I had indeed been walking behind a visiting artist, who de- and re-constructed images to make, and question the idea of, landscapes. My first couple of hours in the school were to be spent observing her working with the arts lead and his Year 9 Photography class.

This field-work anecdote introduces many of the elements that we are going to talk about in this book. The school with a history of engaging with the arts, artists and arts organisations. The school that has developed its own understandings and applications of creativity and pedagogical theory. Key teachers who have developed their own take on arts pedagogy and share it widely. The anecdote doesn't yet introduce the students, but they will feature prominently in the story to come.

This is a research-based story. We begin with the word story because we want to move away from any idea that this is just a report. This book is the result of three years' research into arts education in secondary schools in England, a project that was, to our knowledge, the biggest of its kind in the UK. We thoroughly enjoyed this work and were always encouraged, excited and inspired by the schools we visited. We hope to try to communicate a little of our emotional response to you. So we have chosen a form that uses anecdotes, portraits and images as well as numbers and quotations.

IMAGE 1.4 Watching and listening to the artist

In this introductory chapter, we explain a bit about our research, and why and how we did it. We also outline some of the key ideas you will find in the book. But we begin our story with a little of the history which led to the TALE – Tracking Arts Learning and Engagement – research.

The TALE research

Tracking Arts Learning and Engagement was a three-year project, funded by Arts Council England. It involved 30 secondary schools, 15 nominated by the Royal Shakespeare Company (RSC) and 15 by Tate. The two organisations had different approaches to professional learning, with the RSC working with whole schools, lead teachers and students, and Tate working with teachers and, often, their students. The 30 schools were spread around England and, although we had no intention to claim them as a representative group, they did end up being roughly equivalent to the national spread. TALE schools served rich and poor neighbourhoods, diverse and homogeneous communities, and were located in cities, towns and rural areas, as well the capital, London. They included academies, faith schools, local-authority-run comprehensives, single-sex and special schools. Although they had been chosen for their performing or visual arts engagement, they generally taught both, as well as Music, and often Dance.

The TALE research asked how secondary teachers made their professional development learning into classroom pedagogies, and what opportunities and benefits were then afforded to students. This book draws on the TALE research archive, which consists of transcribed interviews with two teachers in each school for each of the three years of the project (n = 164 interviews) and focus group conversations (n = 323) with Year 10–13 students who had chosen arts subjects (n = 1447), classroom observations, documents and photographic records. We also interviewed senior leaders (n = 30). In the second and third years of the project, we conducted a survey of all Year 10–13 students, regardless of what course they were doing (n = 4477). The survey looked at cultural participation and engagement and had questions in common with the national Department of Culture, Media and Sport survey Taking Part; this allowed us to compare students in TALE schools with their peers across the country. In total, we have some 6000 responses from young people about their experiences of arts education.

You can find details of the TALE data on our website https://researchtale.net where there are full research reports, survey results and blog posts about many of the schools. But you will read about these findings in this book.

The TALE project built on our previous research. We began researching arts in schools in 2003. Our first research project was an ethnographic study of one school, Hollytree Primary. An artist in residence worked with children across the school throughout the year, and her programme culminated in a public exhibition of Year 5 self-portraits. The school had a long history of arts education and it was not surprising that it became an early member of the Creative Partnerships programme. We were particularly struck by the ways in which the arts allowed children to bring their extended family knowledges into the school and offered avenues for all children to explore ideas and express themselves. The arts were integral to the inclusive approach taken by the head, and demonstrated how the ideal of a broad and balanced curriculum could be realised (Hall & Thomson, 2007; Hall, Thomson, & Russell, 2007; Thomson & Hall, 2008, 2011; Thomson, Hall, & Russell, 2006, 2007).

We became interested in Creative Partnerships (CP), a government initiative which placed artists in schools in order to support developments in teaching practice and provide directions for school change. CP is still the largest arts and creativity school reform programme anywhere in the world. CP was underpinned by research and commissioned new research about its programmes. After Pat had completed a CP-commissioned literature review on whole school change (Thomson, 2011), CP funded us to undertake a three-year project investigating how 30 primary and secondary schools across England went about changing pedagogies and whole schools. Not surprisingly, we found enormous diversity among the approaches taken, and different results. We called this 'vernacular school change' to acknowledge that there were both patterns and unique aspects to the approaches schools took to reform (Thomson, Jones, & Hall, 2009).

We developed a strong relationship with CP and undertook two other projects with them. The first examined the RSC's work with schools. Our case studies affirmed the often transformative impact that their rehearsal-room pedagogies had on teachers and students (Franks, Thomson, Hall, & Jones, 2014). The second examined in detail the work that artists did with teachers and students. This research led to the development of our notion of artists' 'signature pedagogies'

(Thomson, Hall, Jones, & Sefton Green, 2012) and a strong view that teachers and artists are not interchangeable, but can form powerful overlapping and complementary partnerships (Hall et al., 2007; Thomson & Clifton, 2012; Thomson & Hall, 2015). We saw a wide range of benefits accruing for students from their involvement with creative practitioners and projects (Thomson, Coles, Hallewell, & Keane, 2014; Thomson & Rose, 2011).

Of course, we did not always research together. Chris developed her relationship with the RSC. Pat established a strong connection with the Tate Schools and Teachers team and became resident ethnographer in the annual summer school teacher professional development programme (Thomson, 2017; Thomson & Pringle, 2020). We continued to see how well-designed professional development which recognised teachers' professional knowledges and know-how could excite and extend their expertise and inspire school change (Hall & Thomson, 2017a, 2017b).

It was hardly surprising, then, when Arts Council England announced a new funding programme to encourage partnerships between universities and arts organisations, that we were interested. Nor was it surprising that we turned to our existing relationships with the RSC and Tate, wondering if this was a way that we could pursue a question that we had been discussing for some time. How could we find out more about what teachers *did* with their professional learning from RSC and Tate? What uses did teachers make of it in school? Did the students benefit, did the school more widely benefit? If so, how?

The TALE project allowed us to explore further how teachers and students made sense of their arts experiences, separately and together. The schools we studied provided arts education for young people across the ability range, with three of the 30 schools in the sample designated as special schools. Across the board, we took both teachers and students as expert witnesses, seeing them as possessing valuable knowledge and being capable of articulating their experiences. We wanted to make sure we didn't simply reclassify teachers' and students' words into singular and pre-determined categories (Smith, 1990); we wanted to acknowledge and value their meaning-making. It is for this reason that we make extensive use of quotations in this book.

We developed key linked concepts through the research process and these concepts form the backbone of this book. Some of these are our own and emerged from analysing the data. Others have been taken from the scholarly literatures but have been used in particular ways to address particular aspects of the analysis. In the book you will find the following key concepts:

1. The arts-rich school. A school which has a strong arts identity and curriculum offer. We build on the work of James Catterall (2009) to elaborate the patterns that existed in the 30 TALE schools (Chapters 2 and 10).
2. The arts-broker teacher. An arts-broker teacher does not simply teach an arts subject but also supports students to engage with arts outside of school, as they do themselves (Chapter 3).

3. Immersive professional development. Arts-broker teachers were inspired by, developed and sustained disciplinary and professional knowledge through immersive engagement with partner arts organisations and networks of peers (Chapter 4).
4. Mood, atmosphere and cultural feelings. We draw on work about affect and mood to analyse impact on students of the distinctive 'feel' of arts classrooms which can be understood by examining their material form and their rhythms (Chapter 5), as well as their
5. Signature pedagogies. Every discipline has a key pedagogical practice through which knowledge, skills, and ways of being, doing, understanding and believing are inculcated (Chapter 5).
6. Artful mediation. Arts-brokers teachers found that they had to simultaneously meet the needs of students and the school to produce good results and their overall aim of supporting students to be and become artists (Chapter 6).
7. Cultural capital. Cultural capital can be understood as the learning accrued through the arts, both the formal and extra curriculum (Chapter 7 and the next section).
8. Cultural citizenship. Cultural citizenship is the aim and the end result of an arts education that is more than a subject. Cultural citizens are informed, critically appreciative audiences and actively engaged cultural producers (Chapters 8 and 9).
9. School ecology. We suggest that the development of students who are cultural citizens is optimal when all of (1) to (8) work together (Chapter 10).

The book is also strongly informed by the work of French sociologist Pierre Bourdieu (1930–2002). So, before we start our story proper, we want to signpost how we use his work.

Bourdieu, education and cultural capitals

Bourdieu understood the world as made up of social fields. He used 'field' as a metaphor which helped explain the ways in which societies worked unequally to benefit some people, places and practices over others. According to Bourdieu, the education field has comparatively modest status within the hierarchy of social fields, where constellations of economic and national and global politics and government fields dominate. However, education's modest positioning is offset by the critical role it plays in the (re)production of capitals and dispositions vital to and in other fields (Bourdieu, 1988; Bourdieu & Passeron, 1977). 'Capitals' is Bourdieu's term for the knowledge and skills that people acquire from home, school and life in general; they can be both social – that is, who you know and what networks you are part of – and 'cultural' – that is the knowledge and skills that are associated with language, religion, the arts and are expressed in 'taste', your preference for particular activities, foods, clothes, music, media and so on (Bourdieu, 1984).

Bourdieu's use of cultural capital is different from that used by other sociologists. Cultural capital can sometimes be used as an important means of producing social capital – the bridging (vertical) and bonding (horizontal) relationships that act as 'social glue'. According to Robert Putnam (1993, 1995, 2000), healthy, democratic and 'good' societies, societies where there is comparatively low inequality, strong communities and overall wellbeing and happiness, have both rich bridging and bonding social capitals. Another approach to cultural capital sits with a form of modern governing which wants to 'see' and include all aspects of society through comprehensive calculations (e.g. see HM Treasury, 2022). Many governments around the world have taken up the theory of human capital – how much value can be attributed to particular kinds of work and how much investing in human capital might enhance productivity (see, e.g., https://www.worldbank.org/en/p ublication/human-capital). Governments now have an interest in 'natural' capital and the measurement of the costs and benefits of investing in the environment (see, e.g., https://naturalcapitalforum.com/about/). There is now policy discussion about whether cultural capital might similarly be measured and how its relative value for money and overall contribution to society might be calculated (see, e.g., https://www.oecd.org/statistics/measuring-economic-social-progress/Saraceno.pdf). This move to attribute financial value to previously intangible social and cultural processes is very different from the Bourdieusian view of cultural capital.

The social and cultural capitals prioritised in the education field, Bourdieu argued, build on the capitals of already culturally and economically privileged families. The correspondence between the capitals of those dominant in society and those recognised, valued and developed further via schooling mean that the educational 'game' is skewed at the outset (Bourdieu, 1991). However, the doxa – the taken-for-granted truth in the field – is meritocracy, the idea that agents advance through the field by virtue of their own innate ability and hard work (Bourdieu, Passeron, & de Saint Martin, 1995). This doxa disguises the 'inheritance effect' of field logics (Bourdieu & Passeron, 1979). The apparently neutral processes of education are in reality practices of sorting and selection which result in different young people being differentially equipped with the symbolic capital (credentials) that they can 'cash in' to obtain further and higher education and work. The end result is the (re)production of an inequitable social and economic hierarchy which seems natural and right to those who reap the benefits (Bourdieu, 1977).

However, Bourdieu wrote, the field of schooling is not simply reproductive. The field is also agonistic (Bourdieu & Wacquant, 1992). Positions and the agents that occupy them are continually moving, engaged in ongoing struggles to advance in the field, but some are simultaneously dedicated to changing the hierarchies within the field (Bourdieu, 1993, 1998). Within the education field, there are a variety of agents and positions which coalesce around questions of equity, social justice and democracy; agents in these positions challenge the doxa, which capitals count and the pedagogical practices of schools and gatekeeping assessment and examination processes.

These ideas about cultural capital and the reproductive practices of schooling underpin our understanding of the broad context in which the TALE research took place. When the Conservative coalition government came to power in the UK in 2010, they moved swiftly to reorganise the field (Ball, 2018). The government redesigned the examination system, the national curriculum and the inspection framework, prioritising a 'traditional', or cultural restorationist (Apple, 2001), approach. As we are writing this book in 2022, the Conservative government operates a system that holds schools accountable for their performance in 'core' curriculum subjects through a school performance measure called the English Baccalaureate (the EBacc) (Maguire, Gewirtz, Towers, & Neumann, 2019). The arts are not part of this accountability measure (Neumann, Gewirtz, Maguire, & Towers, 2020). The policy shift effected by responses to the introduction of the EBacc measure, from schools but also from students themselves and their families, has accelerated already falling enrolments in arts subjects, with Design and Technology being the biggest loser. Looking through a Bourdieusian lens, these policy changes can be understood as strategies designed to regain and consolidate pre-existing advantage (Grenfell & James, 1998). As we have argued elsewhere (Thomson, 2010), when there is an increase in levels of mass education across the field, those in dominant positions move to adjust the rules of the game in order to maintain their (unfair) advantage.

However in 2019, Ofsted, the school inspection agency, adopted and began to champion the term 'cultural capital'. In an update to school inspection guidance, Ofsted announced that 'quality' in educational provision meant that

> inspectors will consider the extent to which schools are equipping pupils with the knowledge and cultural capital they need to succeed in life. Ofsted's understanding of this knowledge and cultural capital matches the understanding set out in the aims of the national curriculum. It is the essential knowledge that pupils need to be educated citizens, introducing them to the best that has been thought and said, and helping to engender an appreciation of human creativity and achievement.
>
> *(Ofsted, 2019, p. 10)*

Elsewhere in the same document, cultural capital is connected with "social justice", "inequality" and "unfairness" (p. 7): "So many disadvantaged pupils may not have access to cultural capital, both in the home and then in their school" (p. 8). According to Ofsted, schools must ensure that all children and young people have access to an entitlement which includes "great works of art, music and literature" (p. 8). Bourdieu (1984) argued that everyone possesses cultural capital (language and accent, taste in fashion, art, music, sport, food, etc.) and these cultural capitals are both embodied and institutionalised (Reay, 2019). There is, however, a social hierarchy in which some capitals are seen as more prestigious and worthy than others, as epitomised in Ofsted's guidance to schools.

This book directly addresses Ofsted's advocacy of elite cultural capital. As we have already explained, half of the TALE schools worked with the RSC, whose main mission is to promote Shakespeare's work, the quintessential case of an elite, canonical cultural oeuvre. The other TALE schools worked with Tate, an art museum dedicated to collecting, conserving and showing British art and international contemporary art, building an archive which includes the 'best' of popular and avant-garde art forms. We don't disagree with Ofsted that all children and young people should have access to elite cultural capitals. As we will show, the schools we studied met this criterion. The RSC and Tate Education teams are committed to the view that Shakespeare and the national museums' art collections belong to everyone, and they are passionate about opening up access and promoting engagement. But the arts pedagogies they promoted, pedagogies which the schools we studied embraced and developed, also saw vernacular, community and popular arts as integral to the curriculum. They took the view, as we do, that all art forms should be equally subject to critical socially situated analysis and appreciative evaluation (c.f. Stevenson, 2010).

We explore the concept of cultural capital, and the critique of Ofsted's position, in Chapter 7 of this book. It takes us a while to get to that discussion because we have done our best to set out the terms of our argument systematically, clarifying the key concepts we have been working with and demonstrating how they have been derived from analysis of the data we generated over the three years of working on the TALE project. We learned a lot from listening to what the teachers, school leaders and students had to say about arts education and we have tried to represent those voices and views in this book. So we set out to build our argument throughout the book, being mindful of the specificity of the schools we researched and attending to the voices of the students and staff who worked in them, while also being alert to the patterns and similarities and overlaps across the sample. This has led us to take the approach we outlined above, focusing each of the first seven chapters on one or more key concept derived directly from the analysis of our data – ideas that seemed to us to have explanatory power and generalisability beyond the immediate context of the schools we were looking at.

Across the book as a whole, though, we set out to build an argument that went a step further: to make the case that the cultural capitals gained from studying the arts provide the basis for what we, and some others, call 'cultural citizenship'. That is, the book proposes that an arts education is not just learning one or more arts subjects, but is about and offers learning for living and life. In Bourdieusian terms, we suggest that the arts provide the capitals, practices and dispositions that are not only useful in other fields besides education, but are also the basis for engaging with and even contesting the status quo, if those who possess them choose to do so.

We set out this argument in Chapter 9, before concluding with what we hope might be a useful heuristic for schools and teachers who want to further develop their own arts offer. In line with the adage that there's nothing so practical as a good theory, we see the ideas in this book, ultimately, as foundations and principles for practice.

References

Apple, M. (2001). *Educating the "right" way: Markets, standards, God and inequality.* New York: RoutledgeFalmer.

Ball, S. (2018). *The education debate* (3rd edn). Bristol: The Policy Press.

Bourdieu, P. (1977). *Outline of a theory of practice*. Cambridge: Cambridge University Press.

Bourdieu, P. (1984). *Distinction: A social critique of the judgment of taste* (R. Nice, trans.). Boston: Harvard University Press.

Bourdieu, P. (1988). *Homo academicus* (P. Collier, trans.). Stanford, CA: Stanford University Press.

Bourdieu, P. (1991). *Language and symbolic power*. Oxford: Polity Press.

Bourdieu, P. (1993). *The field of cultural production: Essays on art and literature*. Oxford: Polity.

Bourdieu, P. (1998). *Practical reason: On the theory of action*. Oxford: Blackwell.

Bourdieu, P., & Passeron, J. C. (1977). *Reproduction in society, education and culture*. London: Sage.

Bourdieu, P., & Passeron, J. C. (1979). *The inheritors, French students and their relation to culture*. Chicago: University of Chicago Press.

Bourdieu, P., Passeron, J.-C., & de SaintMartin, M. (1995). *Academic discourse* (R. Teese, Trans. 1965 ed.). Stanford, CA: Stanford University Press.

Bourdieu, P., & Wacquant, L. (1992). *An invitation to reflexive sociology*. Chicago:University of Chicago Press.

Catterall, J. S. (2009). *Doing well and doing good by doing art*. Los Angeles: I-Group Books.

Franks, A., Thomson, P., Hall, C., & Jones, K. (2014). Teachers, arts practice and pedagogy. *Changing English*, 21(2), 171–181.

Grenfell, M., & James, D. (1998). *Acts of practical theory: Bourdieu and education*. London: Falmer Press.

HM Treasury. (2022). *The green book: Central government guidance on appraisal and evaluation*. https://assets.publishing.service.gov.uk/government/uploads/system/uploads/attachment_data/file/1063330/Green_Book_2022.pdf.

Hall, C., & Thomson, P. (2007). Creative partnerships? Cultural policy and inclusive arts practices in one primary school. *British Educational Research Journal*, 33(3), 315–329.

Hall, C., & Thomson, P. (2017a). Creativity in teaching: What can teachers learn from artists? *Research Papers in Education*, 32(1), 106–120.

Hall, C., & Thomson, P. (2017b). *Inspiring school change: Transforming education through the creative arts*. London: Routledge.

Hall, C., Thomson, P., & Russell, L. (2007). Teaching like an artist: The pedagogic identities and practices of artists in schools. *British Journal of Sociology of Education*, 28(5), 605–619.

Maguire, M., Gewirtz, S., Towers, E., & Neumann, E. (2019). Policy, contextual matters and unintended outcomes: The English Baccalaureate (EBacc) and its impact on physical education in English secondary schools. *Sport, Education and Society*, 24(6), 558–569.

Neumann, E., Gewirtz, S., Maguire, M., & Towers, E. (2020). Neoconservative education policy and the case of the English Baccalaureate. *Journal of Curriculum Studies*, 52(5), 702–719.

Ofsted. (2019). School inspection update. https://assets.publishing.service.gov.uk/government/uploads/system/uploads/attachment_data/file/772056/School_inspection_update_-_January_2019_Special_Edition_180119.pdf.

Putnam, R. (1993). *Making democracy work: Civic traditions in modern Italy*. Princeton, NJ: Princeton University Press.

Putnam, R. (1995). Bowling alone: America's declining social capital. *Journal of Democracy*, 6(1), 65–78.

Putnam, R. (2000). *Bowling alone: The collapse and revival of American community*. New York: Simon & Schuster.

Reay, D. (2019). Education and cultural capital: The implications of changing trends in education policies. In D. Reay (ed.), *Bourdieu and education* (pp. 92–105). London: Routledge.

Smith, D. (1990). *The conceptual practices of power*. Boston: Northeastern University Press.

Stevenson, N. (2010). Cultural citizenship, education and democracy: Redefining the good society. *Citizenship Studies*, 14(3), 275–291.

Thomson, P. (2010). Bringing Bourdieu to 'widening participation' policies in higher education: a UK case analysis. In M. Apple, S. Ball, & L. A. Gandin (eds), *The Routledge handbook of the sociology of education* (pp. 318–328). London: Routledge.

Thomson, P. (2011). *Whole school change: A reading of the literatures* (2nd edn). London: Creative Partnerships, Arts Council England.

Thomson, P. (2017). Nine notes on a pedagogy of not knowing. In L. Turvey, A. Walton, & E. Daley (eds), *In site of conversation: On learning with art, audiences and artists* (pp. 25–34). London: Tate.

Thomson, P., & Clifton, J. (2012). Connecting with parents and the community in an urban primary school: Creative partnerships to build literacy/ies. In C. Hall, T. Cremin, B. Comber, & L. Moll (eds), *International handbook of research in children's literacy, learning and culture* (pp. 54–66). Oxford: Wiley Blackwell.

Thomson, P., Coles, R., Hallewell, M., & Keane, J. (2014). *A critical review of the Creative Partnerships archive: How was cultural value understood, researched and evidenced?* Swindon: Arts and Humanities Research Council.

Thomson, P., & Hall, C. (2008). Dialogues with artists: Analysing children's self-portraits. In P. Thomson (ed.), *Doing visual research with children and young people*. Abingdon: Routledge.

Thomson, P., & Hall, C. (2011). Sense-making as a lens on everyday change leadership practice: The case of Holly Tree Primary. *International Journal of Leadership in Education*, 14(4), 385–403.

Thomson, P., & Hall, C. (2015). 'Everyone can imagine their own Gellert': The democratic artist and 'inclusion' in primary and nursery classrooms. *Education, 3–13*, 1–13.

Thomson, P., Hall, C., Jones, K., & Sefton Green, J. (2012). *Signature pedagogies*. London: Creativity, Culture and Education.

Thomson, P., Hall, C., & Russell, L. (2006). An arts project failed, censored or...? A critical incident approach to artist–school partnerships. *Changing English*, 13(1), 29–44.

Thomson, P., Hall, C., & Russell, L. (2007). If these walls could speak: Reading displays of primary children's work. *Ethnography and Education*, 3(3), 381–400.

Thomson, P., Jones, K., & Hall, C. (2009). *Creative whole school change: Final report*. London: Creativity, Culture and Education; Arts Council England.

Thomson, P., & Pringle, E. (2020). Dancing past categories: Researching a live art project with participants. In C. S. Nielsen & S. Burridge (eds), *Dancing across borders: Perspectives on dance, young people and change*. London: Routledge.

Thomson, P., & Rose, L. (2011). Creative learning in an inner city primary school: England. In T. Wrigley, P. Thomson, & B. Lingard (eds), *Changing schools: Alternative ways to make a world of difference* (pp. 128–139). London: Routledge.

2

ARTS-RICH SCHOOLS

School One

9am: I walk the few minutes from my accommodation to the school. It is a gorgeous day. The sea is flat and the sky is blue. It is sunny and much warmer than I anticipated. The school is on a hill above (the town), in a very suburban area. It is near the beach. The school grounds are leafy and green. The exterior of the school reception area is shale-brick and looks pretty. The rest of the campus is 1960s prefab-looking. The reception area is welcoming. There are lots of posters, work and awards on display. There are Year 7 Cornish landscape paintings, Duke of Edinburgh awards, and 'Business & Enterprise' technicians' academy and surf academy posters. The school motto is: 'Be part of something inspirational'. There are different flags above the glass doors leading from reception to the rest of the school, and a glass case full of awards.

I meet (key teacher) and they give me a quick tour through the art block on our way to drama, through the sixth-form space too. (They later tell me this is because there are GCSE exams going on and so the main corridor between drama and reception is out of bounds, although I can exit at lunch and the end of the day this way.) They show me the music room and then we go through to the drama studio. They explain that Wednesdays is their long day – school begins at 8.45am with registration and doesn't end until 4.10pm. Lessons are 100 minutes (which is long!) so there are only four sessions today, two breaks and a lunch-break half-hour. (Lexi's field notes)

School Two

11am: I arrive at the school which is a large new-build (all grey and large windows), set in a suburban area. There is an extra-curricular drama group outside the school, in the local com-munity centre (later the Year 9s tell me that some of them attend a drama group there). The school is set in large grounds and I cross a pretty, slightly manicured garden to the main

DOI: 10.4324/9781003093084-2

entrance. The school building is bright, with high skylights and lots of natural light. The walls are light but bare – there is not a poster or artwork up unless it is on a notice board (the building was built through PFI [private finance initiative] and it is owned by someone else who won't allow things on the walls).

I am to be based in the graphics room and I chat with one of the 'designers in residence' who is also based there. They used to be a pupil here and then returned after university. They are trying to move to NYC this summer to gain further work experience.

11.45am: I meet the head teacher. We're in a central space in the middle of the school. To one side is a large red cow and to another a small, colourful panda. Above us is a motivational quote and a Bible verse plus a mural with sculptural elements. I notice a collage of the school is up at the end of this space, framed in glass.

The head is having their daily meeting with five pupils. The head says we shouldn't need to make a case for the arts because they are so important. But the school has to be adaptable because of policy changes. The school has traditionally had a very broad curriculum but now they have to think of ways to offer the same programme but not necessarily through the curriculum. I understand that by this they mean teaching/experiencing some of the arts through other means – like extra-curricular activities.

The head asks the pupils if anyone does art – neither of the Year 10s do but there are two Year 9s who are taking Music/Drama on rotation and art. One of the boys says he'll consider taking an arts subject if he does well in it. Later we talk more about the Ofsted inspection and changes to the curriculum. The conversation becomes quite political. The head says that the government seems to be listening to no one, or none of the experts anyway. The head talks about a conference he attended recently with head teachers from all four home countries and about the different ways teachers in Wales/Scotland/NI are approaching teaching and how vastly different this is from what is happening in England. (Lexi's field notes)

Schools are often treated as if they are all exactly the same. But every one of the 30 schools we visited was different. They were in different parts of the country and served very different populations, they were all built at different times and in different styles. Their different histories and current priorities and philosophies were very apparent almost as soon as we came through the school gates. Nevertheless, there were discernible patterns among this special and understudied group of schools. This chapter introduces one of these similarities – and one of the core concepts from our study – the arts-rich secondary school.

We first came across the term 'arts-rich' in the work of James Catterall (2009). Catterall conducted a 12-year national study of education in the visual and performing arts. Based in the US, he used the National Educational Longitudinal Survey, a panel study which surveys more than 25,000 students and brings together data about their schools, educational records and destinations and some activities outside of school. Catterall wanted to know about school 'effects' so he compared 'arts-rich' and 'arts-poor' schools. To do this, he and his team developed a set of variables that included "the availability of various arts programs, whether or not a school has a formal department of arts and/or of music, and the number of arts and music faculty" (Catterall, 2009, p. 109). These characteristics are also important in our research.

Catterall found that arts-rich schools have a positive impact on student attainment and engagement both in and out of school. An examination of the educational pathways of students in arts-rich schools showed that:

> Intensive involvement in the arts during middle and high schools were associated with higher levels of achievement and college attainment and also with many indications of pro-social behaviour such as voluntarism and political participation.
>
> *(Catterall, 2009, p. i)*

He concludes that:

> Arts-rich schools are seen to bear characteristics including a climate for achievement as well as instructional practices that may account for their advantage.
>
> *(Catterall, 2009, p. i)*

Catterall notes that, because his study was at scale, the variables the researchers could consider did not afford a detailed understanding of the beneficial "climate for achievement", or what he elsewhere calls their "zeitgeist" or "coherent arts-based identity" (p. 108). Other US researchers, notably in the A+ schools programme (Adkins & Gunzenhauser, 2005; Noblit, Dickson, Wilson, & McKinney, 2009) and the Ford Foundation's Arts Education Partnership Program (Stevenson & Deasy, 2005), have gone further, and identified coherence of identity and a positive and inclusive school ethos as characteristics of the arts-rich schools they studied.

The findings from these American studies, and the questions they give rise to, resonate strongly with our own research. We set out to try to understand more about what arts-rich schools in England do (their instructional practices, partnerships, organisation) but also how they feel (the school ethos, the mood and atmosphere of the different classrooms, whether there was a 'climate for achievement') and the impact of all this on students.

In this chapter, then, we start by considering the idea of the arts-rich school. We should clarify, from the outset, that 'arts-rich' wasn't a designation the schools claimed for themselves. We chose our sample of schools by asking our research partner organisations, Tate and the Royal Shakespeare Company (RSC), each to recommend 15 schools. They proposed schools they knew and had worked with, or the schools where teachers had been heavily involved with the professional development they offered. We took this professional development connection as indicating the school's interest in, and willingness to commit resource to, arts education. We then considered the sorts of variables Catterall mentions – which arts subjects were offered, staffing levels, inspection reports on the arts curriculum and what the website had to say about arts in the curriculum and in extra-curricular activities. So, we could say with reasonable certainty, as we began the research, that all of the schools in the project seemed to be taking the arts education of their students seriously. This unfortunately, is not something that can be said about all secondary schools in England.

As we got to know the schools and to appreciate their different strengths, histories, challenges and motivations, the value of the concept of an arts-rich school became clearer to us. Our research design involved annual visits to each of the 30 schools over three school years. Over that time the schools evolved and changed, sometimes quite dramatically. Staff moved on, leadership styles altered, new assessment and accountability measures meant that the curriculum had to be rethought. Despite this, in all of the sample schools we witnessed a commitment to arts-richness that seemed to weather the storms. Some schools managed the choppy waters better than others but, across the board, the schools we investigated were proud of their commitment to arts education. They talked about the arts as central to their school's identity, its zeitgeist, its coherence, its place in its community, its DNA ...

The term 'arts-rich' is useful, we think, as a descriptor of these schools, but also as an aim for any school. Arts-richness doesn't depend on finance; all schools could have arts-richness as one of their goals. The elements that make a school arts-rich can be defined and debated; they can differ; their impact can be evaluated. And surely, there are no meritorious arguments for 'arts-poor' schools that deny students opportunities and limit their ways of understanding the world and expressing themselves. For these reasons we decided to start this book by thinking about what TALE-project head teachers had to say about their schools, their beliefs about education and why they saw the arts as enriching and important.

The heads' view of arts-richness

All of the TALE arts-rich schools had strong support from at least one member of the senior leadership team, very often the head. Support from the top is congruent with school change literatures (Ainscow, 2015; Earl & Hargreaves, 2000; Elmore, 2004; Leithwood, Harris, & Hopkins, 2020) which stress the importance of senior leaders in direction setting, in articulating the school's 'vision and mission', and in ensuring that administrative processes and resource allocations support goals and plans. We discuss: (1) the personal-ethical work of leading an arts-rich school; (2) the value of arts-richness in the school; and (3) significant management issues related to arts-richness.

(1) The personal-ethical work of leading an arts-rich school

It is no surprise that vast majority of the heads of the TALE schools were generally interested in the arts. There was a 'fit' between their own experiences, their philosophy of education and the school to which they were appointed. The heads felt comfortable leading a school where the arts were valued, prioritised and were integral to the schools' identity. This was in part because of their own childhood experiences.

Research on teachers' lives and work (e.g. Day, 2005; Day et al., 2006) tells us that, together with school context and policy framing, individual biography is important in the formation of professional values and practices. Bourdieu would agree, suggesting that dispositions formed in childhood are highly influential – such dispositions include interests in the arts, as well as orientations and aptitudes to education. Some heads of TALE arts-rich schools told us that they had 'always' been interested in the arts because of childhood arts experiences at home. Other heads did not have arts experiences and interests at home but had been encouraged and supported during their own schooling by staff and the wider community. Some heads felt very strongly that they had succeeded educationally and professionally against the odds and they had relied heavily on their own schooling to support their growing interest, knowledge and skills in the arts. Peer arts interests were important too, as well as the cultural opportunities available in the local area. And once they got the top school job, TALE heads brought these life experiences and values to the task of creating opportunities for students.

Arts-rich school leaders drew a direct line from their own experience of schooling and their arts education to their own practice as a leader, their expectations of their leadership team and the school arts offer. TALE heads who had succeeded against the odds often had a strong civic sensibility and commitment to equity. *I personally want to contribute towards an education system that has given me quite a lot. My parents didn't have to pay anything apart from their taxes and I benefited greatly from that education and provision. It is saddening that individuals in inner cities and the coastal regions perhaps don't have the same level of opportunity as I did.* For many of the heads, their own arts experiences had become an integral part of their moral purpose. They saw schools as having a duty to provide life opportunities. *We are a girls' school, so it's about empowering women. Our aim is about them taking charge of their learning, being independent women, to meet the challenges of the 21st century, so it's a very positive aim.*

The heads' conversations were strongly resonant with Bourdieusian understandings of the potential for schools to 'produce' cultural capitals and associated dispositions for the children and young people who did not arrive at school with the arts as a birthright. One possible Bourdieusian reading would suggest that heads had uncritically taken up the prevailing logics and beliefs of the educational field through their own apprenticeship as students and teachers – that they believed it was possible for all of their students to do well and that all would equally benefit from their education. Bourdieu called the belief in universalised expectations and capacity a misrecognition of the ways in which schooling selects only a few who have not inherited the capitals necessary for success and supports them to become socially and economically mobile. He suggested that educators possess a necessary blind spot which allows them to do the work that results in such selection. However, we saw that many of the heads were well aware of the ways in which schools reproduced the status quo but felt morally obliged to work for equitable educational outcomes, in full knowledge that this might mean advantaging their students over those from other schools. They rejected any notion that they should teach some students differently simply because of their family circumstances and field logics: *One of the reasons why I love working with this school is because the staff buy into the vision that social background shouldn't make any difference to your progress or where you actually end up.*

The heads often used the familiar policy rhetoric of high expectations and no excuses. In their words we can perhaps hear them speaking to staff meetings, at school assemblies and to parents and governors. These heads re-created in our interviews the ethical narrative which they expected staff to sign up to, which underpinned organisational decisions and which brought and held the school together. *To say that somebody has a difficult home life and to say that I would expect less from them here is to say that I expect them to make less of their life. And that is just not OK for us. So our idea of being academic and traditional is about teaching children the values here that they can take on to use in their future lives if they want to – because they may not want to … We want to have high expectations of our students because we believe that is what they are worth.*

Some heads additionally linked the need to provide all students with a good education to the purposes of schooling. *The function of school curriculum is to lay the foundations of a just democracy. Young people need to have common understandings … it oils the wheels of society. State sector children need this just as much as the private, otherwise democracy falls apart.* Integral to their overall goal of empowerment, many of the heads saw that their school must provide access to the arts, especially for those who don't have easy access, and give those students who are interested in the arts the opportunity to develop their talents and expertise. It is not hard to imagine the family who would want their child to attend this over-subscribed school: *We have a large proportion of students come to us who, if they went to an average school, they would not make it to university or to a career of their choice. They would come out with GCSE grades that are barely acceptable. But that is not an acceptable thing for us. We have this idea of there being a kind of hurdle, and a stretch point beyond that, and the students must reach the point at which university is accessible or a career of their choice is on their doorstep. They must be supported through that journey regardless of their starting point. For the rest, it is about making sure that they are truly challenged to develop and make the leap towards the highest grades of attainment. We have stratospherically high expectations.*

Bourdieu too was strongly in favour of an approach to schooling which saw all students as potentially capable, and where the school took up the challenge to support them to "overcome hurdles and stretch beyond that". While Bourdieu's view might seem paradoxical, it was because he thought that the critical and reflexive thinking and acting inculcated by a strong school system was important inside and outside of the education field and was necessary for any contestation of the status quo. Our reading of our conversations with heads of arts-rich schools was that they understood schooling generally, and the arts in particular, as providing education for life, as well the acquisition of essential qualifications.

(2) The value of arts-richness in and to a school

TALE heads considered that the arts brought four significant benefits to the school: (a) as an essential part of the school identity; (b) as integral to its educational missions; (c) in connecting the school with families and the wider community; and (d) enabling the school to build partnerships with arts organisations.

(a) The arts are integral to the school's identity and culture

Heads often told us that the arts become part of the school's DNA. *We've hung our hat on doing things creatively*. Some heads had been attracted to apply to work at the school because of its arts programmes: *One of the things that attracted me to the school ... was the fact that it was a performing arts school. ... students have music, dance and drama all the way through for KS3 ... that's quite unusual for dance ... we have a stand-alone dance team in the performing arts faculty*. Heads often referred to the long history of arts education which predated them: *This has always been known as an arts school. If you were to read the history, it goes right back to the turn of the 20th century*. Being an arts school meant a specific approach to pedagogy and curriculum: *It has always been an area of its strength and we've been able to have a very innovative and creative curriculum where the arts have supported other faculties and areas with their teaching methodologies and their way of interpreting the curriculum*.

Some heads told us that the arts were beneficial in a competitive school market. The arts were a marker of distinction. While nearly all secondary school brochures feature smiling students in lab coats, playing on sports fields and apparently enjoying art, music and drama activities, heads felt that the depth and authenticity of their school's 'brand' were apparent and a 'unique selling point'. The arts helped to build the reputation of the school: *People send their kids here for the arts and they want them to be part of that*.

Many TALE school heads told us that the arts contributed significantly to making the school a positive and productive place to be. The arts were important in creating and sustaining a purposeful and vibrant school culture.

Heads are particularly concerned with school culture, sometimes called climate or ethos, the 'je ne sais quoi' that visitors can feel when they enter the school foyer and walk through its corridors (Deal & Peterson, 2016). School culture is a complex mix of beliefs, actions, attitudes, values, relationships, motivations and enthusiasms. It is as much unspoken as it is explicit, but can often be partially heard in the ways in which heads, staff and students talk about their school, and seen in the images and texts that populate corridors, classrooms, offices and foyers (Prosser, 1999). School culture shapes the ways in which the school community lives together and makes sense of their everyday institutional life. While a school's history is an important aspect of its culture, heads have a powerful influence on and through school culture (Fullan, 2001; Morris et al., 2020). Their emphases on some things and not others, their priorities, systems of reward and sanction, their interactions and storytelling are key to establishing and maintaining cultural norms (Hobby, 2004). Budgetary, plant and staffing decisions, administrative procedures and regular school routines and rituals are significant materialisations of the ways in which heads see their school and shape its culture (Brighouse & Woods, 1999).

Strong school cultures are characterised by extensive, overlapping and cohesive interactions and affiliations between people (Bridwell-Mitchell & Cooc, 2006). The arts create, support and extend interactions and affiliations as they generate opportunities to communicate, share understandings and build empathy and respect. The arts thus have the potential to be a powerful strategy for school improvement (Hall & Thomson, 2017; Shaw & Bernard, 2022). And if the going gets tough, the arts can help a school turn itself around.

Two of the school heads in the TALE study had had critical moments when they might have abandoned the arts. One head, newly appointed after a public scandal, could have decided to take the school in a different direction but became rapidly convinced that the arts were an essential aspect of the school's identity, culture and reputation. The other head faced a poor inspection rating and academisation. A poor inspection rating typically creates pressure to focus on core subjects and abandon all else. In our earlier study of schools in the Creative Partnerships programme (Thomson, Jones, & Hall, 2009) we saw that heads responded differently to this pressure – some abandoned creative teaching altogether, while others saw it as the heart of the school improvement effort. This head faced a similar crunch point: *The school went into special measures. We are, for the record, very much a good school and very proud of that journey and it was quite serious when the school went into special measures because at that time we were getting additional funding for the arts specialism. But we also had an Ofsted validation that arts was strong for this specialism and it came out with flying colours. Even when the school was in its darkest time, the arts were always a very strong faculty and students did very, very well and they loved the arts.* Why would you abandon a curriculum area that was doing well?

School cultures can sometimes be highly dysfunctional. A negative school culture is characterised by distrust between staff and staff and students (Bryk & Schneider, 2002). Differences are unresolved and become points of simmering tension, bullying and conflict (Woodley & Morrison McGill, 2018). The subsequent the lack of attachment and affiliation to the school fosters acrimony and hinders improvement (Normore & Brooks, 2016). Heads are generally anxious to avoid negative school cultures, and TALE heads were unequivocal that the arts were an important avenue for generating a constructive collegial atmosphere (as with creative education approaches; see Bragg & Manchester, 2011). The arts energised staff and students alike and created new opportunities for "sayings, doings and relatings" (Wilkinson & Kemmis, 2014). *The work with the Royal Shakespeare Company has rekindled a passion for the subject literature and also a passion for teaching, but I think what's important for me is actually that subject knowledge, because as soon as a teacher has passion for subject knowledge – I don't know what it is, but it seems to get passed on to the children… that's actually happening. So the work with the RSC is a double whammy. It is basically enthusing staff and it's enthusing children and then there is a synergy between that and it is just wonderful to see.*

Researchers argue that positive school cultures are strongly associated with both students' (MacNeil Prater, & Busch, 2009) and teachers' (Seashore Louis & Lee, 2016) learning. TALE heads agreed.

(b) The arts are essential to the school's educational mission

TALE heads told us that the arts were an important, and sometimes indispensable, avenue for their school to fulfil its educational mission. Heads tended to take a broad view of the benefits of education in and through arts subjects. They generally took a holistic view, seeing the whole child and the summative effects of schooling. They told us that the arts are about what makes us human; that being engaged in a rich arts curriculum was about being and becoming a person. *There are lots of schools that have academic prowess but it has to be a special school to take that a little bit further, which is about creating that rounded human being. It isn't just about how many A Levels and GCSEs you've got. It's about being a rounded human being who can say 'I've stood on a stage and recited this' or 'I took part in this production' or 'I sang in this festival' or whatever. That is really important here.*

The arts enriched students' lives because they learnt about their diverse local, national and international cultural heritages. Some schools linked the arts to the development of democratic values and national identity. The arts provided access to social and cultural capital that was important for being able to take part in everyday conversations. *The arts are too often seen as the fun bit of the curriculum, which is not how we perceive it. We perceive it to be a facet of a really traditional and well-rounded education where you can hold your own in a discussion about the Renaissance and what that actually means, or you can experience getting up and performing Shakespeare as well as knowing the story in a dumbed-down version from some film or other.* Heads of arts-rich schools often saw themselves bucking the policy-favoured trend to focus primarily on qualifications, and to continue to value holistic and well-rounded schooling. *It is a horrific situation when I know that schools in this area are cutting performing arts from their curriculum because of the need to focus on smashing children through academic qualifications. Because that is a nonsense and it will come back to bite society in five, ten or 15 years from now.*

All the heads we interviewed were very clear about the contribution that the arts made to the development of meta-cognitive skills: the arts encouraged questioning, reflection and interpretation. Important life and vocational skills were formed through the arts. Students were able to work independently and also work collaboratively. And because the arts offered different and varied ways to communicate, they allowed students to practise conveying their ideas, interpretations and opinions. The performing arts in particular offered opportunities to communicate more confidently in a variety of public settings and to a range of different people. *It's about self-confidence. If you can stand and express yourself to other people, whether that's music or speech or movement ... people are looking at your revealed self in your photography or art work ... you are putting yourself on the line and articulating. That's why I put an extra post in our staffing structure, Head of Communication and Performance, in order to make sure we have the relationship between the arts and more traditional subjects – there are huge opportunities for cross-curricular work.*

The arts also fostered self-management, developing what Bourdieu would call a disposition for self-management. Students became enterprising and resourceful problem-solvers. They developed persistence and patience, they could work through difficulties and stick at things. *If they overcome a problem at school they can overcome a problem in their own life.* Some heads told us that there were also wider implications for students' increased self-awareness and self-control. *They become less self-centred and more socially aware. What the arts gives to students is the opportunity to self-actualise and to work through their issues outside of themselves. It gives them a contact with a richness in cultural terms that they would otherwise be denied.*

The inclusivity fostered by the arts was also important. Because every child can participate and contribute, the arts supported *the ethos of the school … every child matters and we want to bring out the best in students regardless of what that best might mean for every individual student.* Heads connected inclusivity to their overall commitment to equity: *Art and the arts including music, drama, I see it as a real leveller. We have quite a breadth in terms of students' abilities. Something like drama, art, photography are real levellers because everyone can contribute.* Heads were clear that the arts allowed students who often struggled with the curriculum to find new ways to acquire important knowledges and skills. *Some children will do very well at the arts where they won't in other subjects and so it allows them to have that self-esteem and respect for themselves.* The RSC rehearsal room approach to Shakespeare, for example, allowed all students to engage with difficult texts. *We've got EAL [English as an Additional Language] kids who are not scared to play with language and actually try out new things. They are just basically flying because of it. So we love it.* By valuing individual creativity, talent and self-expression the arts were, according to the heads, an important avenue for nurturing children. In turn this led to more varied and better teaching across the school. The arts were a 'flag' to encourage aspiration and social mobility. *We talk about the footsteps the children are going to leave behind … a few years ago a girl in her GCSE Art did a pair of shoes and her rationale was 'your shoes are your footprints of the past'. I just love the fact that's what she did. She had two child's shoes, her own childhood shoes, and I talk about the fact that it is about your impact. What are you going to contribute to the world, to the people around you, to your family?*

The interpersonal and cognitive skills emphasised by TALE heads are supported by research. For example, a randomised control trial into the Houston Arts Access Program, involving over 10,500 Year 4–8 students in elementary and middle schools, found that engagement with the arts

> significantly reduced the proportion of students receiving disciplinary infractions, improved writing achievement, and increased students' compassion for others. For students in elementary schools, which comprised 86 percent of the sample, arts educational experiences also significantly improved school engagement, college aspirations, and arts-facilitated empathy
>
> *(Bowen & Kisida, 2019, p. 2)*

Like the TALE heads, the Houston study did not make claims about transfer to other core subject areas: the researchers "did not find significant effects overall on math, reading, or science achievement" (p. 5). Other researchers have also noted the importance of the arts for the development of what are sometimes called 'soft skills' (e.g. Harland et al., 2000; Thomson, Coles, Hallewell, & Keane, 2014) and emphasised, as did the TALE heads, the contributions made by the specific disciplinary particularities of the arts to inclusion and an overall well-rounded education (e.g. Catterall & Peppler, 2007; Harland et al., 2005; Hetland, Winner, Veenema, & Sheridan, 2007; Winner, Goldstein, & Vincent-Lakrin, 2013).

(c) The arts connect families and the community

Heads saw that their schools' arts activities helped to create traditions and a legacy, because the arts are memorable for students, and for their families. They told us that the arts create opportunities for families to come into the school to celebrate their children's successes. The wider community also connect with the school, particularly if the school's arts programmes reach beyond the school gate, which many did. Through the arts, students were able to work in and out of school: *There's lots of outreach into the local area and we have relationships with a local art studio and they have exhibitions there. And the textiles department did a catwalk with lots of t-shirts that were created in Year 9, which was part of the process of getting them all engaged.*

Heads told us that the arts provision in the school not only helped the school but also the general locality to be seen as somewhere of value. *We had a production of The Taming of the Shrew in here and people from the community came who had never been to a Shakespeare play. Also, because of the Royal Shakespeare Company programme, teachers have gone out and been able to talk to other teachers and we've been able to create a hub network and that has been amazing. And just the whole culture in terms of staff who have been here for quite a long time and who were included. And the students feel that too – that they are cared about and we are connected – and the parents get the fact that the school is not right at the end of the world in terms of what we are giving our students.* Some TALE schools had become a cultural hub for the area, opening up space for local arts organisations and activities, but also supporting and leading the development of local arts programmes: *[The drama teacher] plays a really huge part in community work. For instance, every summer he runs a Youth theatre that we part-subsidise as a school.*

The arts create and strengthen neighbourhood bonds as students and staff work in and out of school and build networks with other schools in positive strengthened relationships, and in developing partnerships between schools and other cultural organisations. *I like the idea of the collaboration with other schools and I like the fact that we will be in the Arts Mark family and we will have their logo on our website and all the rest of it. And some of the local primaries that we didn't even know were involved have approached us and asked for our help to get Arts Mark, and that has encouraged us to spread our wings a little bit and work within our community. Our Music teacher runs a choir for some of our local primaries. Our Art department does a lot of work with local old people's homes and they've produced work for Remembrance Day and we had it mounted and presented it to the old people's home. And we had a tea and cocktails afternoon and the girls went down and played music from the twenties and thirties for them. I like working with people in the community.*

Bourdieu might note that the arts are a way of building local social and cultural capitals as well as ensuring a harmonious relationship between the school, its community and the wider neighbourhood. Ensuring that the school had some characteristics which differentiated it from competitors made it attractive to particular parents and students. The shared family–school interest in the arts was supported through opportunities for families to act as engaged audiences for exhibitions and performances. The openness of the arts-rich school worked to enhance its reputation and garner local affection.

(d) The school can build partnerships with cultural organisations

TALE arts-rich schools were initially chosen because of their association with either the RSC or Tate. However, they all had more than one partnership. One of their shared characteristics was the thick web of connections they had with cultural organisations locally and, often, further afield. The heads saw these partnerships as bringing benefits for students, staff and the school.

Arts partnerships brought new and different people into the school. Students had new experiences. *I think it's good in the sense that they are being spoken to by somebody who isn't us. They learn their safety and their comfort zone with us and the boys will speak to me like I'm their mum. We have very good relationships with our children and when we talk to them we do it in a very kind way. But I think that when they have to speak to outside organisations, they have to mind their Ps and Qs. And they do and it makes them use respect and kindness, and I think it is just so worthwhile. And you can see the difference.* Engaging with professionals allowed students to see new career possibilities and pathways but also work of a high professional standard. They not only saw that work and effort were required to achieve excellence but also that it was important to develop a sense of what was good and excellent in order to critically evaluate your own work. *It's the same with the Olympic Games. You see these runners and these athletes and you think – oh wow, this is all terribly glamorous. What you don't see is the hours and hours of slog behind it, the boredom at times, going out running in the winter and many things worse. But that's really good for our students, especially for a secondary modern school in a grammar school environment, aspiring to be an outstanding school.*

Working with cultural organisations contributed to teachers' professional learning but, as importantly, recharged their batteries. *Being in school is very fatiguing and teachers work very hard, so they need to recharge their batteries and they need to re-engage with the subject they love. So going out and working with a theatre group or in a gallery for a day will do that for people. I've just had a note from the head of Music wanting to take a group to a premiere performance in (the city) and I could tell from the note that they just couldn't wait to get there. Now they will come back so fired up from that and it will inspire them.* Teachers' passions for their subject were rekindled. Engagement with cultural organisations often meant that teachers worked collaboratively across departments; this collaboration helped departments cohere. Coherence and shared endeavour are important for school morale, for generating intra-organisational trust and for creating affiliations within the school itself.

Over time, work with partners contributed to enhanced reputation within the profession and thus to improved recruitment and retention of staff. *Recruitment and retention have got much better and there are a number of reasons for that, one of which is our success and another is our reputation for looking after staff. And, locally, that reputation is important but the other part of that is our connection with cultural institutions. Because teachers want to have access to these things. And the fact that the school is near [a major gallery], and [the local towns] are on the up in terms of all the stuff that they are offering. And it's brought in tourism but also the school is forward-thinking enough and interesting enough to be part of the Royal Shakespeare Company and that is a draw.* Work with cultural partners often went beyond decals to positive media coverage and awards. *The work with the RSC is a double whammy. It is basically enthusing staff and it's enthusing children and then there is a synergy between that. It's no surprise that this fantastic department has won [a national newspaper's] English and Literacy Award three years running, which hasn't ever been done before.*

The competitive nature of the schooling field in England leaves heads little choice but to compete with others if they are to serve their students. Heads brought together their commitment to a broad and balanced curriculum with the desire for their school to be ahead of others. *It is very helpful to us to be associated with the Royal Shakespeare Company because it is a global brand. It is also important for us because it is the right thing to do to be part of a network that not only services other schools but the community as well, because that is also what education should be about.* Heads juggled external pressures with their own commitments to equity and to holistic education and this juggling act was a key logic of their everyday leadership practice.

(3) Significant management issues related to arts-richness

Key to ensuring the school's reputation was its capacity to ensure that students left the school with the qualifications that counted. Although the heads and governing bodies of arts–rich schools were committed to a broad and balanced curriculum and a holistic approach to teaching and learning, students still needed to achieve and be seen to be successful in the core national curriculum. Because the arts had been removed from the core, school audit measures had been strengthened and inspections were tightly focused around the attainment in the core subjects, heads had no choice but to meet these requirements. Schools that fell foul of audit and inspection could be forced into academisation, re-brokered if they were already academies, and heads were likely lose their jobs. Stakes were high and punishments for deviation from policy directions could be severe (Ball, 2018; Thomson, 2020).

Keeping the core curriculum and the optional arts curriculum in balance required considerable effort. As one head put it, *It's really tough because you want to give students the opportunity to understand what their talents may be but you are under the cosh with really rapid change.* Heads saw a fundamental contradiction at the heart of public policy which they had to mediate and manage at the local school level. *What I would describe as the dichotomy at the heart of government policy that comes from a complete mismatch between the agendas of the Department of Innovations & Skills and the Department of Education is probably the biggest challenge. Because, on the one hand, we are supposed to be doing the English Baccalaureate and, on the other hand, the government wants three million apprentices. And the two things don't match up, because the curriculum of the English Baccalaureate is not what is needed to develop those young people to be future working people – although I should make it really clear that I don't view any school as a servant of employers because I think that is a very unhealthy thing for education. Our priority is their fulfilment as a person.*

Heads often told us that policy was forcing them to choose between the young people and the school. *If you gave kids completely free choice and they chose art, music and drama, that wouldn't fill all the elements of Progress 8. On a personal level, I find that very, very difficult. And when I speak to parents about it, I find it even more difficult because effectively we are defending something that we don't agree with. I think it's important that kids have a balanced curriculum but I think it's probably more important that they do things that they're good at and can thrive in. And making them do a modern foreign language that they hate and might not do well in, but not letting them do a second arts subject that they love and could really thrive in – because the modern languages thing helps your Progress 8 score, and the arts doesn't – that doesn't feel good. But all schools are facing that challenge.*

Heads often found themselves dealing with the fear and pressure brought about by audit measures, inspections and exams, and debating how much time should be given to arts subjects. One of the effects of students making 'safe choices' to study the EBacc were problems maintaining subject options and building and retaining decent sized arts departments. *We've almost got a reverse challenge, which is that for some parents, they are keen for children to adopt an unbalanced curriculum too early.* Ironically some TALE heads also reported difficulties recruiting arts specialists, a consequence of the overall reduction of numbers of qualified specialist arts teachers in the system, the direct result of falling enrolments due to the government's accountability measures.

Heads made various decisions about how to retain the arts and how much of an arts curriculum they offered. TALE heads fell into three camps:

- those who openly went against the policy grain. *We've stood against [the EBacc] and gone the other way, art and music and drama and media … It's important to support what teachers are doing … and those subjects are as important as English, maths and science. We say, like every school in the country, that we believe in a broad and balanced curriculum, but we've actually put our money where our mouth is.*
- those who managed to balance external pressures and their own philosophies of education. *We managed to put emphasis on the EBacc subjects, but without losing the emphasis on the arts. That comes with the breadth and depth in Key Stage 3. And during the option process we also highlight student pathways and encourage them towards some of the EBacc subjects but we also encourage them to take an arts subject as well.*
- those who initially conformed with policy but then changed their minds when they saw the effects on students. *A few years ago, because of the pressures of accountability measures, we went from four arts options to three. They needed to do less*

but get better grades … The unintended consequence was a drop in the arts at GCSE. Therefore, we've taken the decision to change our curriculum … Staff went to investigate the arts in other schools with a similar profile and we've decided to change back to four options.

Cuts in resources were also a serious issue. *There is a financial issue because we obviously have to ask parents. Every school has a charging policy and you are not allowed to demand that parents cover the cost of curriculum activity and you have to ask for a donation. Going to the theatre can be expensive – art galleries not so much – and of course the cost of coaches is very expensive these days. You do your best to manage. For example, if an activity is going to take place which is going to be quite expensive, we have an unwritten practice – the staff know that they must give parents maximum notice, and so you never ask for a donation just a week in advance because that is unfair. Some of our parents are relatively affluent and could find the money but others are not and then you'd have only the more affluent ones that were going. Within our culture there is an understanding that if there is a cost attached to an activity, we give parents the maximum time. Now it is sometimes difficult to do that with a play because you might only get notice of the play within a couple of months but that is what we try to do.* Most TALE schools were in receipt of additional funding for students whose families were officially judged to be financially in need. *We use Pupil Premium quite wisely and so young people who are entitled to Pupil Premium we don't ask their parents to make a contribution and we pay for the activity because it is even more important that children who are entitled to Pupil Premium get these opportunities, because they might come from family backgrounds where it is not part of their experience to go to a theatre or a gallery.*

The challenges that leaders face are a direct result of the competing logics of the field. The arts bring distinction to the school. Through their unique cultural offer and associations with a range of arts organisations, including elite national companies such as the RSC and Tate, the school promises particular benefits to students. School leaders' commitments to equity and to a broad and balanced curriculum provide a powerful rationale for the arts, and their practices invite families and the wider community to enjoy the results of students' learning. However, the policy emphasis on core subjects, supported by school audit measures, inspection regimes and punitive consequences for not doing well enough in other academic areas, create continued tensions and juggling within the school. Senior leaders must continually revisit their decisions about the arts in order to ensure that neither students nor the school are suffering as a result of making the arts a priority. Artsrichness is not static and immutable. Even if it is what the school has been and has had for some time, arts-richness is vulnerable to external pressures and relies heavily on continued internal commitments.

In sum: what is an arts-rich secondary school?

When we look through what the heads told us, and anticipating some of what is to come in the book, we can identify some patterns in the TALE schools which indicate arts-richness:

1. The arts are part of the school identity and school culture. They are integral to what the school is and what is done each day. The schools have a (sometimes long) history of arts and cultural education. The arts are not used simply for promotion. Students, families and the wider community understand the arts to be important.
2. There is a broad and balanced curriculum in which the arts are taken seriously – the arts are integral to the curriculum on offer to all children. The school may specialise in one arts subject, but it does not ignore the others.
3. There is a coherent and explicit philosophy for teaching the arts which underpins the selection and nature of key concepts and skills. There is regular and separate teaching of arts subjects. There is a curriculum plan which shows the sequential development of theory and practice (knowledge and skills). There are regular opportunities for the arts to be combined with other subjects.
4. Arts-rich schools have strong arts leadership. There is an effective, supportive senior management team who can communicate vision and mobilise resources; there is strong arts leadership at department level supported with time and resources.
5. There are dedicated arts spaces. Resources are allocated to the arts and time is made for them. There is visible 'kit'.
6. Departmental staff have continuing professional development in the arts.
7. The school has productive partnerships with arts organisations, including galleries and museums, local artists, and arts in the parent community and neighbourhood. The school is permeable; it acts as a hub. There is consistent access to arts expertise (bought in, artists in residence).
8. The school is connected to local, national and/or international networks which bring arts resources, conversations and practices. Post-pandemic these may be strongly geared to the digital.
9. There is a wide range of educational arts and cultural visits and experiences that are accessible to all. The school offers specialised extra-curricular arts activities.
10. The arts are included in work and careers focused education and activities.

As the book unfolds, we will address each of these in more detail.

References

Adkins, A., & Gunzenhauser, M. (2005). West Hollow School and the North Carolina A +Schools program: Integrating the arts, creating a local agenda for reform. In W. Pink & G. Noblit (eds), *Cultural matters: Lessons learned from field students of several leading school reform strategies* (pp. 63–86). Cresskill, NJ: Hampton Press.

Ainscow, M. (2015). *Towards self-improving school systems: Lessons from a city challenge*. London: Routledge.

Ball, S. (2018). *The education debate* (3rd edn). Bristol: The Policy Press.

Bowen, D. B., & Kisida, B. (2019). Investigating causal effects of arts education experiences. Experimental evidence from Houston's arts access initiative. https://kinder.rice.edu/sites/

default/files/documents/Investigating%20Causal%20Effects%20of%20Arts%20Education%20Experiences%20Final_0.pdf

Bragg, S., & Manchester, H. (2011). *Creativity, school ethos and the Creative Partnerships Programme*. London: Creativity, Culture and Education.

Bridwell-Mitchell, E. N., & Cooc, N. (2006). The ties that bind: How social capital is forged and forfeited in teacher communities. *Educational Researcher*, 45(1), 7–17.

Brighouse, T., & Woods, D. (1999). *How to improve your school*. London: Routledge.

Bryk, A. S., & Schneider, B. (2002). *Trust in schools: A core resource for management*. New York: Russell Sage Foundation.

Catterall, J. S. (2009). *Doing well and doing good by doing art*. Los Angeles: I-Group Books.

Catterall, J. S., & Peppler, K. (2007). Learning in the visual arts and the world views of young children. *Cambridge Journal of Education*, 37(4), 543–560.

Day, C. (2005). *A passion for teaching*. Buckingham: Open University Press.

Day, C., Stobart, G., Sammons, P., Kington, A., Gu, Q., Smees, R., & Mujtaba, T. (2006). Variations in teachers' work, lives and effectiveness. Research report 743. London: Department for Education and Skills (DfES).

Deal, T., & Peterson, K. (2016). *Shaping school culture: The heart of leadership* (3rd edn). San Francisco, CA: Jossey-Bass.

Earl, L., & Hargreaves, A. (eds). (2000). *Learning to change*. San Francisco, CA: Jossey-Bass.

Elmore, R. (2004). *School reform from the inside-out*. Cambridge, MA: Harvard University Press.

Fullan, M. (2001). *Leading in a culture of change*. San Francisco, CA: Jossey-Bass.

Hall, C., & Thomson, P. (2017). *Inspiring school change: Transforming education through the creative arts*. London: Routledge.

Harland, J., Kinder, K., Lord, P., Stott, A., Schagen, I., & Haynes, J. (2000). *Arts education in secondary schools: Effects and effectiveness*. Slough: National Foundation for Educational Research.

Harland, J., Lord, P., Stott, A., Kinder, K., Lamont, E., & Ashworth, M. (2005). *The arts-education interface: A mutual learning triangle?* Slough: National Foundation for Educational Research.

Hetland, L., Winner, E., Veenema, S., & Sheridan, K. (2007). *Studio thinking: The real benefits of visual arts in education*. New York: Teachers College Press.

Hobby, R. (2004). *A culture for learning: An investigation into the values and beliefs associated with effective schools*. London: Hay Group Management.

Leithwood, K., Harris, A., & Hopkins, D. (2020). Seven strong claims about successful school leadership revisited. *School Leadership and Management*, 40(1), 5–22.

MacNeil, A., Prater, D., & Busch, S. (2009). The effects of school culture and climate on student achievement. *International Journal of Leadership in Education*, 12(1), 73–84.

Morris, J. E., Lummis, G. W., Lock, G., Ferguson, C., Hill, S., & Nykiel, A. (2020). The role of leadership in establishing a positive staff culture in a secondary school. *Educational Management Administration & Leadership*, 48(5), 802–820.

Noblit, G., Dickson, C. H., Wilson, B. A., & McKinney, M. B. (2009). *Creating and sustaining arts-based school reform: The A+ schools program*. New York: Routledge.

Normore, A. H., & Brooks, J. S. (2016). *The dark side of leadership: Identifying and overcoming unethical practice in organisations*. New York: Emerald.

Prosser, J. (ed.) (1999). *School culture*. London: Paul Chapman Publishing.

Seashore Louis, K., & Lee, M. (2016). Teachers' capacity for organizational learning: The effects of school culture and context. *School Effectiveness and School Improvement*, 27(4), 534–556.

Shaw, R. D., & Bernard, C. F. (2022). School culture change through the arts: a case study of the turnaround arts program. *Arts Education Policy Review*, https://doi.org/10.1080/10632913.2021.2023059.

Stevenson, L. M., & Deasy, R. J. (2005). *Third space: When learning matters.* Washington, DC: Arts Education Partnership.

Thomson, P. (2020). *School scandals: Blowing the whistle on the corruption of the education system.* Bristol: Policy Press.

Thomson, P., Coles, R., Hallewell, M., & Keane, J. (2014). *A critical review of the Creative Partnerships archive: How was cultural value understood, researched and evidenced?*Swindon: Arts and Humanities Research Council.

Thomson, P., Jones, K., & Hall, C. (2009). *Creative whole school change: Final report.* London: Creativity, Culture and Education; Arts Council England.

Wilkinson, J., & Kemmis, S. (2014). Practice theory: Viewing leadership as leading. *Educational Philosophy and Theory*, 47(4), 342–358. doi:10.1080/00131857.2014.976928.

Winner, E., Goldstein, T., & Vincent-Lakrin, S. (2013). *Art for arts' sake? The impact of arts education.* Paris: Educational Research and Innovation, OECD.

Woodley, H., & Morrison McGill, R. (2018). *Toxic schools: How to avoid them and leave them.* Melton: John Catt.

3

THE ARTS-BROKER TEACHER

Maria enjoyed art as a child and went to art classes. She remembers going to a big Manet exhibition but says that it was her A-level experience that made her want to be an artist. She took a "slightly circuitous route" through architecture and social and political science, then worked supporting young people with serious illnesses. "There were a lot of young people that I met who were dying and I thought if I only had a year left to live what would I do? And I thought that I would go to art school." Maria then found a Foundation Art course, her future work and her identity.

Maria trained as a painter but switched to sculpture. She was initially a self-employed artist but also did a lot of work in schools through Creative Partnerships. She then did an artist-teacher PGCE and worked part time as a supply teacher, before taking on a permanent part-time position in a large London school. Being part-time allows her to do her own work, which she regularly exhibits. But for Maria, the arts and teaching are inextricably linked: "My practice is a lot about discovering new ways of working and I will feed that back to the kids. And they might try something that will make me think about something in a different way."

Maria wants her students to be as familiar with the visual arts as she is and to love them as she does. She sees this as being centrally about the cultural assets available in the local area: "How do we engage the students with what is going on around us? Because we are a central London school." Early in her time at the school she wanted to take students to a blockbuster exhibition at a national gallery but realised that the entry charge was too high. She wrote to the gallery to ask if she could discuss the question of payment and whether a form of part-nership might be possible. The result was the formation of a School Ambassador group, which mirrors the gallery's Youth Collective. The gallery–school relationship brings mutual benefits: "If we can help them with anything we will and they will assist us, so we have this reciprocal relationship. They will give us tickets and I give those to older teenagers on the condition that they take another teenager."

Maria argues that this relationship, one of many that she and her colleagues have established, fulfils an important aim "to create an art-loving population" but one that is not in awe

DOI: 10.4324/9781003093084-3

of apparently elite institutions: "We can walk in a double lesson to [gallery] … Our big argument is that this is your collection and you own it. … It helps students feel that they are part of an establishment … and that gives them an enormous amount of cultural capital." Maria sees herself breaking down barriers to arts institutions that could remain out of reach for reasons of generation, cost and class. There are also immediate educational benefits, as students learn from what they see: "You can see it in the art department, they make contemporary art, video work, installations and quite conceptual pieces of work." Maria's students are not simply a more educated audience for other people's work but are also engaged in current artistic conversations and debates.

Maria's story introduces the second of our key concepts, the arts-broker teacher. Although Maria's story is particular to her own location, background and interests, Maria's approach to her work resonates strongly with the way many of the other arts teachers we interviewed talked about their lives and work. In the TALE research project, we interviewed 60 arts teachers each year for three years. They weren't all engaged in creative practice themselves as Maria was (though many of them were), and most didn't work within walking distance of a major gallery. But they had a lot in common in other ways: namely, a passion for their subject and an intense interest and engagement in arts and culture. Nothing surprising about that in a good arts teacher, you might well think. What struck us though, as we listened to more and more of their accounts of their work, was the degree of – what we came to call – *brokerage* involved in their teaching.

In Maria's account, she talks about her role in making connections for her students: to her own artistic practice, to cultural events and activities in the local area, to a prestigious national gallery. But the connections are not all one-way (out of the school); they are also about bringing ideas and experiences back into school, re-contextualising them and encouraging students to make them their own. In these ways, we see Maria as engaged in arts and cultural brokerage – a distinctive, vitally important and generally undervalued aspect of arts teachers' pedagogy that we discuss and exemplify in more detail in the rest of this chapter.

Defining arts-brokerage

A broker is usually understood as someone who acts as an intermediary in negotiations; they 'broker a deal'. The notion of brokerage is used in academic writing literatures to describe the role and actions of a knowledgeable, and usually senior, academic who mentors and supports the publication activities of less experienced colleagues (Thomson & Kamler, 2013), or those new to English-language publication (Lillis & Curry, 2010). The senior colleague has expertise and experience that they share. The term cultural brokerage is usually applied to people who work in intercultural settings: it has, for example, been used in health (Jezewski, 1995; Willis, 1999) and in education (Wyatt, 1978–79) to describe nurses and teachers who mediate across cultural boundaries in order to prevent misunderstanding and discrimination and promote mutual and reciprocal learning. In this context the notion of brokering culture has been critiqued for lack of reciprocity and implicit paternalism and colonialism (McKinley, 2001). However, the idea of boundary crossing and mediating is one that became highly relevant to our research with arts teachers.

In thinking about arts teachers as brokers, we have taken something from each of these versions of brokerage. We start from the position that a teacher who is an arts-broker has expertise and experience in the arts. They provide mentoring and support to students to engage with the arts and encourage students to cross borders into arts territories they do not know. However, they do not assume a lower status for the students' own arts interests, experiences, practices and knowledges. We also extend the notion of the broker to include a more active pedagogical dimension of encouragement, enthusiasm, explanation and support. The actions of a teacher arts-broker are thus more than simply organising an excursion or inviting an artist to give a talk or two. A teacher who is an arts-broker not only makes available to students arts and cultural media, genres, events, disciplinary norms and professional practices, but also shows through their own everyday passions and pastimes what engaging with the arts can mean – arts as integral to living every day.

The concept of the arts-broker teacher has something in common with the notion of the teaching artist, or artist-teacher, common in the visual arts sector. There is much debate about the two terms and their overlap. One view is that teaching artists are often understood as identifying as professional artists who teach, integrating their studio practices with their pedagogy. Artist-teachers on the other hand are qualified teachers who also have artist training and maintain an artistic practice. Artist-teachers often come to teaching via art and see that their teaching is an extension of their artistic practice, as did Maria. The production of art is central to both teaching and their own work; classrooms are modelled on studio practices, and teaching is seen as an aesthetic practice which supports students to develop artistic dispositions (Daichendt, 2010) – "studio thinking" as Hetland, Winner, Veneema and Sheridan (2007) have called it.

These debates about the terms teaching artist and artist-teacher are instructive for thinking about our concept of arts-brokerage. There is no agreement among researchers and professionals about whether having an arts practice is a necessary prerequisite for teaching, or whether being immersed in arts practices and discourses is sufficient (Thornton, 2011). Or, indeed, whether arts and education are easy to put together: as Baldecchino (2019) points out, contemporary art practices are committed to openness, paradox and unlearning, whereas contemporary schooling is concerned with the acquisition of predetermined skills and knowledges. Atkinson (2011, 2017) sees this tension as having potential for productive disruption and critique, particularly as the arts afford global and historical connections which support highly diverse identities and experiences (Vella, 2016). Sayers (2019) argues that fostering openness, developing critique and supporting diverse identities, means that artist-teacher pedagogies should "treat arts and culture as a lived experience not simply something from the past to be found in galleries and museums or copied in the art classroom". Sayers' point can be widened to include theatres, screens, workshops and studios. As Sayers puts it, "Young people should be encouraged to understand the idea that they are part of culture, it doesn't just happen to them, they create it in many different forms."

The notion of being part of the culture and of being an active participant and cultural creator is central to arts-brokerage. This notion of cultural engagement is more significant in arts-brokerage than whether the person identifies as an artist or creative practitioner of some sort and has a well-developed creative practice. Maria's story illustrates what cultural engagement means for her: that students have the right of access to cultural institutions, to participate in contemporary debates, genres and platforms. These commitments not only underpin her teaching, but also her advocacy on behalf of her students.

TALE and arts-broker teachers

The 60 arts teachers we interviewed over the three years told us a lot about their own initial arts experiences. Like their headteachers, many of the TALE teachers had been encouraged to engage with a range of arts forms at home. *I have a very strong memory from when I was eight and we went to see A Midsummer Night's Dream in Stratford and there were all these pink umbrellas in light bulbs in the park. And I was like, "This is what I want to do". I suppose because it was just so magical and I just always understood it ... Because I did a lot of drama outside of school I knew a lot about it when I came into school because I'd been doing it since I was five.*

Most of the TALE teachers had had positive experiences with the arts at school and they wanted this for their students. They were strongly committed to ensuring that their students' arts experiences would be rewarding. *I always remember myself as an 11-year-old student whose passion was the performing arts but who didn't particularly get a great experience from school, because the focus was on the more academic subjects. And many people didn't see the performing arts as an academic subject which it definitely can be. So I just want the students I teach to have a better experience of it from somebody with a real passion for the subject, rather than it just being an add-on. I just want to inspire students and for them to feel like it's a decent passion and aspiration to want to perform.* Arts-broker teachers are particularly concerned with widening access to meaningful arts experiences. *One of the greatest privileges of teaching is taking somebody to the theatre for the first time. We do that a lot with kids who are from families that don't access theatre. To be sat alongside a student who is watching a play for the first time is brilliant.*

TALE teachers maintained a strong interest in the arts outside of school and were well connected to local arts communities within their city, town or county, as well as with national arts organisations. They were frequent visitors to theatres and galleries. *I go to the [local theatre] quite a lot and I think it has an extensive and comprehensive programme. You can see stand-up comedy or the Royal Philharmonic Orchestra or Shakespeare. They get many of the big West End shows coming down here, like Warhorse. So I always enjoy going there quite a lot. I love the [contemporary art gallery] because there always seems to be something different there. There is a vibrant music scene down here too and we have many festivals ... there is a lot more here than meets the eye.* In these few words, this teacher conveys something of her lifestyle and her familiarity with the local arts 'assets'; she offers a positive evaluation of and exhibits something like local pride in the variety of arts events that are available in her town. It is not surprising, then, that she wants to bring this into the school. *I went off into the [town] cultural scene looking for a storyteller. I went to a very interesting local group in a café where local amateur writers meet and it was there that I found a storyteller. And so I've got her in and she's skilled up a group of Year 9 pupils who are now storytellers ...*

Arts-brokers actively breached symbolic institutional borders; they made the school permeable, finding ways to connect with local artists and arts organisations that brought new practices and experiences to students. Arts-broker teachers kept up with arts debates, events and key figures and regularly updated their own knowledge of who-is-who and who-is-doing-what in the arts field. They saw this as just part of who they were and what they did. Their arts engagement was as familiar and natural as breathing.

We can understand this 'naturalness' by turning to Bourdieu, whose notion of social fields we sketched out in the introduction. Here, we reprise some key points and elaborate, in particular, on arts-broker teachers as agents in two fields. We then go on to outline the logics of their pedagogical practice.

Fields, dis/positions and agents

Field is a heuristic which can be used analytically to better understand the ways in which, for example, education (or other fields like science, art or literature) produces and reproduces variously inequitable social relations, practices and truths (Bourdieu, 1988; Bourdieu & Passeron, 1977, 1979). A field is social, cultural and material and is occupied by people and things which are, and act, in relation to each other. Here, we are concerned with two fields: education and art.

Fields are populated by agents (institutions and actors) who occupy social positions (in education, we might think of positions such as headteachers, teachers, business managers and so on). Agents are continually engaged in field practices, and their actions generally follow a dominant logic designed to acquire capitals (social, cultural, symbolic and economic) through which they can advance, or at least maintain their position relative to others (Bourdieu, 1977). We are not suggesting that arts-rich schools are one position, as this is determined more by the school's location, population, system distinctions (inspection rating and exam results) and sector (academy, grammar, local authority, etc.). However, within each position, arts-richness might confer particular status and distinctiveness.

Even though fields are reproductive they are also not uniform. They are chiasmatic − that is, they are marked by continued struggles for position. Within any field, there are agents acting counter to dominant modes; oppositional doxa (beliefs and truths) support resistant and counter status-quo practices. Change in a field is thus not only possible but inevitable; fields are not homogeneous but are continually conflicted. This lack of uniformity/conformity is why change occurs. Bourdieu's study of the field of European art (Bourdieu, 1991), for instance, documented how avant-garde art eventually gained dominance in the field:

practices that were once oppositional became prominent, in part through a new economics (the art market) homologous with the wider field of capital.

Field relations are hierarchical, both vertically and horizontally. So a headteacher has more status and more highly valued capitals than a teacher (vertical) and a head in a pupil referral unit has lower status and less highly valued capitals than a head-teacher of a selective grammar school (horizontal). While fields operate in similar ways (they are homologous), in that they are concerned with the logics of differ-entiated positions, each has its own particular set of capitals and its own ways of explaining their value (doxa). Doxa often misrecognise the ways in which field practices produce and reproduce inequitable hierarchies of position and capitals (Bourdieu, 1998).

Agents learn how to act in the particular fields in which they have a position. This learning becomes a kind of embodied second nature (Bourdieu called this habitus). Agency – what agents do – can be understood as a continued interaction between the embodied understandings of action and temporal/spatial contexts. Habitus, understood as a constellation of dispositions, is formed in the ongoing interactions between field, capitals and field positions. Arts-broker teachers pos-sessed dispositions from both the arts field and education.

Agents are disposed, by virtue of who they are, where they have been, and their life experience in positions, to act and be in particular ways. It is an illusion, Bourdieu suggests, to think that any one actor is an individual: we are all socially situated and act in relation to others in the field (Bourdieu, 1987). Thus, arts tea-chers in part prepare students taking arts subjects by ensuring that they have the relevant capitals, doxa and dispositions for the arts field(s) and wider cultural life as well as those valued in the education field.

Bourdieu notes that field change is often driven by agents who experience a deep rift between their habitus and the dominant strategies in the field. It is possi-ble for such agents to act in ways counter to the dominant logics of practice and/or doxa of the field in which they occupy a position, drawing on subjugated strategies and capitals. In chiasmatic fields we can therefore expect to find positions and agents that act according to different logics, logics which are opposed to the dominant. So, because of their positioning in two fields with different capitals, practices, logics and dispositions, agents who are arts-broker teachers are potentially positioned as opposed to the dominant logics of the education field (see also Chapters 5 and 6, which discuss pedagogy in more detail.)

The arts-broker teacher position

We look now at the arts-broker teachers' actions; these are key to both the peda-gogical logics of the arts-rich school and the formation of arts-participation dis-positions in students. As previously noted, the TALE study provides strong evidence about shared aspects of arts teachers' practices. Here we discuss two key interrelated practices that were common to teachers in our study, regardless of whether they were working with performing or visual arts and regardless of the school they were in. The practices were (1) working with a 'students as artists' perspective, and (2) using a repertoire of core arts-brokerage strategies.

(1) Working with a 'students as artists' perspective and pedagogy

Students in English schools are very often treated as 'becomings'; that is, teaching is organised around exams, course entry and jobs, preparation for the future. In contrast, the visual and performing artists teachers that we observed and interviewed started from the position that students were, in their rooms, 'beings', already artists.

It just seems sensible and obvious that you would want students to embody the behaviours, practices and thinking of professional artists. If they made it to that professional status by being immersed in it every day and, even if you only have your students for an hour a week, if they can take on some of that attitude, then surely that is a more authentic way to learn to do that discipline.

In the performing arts, supported by the RSC, TALE teachers used professional practices – ensemble (Neelands, 2009), and rehearsal room (Franks, Thomson, Hall, & Jones, 2014). They engaged students in dramaturgical discussion about possible interpretations and directorial decisions about the translation of ideas into action and staging. In the visual arts, teachers worked through topic-focused modules which offered students the opportunity to work separately and together to design and complete ambitious projects. Such visual arts projects extended students' interests and prior understandings, referred to and intertextually used work of other artists, and required continuous documentation of their thinking and experimentation. We say more about these pedagogies in Chapter 5.

In both art forms students were able to bring the 'texts of their lives' (Fecho, 2011) into the classroom, connect activities with 'big ideas' and bring knowledges from other disciplines to the realisation of their projects (Beane, 1995). The teachers carefully steered students' learning, providing leads to relevant intellectual and material resources, setting milestones, challenging students to take risks and make mistakes from which they could learn. They used whole-class instruction and skills-oriented and practice exercises to support the development of understanding, knowledge, expertise and craft. Senior students were expected to use their initiative, work very independently, research extensively and to explain their artistic choices. Teachers thus had to have deep knowledge of each students' interests, strengths and weaknesses in order to 'negotiate' the curriculum (Boomer, Lester, Onore, & Cook, 1992) in ways that pushed students to do more than they had originally imagined. Teachers used their disciplinary lexicon, and norms and expectations derived not only from the education curriculum frameworks, but also from professional theatre and visual arts arenas.

(2) Using a repertoire of arts-brokerage strategies

The TALE teachers who acted as arts brokers generally used all, or a majority, of the following seven strategies:

(a) Teachers embodied what it means to be culturally engaged

Teachers in our study were deeply engaged in the arts. They regularly attended a wide range of events, exhibitions and performances. Some also directed, acted, made and showed their own work. They were part of local, regional and national artistic networks. Their art-field capitals included knowledge of a wide range of artists, works, genres, galleries, theatres, festivals and studios and, thus, some understandings about the visual and performing arts markets. Teachers shared their out-of-school experiences and knowledge with their students, routinely talking about what they had seen and done and what they read, creating an ongoing classroom conversation. Teachers' experiences and arts knowledges were resources used to make the formal curriculum current.

(b) Teachers ensured students regularly visited local and national cultural events, institutions and organisations

Despite the paperwork associated with excursions, and within the restrictions of school funding, teachers saw visits to cultural institutions as integral to their classroom programme, not a treat or a special occasion. *For us as a creative department we think that the arts are so valuable that we cannot explain the feelings you get from walking into a gallery space and seeing a large sculpture or viewing a piece of work or going to the theatre and actually seeing somebody perform. We have drama shows and music performances but there is always the opportunity for our students to see what the next step could be.*

Whether it was a trip to a local theatre to see a play for drama or English, or to a gallery or museum to look at artwork or artefacts, teachers viewed visits as offering a range of benefits. These included changed social relations with peers and understandings about arts work, accessing a shared culture and new levels of aesthetic experience. *The students are constantly looking at things. And you are giving them artists to look at in books and on the internet but they are not really experiencing what the artwork is about and they haven't got a clue about the texture or the feel of the actual art work, or the scale of the work and how that makes you feel. I know myself that I've seen things in the past in a book, but when you actually see the piece of artwork sometimes it really speaks to you …* *Sometimes you take them out to see things and that can be a turning point for these students in terms of where they go in their life.* Visits extended students' horizons and offered the opportunity not only to see and understand a new place but also to see their own place afresh.

(c) Teachers actively sought out and used students' and communities' cultural resources

It was important to arts-broker teachers that students did not get the idea that the only arts worth engaging with were those that they did not do or have. Arts-broker teachers understood neighbourhood and students' arts practices as cultural participation and as learning resources. *They can choose a project that they want and they say that they've*

got materials at home that they use. They say 'My dad bought me this' or 'My nan does draw-
ing' and I say 'Bring them in and we can photocopy them and you can put them in your book'.
They like having that creative freedom and having that nurturing. And they come up to you at
break time and say, 'Miss, I did this last night'.

Visual-art teachers filled their rooms and corridors with students' artwork, and often created gallery spaces within the wider school. The visible intertextuality (references to a wide range of advertising, youth cultures and current events) in these works attested to the inclusive approach taken by their teachers. *We are going to express what we think about things and we are going to really think about who we are as people and what is important to us. And we are going to express that through the art that we make. That is what we are doing with Year 9 and they absolutely love it. So they are making statement t-shirts and screen printing statements that they believe in onto t-shirts. And even the ones who are usually cynical are so engaged. And they are making really lovely statements about being original and loving yourself and all of these things. Not one of them is doing anything stupid. They are all thoughtful and meaningful.*

Performing-arts teachers encouraged discussion and improvisation around com-munity events and concerns and pressing social issues. *Our students will come and see me if they want things changed. We did something for the Nigerian Chibok girls because we were so angry about it and we wanted to empower our girls and give them a voice. We feel that part of our arts curriculum enables our students to ask those questions about what is happening in the world.* Students' concerns often appeared in interpretations of canonical texts, including Shakespeare's.

(d) Teachers arranged for artists and cultural organisations to visit their schools

Despite the expense, arts-broker teachers saw the importance for students of regular contact with professional artists and their work. *We always bring artists in and we have very good links with several [city] artists. The pupils are always up for working with artists who come in. The value of the museums and galleries is invaluable within education because it's like saying to someone 'What are you going to do?' and they say 'I'll write a short story' but we don't show them what a short story looks like. We're trying to get our pupils to buy into the idea of creating something and yet if we are just telling them how to do it, it's completely different to them seeing something that is going to inspire them. For me, if they are not inspired and they don't see things in a real space, then we are doing our pupils a disservice.*

Working directly with artists and practitioners presented the teachers with a variety of teachable opportunities, ranging from the substantive topic of the event/practice and meaningful encounters with working professionals, to consideration of disciplinary norms, habits, ways of working and the language and terminology of the discipline. Teachers took advantage of travelling theatre productions and workshops specifically aimed at schools, and they welcomed artists-in-residence to create artworks and engage with students. Visiting artists were often asked to make work with students about local lives and the local environment. *We network really well – if it's the National Theatre's Connections festival or the Shakespeare festival, we are part of those professional networks and, where we can, we will use professionals with the kids. So we'll have visiting artists and actual practitioners coming into school or we'll take the kids out to galleries, museums and theatres.*

Extra-curricular and the formal curriculum were blurred through visits, everyday life and school joined together, and the substantive arts experience formed a bridge between home and school.

(e) Teachers provided opportunities for students to exhibit and perform for wider audiences

Performing and exhibiting created an interlinked set of learning opportunities. Students made work not simply for assessment but for wider and public audiences. Students' immediate families were often able to attend, view and understand what their children were doing, and perhaps become more connected to the school. *We have some of our Year 11 artwork on display at the Hepworth Gallery and we do 'Create Ed' which is linked to the University of Falmouth around creative writing and design work and art. And that gets displayed at the university. We have got a lot of those links going on and actually some of the work on display at the galleries gets sold, so those things are highly motivational because they can actually see a career path with it.*

Sometime the arts-broker teacher had to take an active advocacy role with artists and arts organisations and had to be persistent in the pursuit of opportunities for students. *We worked with a local photographic gallery and they hadn't shown pupils' work before. It was a little bit rocky in the first instance because the original director of the gallery wasn't keen on having students' work on show, but there was a change of director and the new one had a very forward notion of where they should be going. They were incredibly supportive and so we ended up with three days' proper exhibition in the gallery. It was a remarkable set-up because the pupils were part of the curatorial team and it was an incredibly fruitful learning opportunity for them. It demystified the whole process of how things happen.*

Through exhibition and performance other faculties in the school saw and understood what happens in the arts; their value was on view. Opportunities for joint work with local and national arts organisations allowed students to experience arts disciplinary processes and norms in semi-professional contexts. Through exhibitions and performance students moved from the position of consumer to that of producer. They learnt that artists make work which asks and receives audience response, communicates ideas (some of which might be highly critical of the status quo), is marketed and sold. They began to understand that the arts are 'institutional' – theatres and galleries have their own particular modes of operation, places in the market and so on (they are positions in the art field). Teachers used exhibition and performance as occasions to clarify and begin to instil professional norms.

(f) Teachers connected students to arts workplaces

Teachers often used their own personal networks (social capital) and went out of their way to build new connections that could bring their students into contact with the arts and cultural industries. They saw the obvious connection between work experience and choosing to study an arts subject. But they generally viewed workplace programmes not as suggesting possible career pathways to students, but more as showing students what working in the arts, other than teaching, could be like. *Our remit it about connecting with creative practices within the South West and so, over this year alone, we've had our students out about six times. The kids are either going out or someone is coming in. We've had an illustrator in this week and, because of the way our timetable works, five times a year we spend time on project-based learning, and that basically is bringing in the sector into the school and looking at real-life projects. For example, today our product design students are looking at package design for a large bakery in the South West and the managing director has said that if they like the designs we make they will use them. And the students went to the factory yesterday and looked at the packaging that they've had in the past and they've thought about how they might improve it. So this is different from working in a more traditional school where you might go up to London and visit the Tate but wouldn't have those explicit links with the sector.*

Arts workplaces are steeped in (often inexplicit) professional capitals – ways of talking and doing things. *We are working very closely with the digital industry in Manchester to make sure that our curriculum is fit for purpose. We've just been to New York as well and we went to visit McCann's which is a design agency that we work with over here and we also worked with the London office on a big project last year on mental health. When we were in New York we took students to visit their studio which is right next to the Chrysler Building and they got to see how a design is produced right from the concept.* Not all schools are able to afford such trips. However, arts-broker teachers were keen to use what resources were available to them.

As well as the more general work-related acts of meeting deadlines, being accountable and working collaboratively, arts workplaces generally have ways of allocating time and space for ideas generation, exploration and critical evaluative 'quality' conversations. The dispositional and the doxic were available for student apprentices. They could learn how to behave, speak, think and 'play the game' of the arts and the arts field.

(g) Teachers worked to enhance arts participation in their communities

Bringing artists and theatre companies into school to perform created a cultural experience for the local community. Teachers in rural communities, or in communities without well-developed theatre cultures, saw this as an important access strategy. However, teachers often went much further. Teachers were often engaged in local arts initiatives which would bring substantial benefits to their schools and their cities and towns. *We have quite a close partnership with a local theatre which is in the old town and we have done for many years. One of the things I've done every summer is I volunteer to run a summer workshop for kids right across all the schools in (local towns) for students aged 14 to 19. I've done it every year for the last ten or so years.*

Engagement with community arts development was not divorced from school; students clearly benefited from enhanced arts activities in their area. Nor was it removed from the arts-broker teachers' own lives; they and their families also benefited from a wider range of local arts. *We were literally bringing the plays out into sites in the community where people could access it easily. And last year when we did A Midsummer Night's Dream I think [the local theatre] had something like 43% of people attending who had never been to a theatre before.*

Teachers brought an understanding that the arts involve 'place-making' practices; they enhance local social bonds and build and strengthen social and cultural capital. Arts-broker teachers often took a 'big and integrated view' of community and the arts, as this extended quotation shows: *We talk about education being part of the community so we try to make the school building a part of the community. Because [the town] has got a theatre, but having another theatre is a good thing. So we can offer touring plays another venue in which to perform. We've got certain companies who use our space and they attract quite large audiences. So there is that further opportunity for our students to see theatre on their doorstep, because money is an issue.*

Also it is important to get the community behind the young people: demystify young people for the community but also capitalise on what the community can offer those young people. We are now established as part of the rural touring circuit and companies have come to [our town] recently to do outdoor productions, which I can't remember ever happening before. But I think the message has got out that actually [town] is somewhere that will support theatre and we are definitely part of that.

I am now also fostering a relationship with the Eden Project so we might organise a 'youth takeover day' where young people are performing around the Eden Project for a day. For me, from a personal level, it is just great to have those connections because it gives the students a chance to get that first-hand experience of working in theatre, and I think we've raised their aspirations.

In sum, then, the arts-broker teacher does more than simply organising the occasional excursion or inviting artists to give talks. They make a wide range of capitals − elite and vernacular arts and cultures, various genres and events, disciplinary norms and professional practices, new networks − available to students. They also embody, through their own everyday arts passions and pastimes, an *arts world disposition*, as we now go on to explain.

Arts-world dis/positions

We have argued that the arts-broker teachers we studied occupied a dual position, being in both the arts and education fields. We see arts-broker teachers as possessing a 'hybridised' (Adams, 2006) arts-world disposition; that is, they take as natural and right the practice of making pedagogies from embedded and embodied understandings of arts world practices. They adhere to art-field doxa about the importance of arts activities, and work to produce arts capitals and an arts disposition, just like their own, in their students.

In other projects (Thomson, Jones, & Hall, 2009), we have explored the practices of arts teachers in 'arts-poor' or arts-indifferent schools who try to maintain arts-broker pedagogical practices. This can be an uphill battle in an arts-hostile educational field and in a school keen to maintain its position in the current field but needing to contend with arbitrary accountability measures, inspection, funding cuts, enrolment and reputational struggles. However, the vast majority of TALE teachers in our study were not experiencing crippling difficulties. They were able to make their arts-world disposition into practice; the conditions in their corner of the school as field were largely favourable. They were not, however, exempt from the effects of the wider education field, as we discuss in Chapter 6.

There is a productive synergy between arts-broker teachers and the arts-rich school. Arts-rich schools need arts-broker teachers in order to become and be arts-rich. Arts-broker teachers thus generally feel valued. Their subjects are given time and resources and their partnership work with practitioners and arts organisations is recognised as important. Their work is integral to the school's identity and is frequently and meaningfully represented in school publications, websites, assemblies, open nights and so on. Many arts-brokers teachers had warm relationships and ongoing conversations with their senior leaders. Many, but not all, senior leaders also encouraged arts-broker teachers to be active learners. *I think the arts are valued here and we are very lucky in that we don't take knee-jerk reactions to things. We still have to counter-balance things all the time and it is not made easy for us. It's about keeping that morale as well, because sometimes it feels like certain things are getting a battering in the press or in the media. But when you are a school like ours everything is about the students and the students' experience, and as long as we keep that at our core we will win that fight – because it does feel a bit like that sometimes. I wouldn't be where I am without my cultural experiences and my theatre studies at A Level and things like that, which give you something that other things can't. We have got some really talented students and we want to make sure that we showcase that talent.*

In interviews, TALE teachers often spoke about the 'fit' between their arts-rich school and their own beliefs and practices. Some had chosen the school because of its commitment to the arts; in other instances, the school had chosen the teachers because of their practice. The harmonisation of teacher and school is important as it not only demonstrates the correspondences in position between institution and agents, but also points to the ways in which it felt, and was, both 'right' and possible for teachers in arts-rich schools to use their art-world positional capitals and practices. The logics of the field strategies used by the arts-rich school – forming and maintaining a particular identity, developing an explicit philosophy about a broad and balanced curriculum, recruiting students and locating the school in the market on the basis of its arts offer – depended on the practices of arts-broker teachers. While core subject teachers were responsible for keeping the school in line with audit and test results, arts-broker teachers were supported to ensure that the school was well connected with local, regional and national arts organisations and events, and students engaged in ambitious projects that demonstrated their, and their teachers', expertise. The arts cultural capitals of the school were also instantiated through extra-curricular activities, excursions and public events.

The arts-broker teacher made their school arts-rich. They translated the cultural goals of the school, animated and made them material, vernacular and specific to the local area and school mix. Reciprocally, the arts-rich school recognised and resourced the arts-broker practices of the teachers. Together, an internal arts-rich school field was produced and reproduced, a field in which the arts had sufficient distinction for students to continue to choose arts subjects in large numbers, despite the external, wider, field trends in the opposite direction. The higher rates of students' cultural participation reported in our survey (see Chapter 8) attest to the likelihood that at least some of the parents and students chose the school on the basis of fit, and that the reciprocal field work of school leadership and management strategies and teachers' arts-broker dis/positional practices complemented family (primary habitus) capitals.

We now turn to consider what this analysis might mean for social justice. Do the arts-rich school and the arts-broker teacher positions and logics of practice simply reproduce hierarchies in the education field and beyond?

Reproducing dis/positions

The TALE study suggests that being an arts-rich school can be a successful field strategy. However, as field success is now dependent on exam results which exclude the arts, the onus of maintaining field position largely falls to other subject teacher positions and practices, and management and leadership strategies. The arts per se are perhaps currently more connected to parental aspirations and enrolments than the official policy logics. But although there may have been a majority of students whose parents possessed particular arts cultural capitals in harmony with those on offer in the arts-rich school, this was not the case for a significant minority. A quarter of students told us that it was their school that introduced them to the arts and one third reported that they depended on their school for ongoing arts engagement (see Chapter 8). We can assume with some confidence that the arts-rich school position did reproduce cultural capitals for the majority of students, but at the same time it also produced new cultural capitals for the rest.

This leads us to ask whether the arts-rich school and the arts-broker teacher are simply inculcating middle-class tastes, capitals, disposition and practice. This must, to some extent, be the case. But one of the key practices of arts-broker teachers was to recognise, seek out, make connections with and promote in the curriculum local vernacular cultural practices and local arts and cultural organisations. While schools in poor areas were particularly keen that knowledge and experience of elite cultural institutions were not left only to students whose parents could afford to take them there, they did not ignore the students' own everyday cultural practices and their particular arts interests. They were also very often keen to include youth cultural practices in the formal curriculum. Both the visual and performing arts curriculum approach was more 'omnivore' than partial: Shakespeare and rap, three-dimensional objects and Instagram and so on.

The 'omnivore' is arguably now the constellation of cultural capitals that dominates the cultural industries and the marketised arts and culture field (Friedman, 2012; Peterson & Kern, 1996). While only a minority of students in our survey and focus groups intended to go on to work in the creative industries, a highly classed, raced and gendered sub-economic field, all of them did intend to continue to engage in the arts. The arts were, almost all of the students in focus groups told us, part of the way that they wanted to live their lives. In other words, by the time they were in senior school, students who chose the arts had an arts-world disposition. Continuing with an arts practice seemed natural and desirable. We can be relatively confident in suggesting that an arts-rich school does reproduce, but also produces, a highly contemporary arts-world disposition, in keeping with the overall role of the education field in producing capitals and dispositions for other fields.

However, arts-broker teachers did not simply reproduce an elite art-field disposition. They did not simply produce artists destined for employment in the creative industries and arts consumers. They saw all students as artists, and thus capable of critical and reflective practice. In the performing arts, students were encouraged through rehearsal-room approaches and dramaturgical and directorial practices to see a Shakespearean text as socially constructed, as an elite art form which nevertheless raised important questions about power and the workings of social institutions. In the visual arts, students were encouraged to focus on the ways in which the world worked, the art world functioned and their position in it. In both art forms, and in keeping with arts-brokers teachers' art-field dispositions, students were encouraged to be reflective and reflexive about their own positioning and practices. The arts-broker practice was one which was not simply reproductive, but also produced counter art-field resources – capitals and strategies. Chapter 6 addresses these tensions and possibilities. The next chapter discusses the ways in which arts-broker teachers were professionally sustained and developed.

References

Adams, M. (2006). Hybridizing habitus and reflexivity: Towards an understanding of contemporary identity? *Sociology*, 40(3), 511–528.

Atkinson, D. (2011). *Art, equality and learning: Pedagogies against the state*. Rotterdam: Sense Publishers.

Atkinson, D. (2017). *Art, disobedience and ethics: The adventure of pedagogy*. London: Palgrave Macmillan.

Baldecchino, J. (2019). *Art as unlearning: Towards a mannerist pedagogy*. New York: Routledge.

Beane, J. (1995). Curriculum integration and the disciplines of knowledge. *Phi Delta Kappan*, 76, 616–622.

Boomer, G., Lester, N., Onore, C., & Cook, J. (eds). (1992). *Negotiating the curriculum. Educating for the 21st century*. London: Falmer.

Bourdieu, P. (1977). *Outline of a theory of practice*. Cambridge: Cambridge University Press.

Bourdieu, P. (1987). The biographical illusion. *Working Papers and Proceedings of the Centre for Psychosocial Studies (University of Chicago)*, 14, 1–7.

Bourdieu, P. (1988). *Homo academicus* (P. Collier, trans.). Stanford, CA: Stanford University Press.

Bourdieu, P. (1991). *The love of art: European art museums and their public* (C. Beattie & N. Merriman, trans.). Cambridge: Polity Press.

Bourdieu, P. (1998). *Practical reason: On the theory of action.* Oxford: Blackwell.

Bourdieu, P., & Passeron, J. C. (1977). *Reproduction in society, education and culture.* London: Sage.

Bourdieu, P., & Passeron, J. C. (1979). *The inheritors, French students and their relation to culture.* Chicago: University of Chicago Press.

Daichendt, J. (2010). *Artist teacher: A philosophy for creating and teaching.* Bristol: Intellect Books.

Fecho, B. (2011). *Writing in the dialogical classroom: Students and teachers responding to the texts of their lives.* Urbana, IL: National Council of Teachers of English.

Franks, A., Thomson, P., Hall, C., & Jones, K. (2014). Teachers, arts practice and pedagogy. *Changing English,* 21(2), 171–181.

Friedman, S. (2012). Cultural omnivores or culturally homeless? Exploring the shifting cultural identities of the upwardly mobile. *Poetics,* 40(5), 467–489.

Hetland, L., Winner, E., Veenema, S., & Sheridan, K. (2007). *Studio thinking: The real benefits of visual arts in education.* New York: Teachers College Press.

Jezewski, M. A. (1995). Evolution of a grounded theory: Conflict resolution through culture brokering. *Advances in Nursing Science,* 17(3), 14–30.

Lillis, T., & Curry, M. J. (2010). *Academic writing in a global context: The politics and practices of publishing in English.* London: Routledge.

McKinley, E. (2001). Cultural diversity: Masking power with innocence. *Science Education,* 85(1), 74–76.

Neelands, J. (2009). Acting together: Ensemble as a democratic process in art and life. *Research in Drama Education,* 14(2), 173–189.

Peterson, R. A., & Kern, R. M. (1996). Changing "highbrow" taste: From snob to omnivore. *American Sociological Review,* 61(5), 900–907.

Sayers, E. (2019). The artist teacher. In *Oxford Research Encyclopaedia of Education.* https://doi.org/10.1093/acrefore/9780190264093.013.401.

Thomson, P., Jones, K., & Hall, C. (2009). *Creative whole school change: Final report.* London: Creativity, Culture and Education; Arts Council England.

Thomson, P., & Kamler, B. (2013). *Writing for peer reviewed journals: Strategies for getting published.* London: Routledge.

Thornton, A. (2011). Being an artist-teacher: A liberating identity?. *International Journal of Art & Design Education,* 30, 31–36.

Vella, R. (ed.) (2016). *Artist-teachers in context: International dialogues.* Rotterdam: Sense Publishers.

Willis, E. (1999). From cultural brokers to shared care: The changing position of literacy for Aboriginal health workers in Central Australia. *Studies in Continuing Education,* 221(2), 163–175.

Wyatt, J. D. (1978–79). Native involvement in curriculum development: The Native teacher as cultural broker. *Interchange,* 9(1), 17–28.

4

IMMERSIVE PROFESSIONAL DEVELOPMENT

We are in the fifth year [of the partnership] now and it seems more like a three-way partnership with the RSC, the [local] Theatre and us as the school. We get a lot from the RSC and they get a lot out of us, so it does seem like a very good relationship ... we've been able to work with them to tailor the in-service to what we think our needs are and what can really support the work that we are doing ...

Partly I think it's a trust thing. Before we were probably seen as the lesser of the three [partners] because we were a school. But now there is more of an understanding of the level of commitment that we make to the programme in order for it to be successful and the achievements that we've secured over the course of the five years that we've been working with them. Those things haven't just happened because of the RSC and the [Theatre] but it's been down to all three partners. I think they've learnt to appreciate us and to understand how much time and resources we've put in. For me that has been the biggest thing and it seems that we are now being seen as an equal partner rather than the lesser of the three.

It [the professional development] is really exciting and varied and there is something in there that you can get out regardless of what you do. When we've had them down here for our in-service some of our staff said that it was the best CPD [continuing professional development] sessions that they've ever had. It is definitely relevant, and it is having an impact on those staff. They've got a variety of resources and packs that are available and, depending on what we are looking for, they are able to tailor their workshops to our needs as a cluster.

[At first] ... it felt very kind of prescribed but now it is much more open. We have identified that written approaches are really important to our cluster and so, therefore, we need exercises that are going to help the teachers to bring things back into the classrooms, because that is ultimately what teachers do. I mean, performing at the [Theatre] is great but it's the cherry on the cake and not the cake itself, which is all the teaching that goes on. Unless those activities are really easily transferable without a huge amount of work from the teachers within the class, they are not going to be able to use them.

DOI: 10.4324/9781003093084-4

We've looked at a number of texts and the confidence is developing. We were very clear that we didn't just want to look at the mainstream texts – Romeo and Juliet, A Midsummer Night's Dream and Macbeth – but we wanted to open people's eyes a little bit and make them realise that the RSC techniques are transferable ... so people had more confidence to feel independent and to go away and have a go at things. I hope it's made people feel more capable and confident ... I think they've been really good and certainly our cluster schools have got an awful lot out of it.

It's more immersive when you go to Stratford. We had a training weekend in January last year where all but two of the Associate Schools were able to attend. So we were up there for two days and they really felt special because they were in Stratford working directly with the RSC. They were completely immersed in the world of the RSC. That has been one of the highlights from the feedback that we got from the staff. The local CPD sessions are really good when you've got a particular focus that you need to work on, but the RSC weekends in Stratford are more enriching. And having the two days instead of one gives them the opportunity to throw themselves into it and to relax and to switch off from school a little bit more than they can with the one day. I think they get more out of it. And the fact that they are all there together as a cluster was really great for them because they were connecting with each other and sharing their practice. I know some of them have become quite good friends, so that is a really nice outcome for the school and that wouldn't have happened necessarily at a local in-service because it's just about the time that people have to commit to it.

These comments from Lucy, a senior teacher who oversees her school's partnership with the Royal Shakespeare Company (RSC), introduce the themes and some of the critical perspectives we explore in this chapter, which is about the nature and potential of partnerships between schools and arts organisations, and about the professional development of arts teachers. We have used her word, "immersive", an adjective used by other teachers we interviewed too, to name the key concept developed in this chapter – immersive professional development.

Lucy is clear about the benefits of partnership to the teachers and students in her school; her account also serves to illustrate some of the work that goes into developing and sustaining mutually beneficial and equitable partnerships and professional development that is really responsive to teachers' needs. We return to Lucy's comments as we develop our discussion.

Our research in the TALE project involved in-depth investigation of the different models of teacher professional development offered by the RSC and Tate. We set out to understand the particularities of the ways in which these differing models worked, but we also had the wider aim of throwing some light on the general question of what, and how, arts teachers learn from close engagement with cultural organisations. So we move in this chapter from a focus on what we learned from studying the specific RSC and Tate models of professional development, to a more general discussion about approaches and principles. In the final part of the chapter we focus on partnerships, reviewing some of the literature in this area.

We begin by outlining the two professional development models we studied and then report on what the teachers made of them.

Two models of professional development

Tate and RSC adopted innovative but different approaches to teachers' continuing professional development (CPD). Tate's Schools and Teachers team offered individual teachers the opportunity to engage in immersive experiences, either through a network, through single CPD events or through an intensive Summer School that took place at the gallery. Through encounters with artists and artist-mediated materials, teachers were encouraged to experience, as learners, the pedagogical principles of open-ended, critical aesthetic enquiry. They were supported to consider how they might create learning experiences that encouraged questioning, exploring, challenge, play and interpretation.

The RSC's professional development offer involved key teachers in working alongside RSC professionals to embed active 'rehearsal room' approaches to studying Shakespeare's texts across a national network of schools. This offer was rooted in the real-world work of actors and directors committed to working together as an ensemble to explore the interpretive possibilities of the texts they were performing. The slogan 'Stand up for Shakespeare!' encouraged teachers to get out of their seats and use their bodies, minds and emotions to interpret, voice and get involved in staging Shakespeare's plays. The RSC then actively supported the teachers to use these approaches in their classrooms: RSC Education team professionals visited schools to work alongside teachers with students; they offered extra in-service training in school; they encouraged the sharing of the ideas and approaches and helped the teachers build clusters of schools in the same locality. These clusters were often linked with a local theatre partner as well as the RSC (as in Lucy's description, above).

Both the RSC and Tate offered extra support, materials and resources for teachers. Both offered engrossing and engaging group experiences, in the Tate gallery spaces or in the rehearsal spaces at Stratford-upon-Avon. Both offered teachers the chance to work directly with professional artists. For the RSC, where the main aim was to promote a single playwright whose work the national curriculum already required students to study, the agenda was perhaps more narrowly focused. Through their Learning and Performance Network and Associate Schools Programme, they followed through on the 'Stand Up for Shakespeare' agenda, offering longer-term and more sustained support to individual teachers to build localised communities of practice.

Teachers' experience of professional development

There is an overwhelming amount of evidence in the TALE interview data to suggest that teachers generally found their CPD experiences with the RSC and Tate extremely rewarding. Lucy's response, quoted above, in which she describes the CPD as "really exciting", is replicated hundreds of times throughout the dataset. A strong and consistent theme across the data is the teachers' perception of the professional learning with the arts organisations as transformative. Typical comments were:

- *It was their training and CPD that changed my career.*
- *Because it is all practical, it makes a big difference.*
- *For myself, it's definitely changed the way I teach, because it has changed the way that I teach everything.*
- *I suppose the biggest thing is the change of mind-set for myself. Because I come back to my school and I say, "What about this?"*
- *It's been transformative in terms of my own practice.*

How do we account for this extremely positive response? Although the RSC and Tate models of professional development are different, our analysis revealed congruences in key principles and approaches, which are key to the success of both. These key principles are:

1. **The experience is immersive**. There is time to develop focus and flow, to tackle problems and allow ideas to grow. The experience has intellectual and embodied, physical and emotional, aesthetic and pedagogical dimensions.

    - *The training courses at Stratford with the RSC initially were the most inspirational training that I've ever experienced because you put yourself in the position of the student so you are fully immersed in the activities but, at the same time, reflecting as a teacher.*
    - *You realise that you have to be inspired yourself to teach anything interesting, so I did the Summer School, which was really intense. Within an hour there were people crying! I got to meet lots of interesting people and I did some bold things and ended up – we were doing performance pieces and I'm a swimmer and I'd been swimming that morning and we had to take selfies. I can't remember the artist who was running it, but I had my goggles and I had my swim kit with me. And I made a video piece where I walked throughout the Tate Modern in my swimming kit for about half an hour, which was actually really liberating. The whole thing was more than I thought it would be.*

2. **Teachers work with highly skilled professionals whose disciplinary norms and identities are different from their own**. Teachers engage with the ways theory and practice are combined within the specific discipline. They experience the way practice brings together language, thinking and different artistic perspectives (for example, curatorial, dramaturgical, art historical); they have opportunities to consider how these might be taken into the classroom.

    - *[The RSC team are] very relaxed and it feels like you're doing things really slowly and then, all of a sudden, they take you to somewhere where you think "How did we get here? How did they cover this much material?" They do it with such ease and it's unbelievable actually. It's been really useful for me to bring back and try and copy that practice. It is really impressive stuff but they just make it look easy. Everyone in the room makes so much progress without having a clue about how far you are being pushed. Every time you go down you meet different professionals who work in completely different ways.*

- *I went to Tate for the pop-up summer school and that was the best experience I've had. It brought everything into this idea of, as a person, you've got everything you need; you just stand up and you can make art. The people teaching on that were just awesome and they just inspired me to try performance with everything that I do and so every painting becomes a "Why am I doing this" "Why am I working from top to bottom?"*

3. **The professionalism of both teachers and artists is recognised and respected**. These professional spheres are understood as distinct but complementary. It is assumed that each group has something to learn from the other.

    - *I'm not a drama person but what I really like about the RSC in this school is that you are always asked for your opinion. Even though I am not trained in the dramatic arts I can always make a comment that will be listened to. It was absolutely brilliant.*
    - *The Tate has worked with teachers over many years and they've invested a lot in those relationships. They build in unique opportunities for schools to attract them in the first place and it means that it's easy for us to work with them. And they think about schemes of work and how things might fit in with the exams. They have a vision about education and I think that is pretty much unique.*

4. **There is an investment in building sustained relationships.** Individual teachers feel they have a personal relationship with the arts institution. Careful attention is paid to building group dynamics and to establishing the expectation of a continuing relationship.

    - *It's a highlight of the year because there is a great group of people that do it who we've worked with for a long time. It's really motivating and there is overlap from year to year in terms of what we do but there is always new stuff. And the RSC are amazing hosts who make you feel like a valued professional so that feels like a real treat.*
    - *It's been a five-year journey which started at my last school but has completely changed my whole pedagogy and my whole attitude towards teaching.*

5. **The importance of place is recognised**. The affordances of the arts buildings and spaces are used: the design, the symbolism and status. The location and the local connections of the schools are also seen as important resources to be drawn upon and celebrated.

    - *That really was something special because you are up there and you are in Shakespeare's country and seeing the productions and working with experts in their field and talking to other teachers from other schools about how they are working.*
    - *It was just amazing. It was really fun and it was also in the year after I had my kids so I'd spent a year being very enclosed and just doing baby things. And then I got to go to London for a week and do art at the Tate, and it was amazing.*

These principles were evident, though differently operationalised, in the CPD offered by both the RSC and Tate. Both institutions offer initial immersive experiences that give teachers privileged access to prestigious arts venues, highly skilled professionals and top-quality resources. The immersive experience involves working together, as a group of teachers (sometimes from the same locality, as in Lucy's account) and as a cross-professional group of teachers and arts practitioners, to develop understandings about how national resources can be made meaningful to school students through the mediation of the teacher. The immersive nature of the experiences focuses the participants on learning in the present moment, but there is always an implied future for using this learning, back in school with pupils.

For teachers the immersive CPD experience allows them to re-engage with their own earlier disciplinary identities, as art or drama students; for all the teachers there are connections to their out-of-school identities and interests in the arts. Importantly, though, the connections here are not just to gaining knowledge about systems in and for schools. The CPD builds specialist disciplinary knowledge about the possibilities of the art form, and the criteria for making judgements and critical distinctions. These experiences provide a rich web of social and artistic connections within which to develop professional learning and identity. The teachers we interviewed spoke about their high levels of personal motivation to engage in the CPD activities, their commitment to the particular organisation they were working with, their enjoyment of learning alongside other teachers from a range of schools and their determination that their own students should benefit from the experiences they themselves were having. For arts-broker teachers in particular, the CPD was a powerful re-encounter with an art world they had been involved with in their undergraduate education, and for some it supported and strengthened links with the art form they were involved with outside of school. The CPD was an important affirmation of arts-brokerage or a stimulus to move in that direction.

The teachers' levels of engagement, intrinsic motivation and commitment to ongoing professional learning with Tate and the RSC stood in marked contrast to their responses to the one-off training courses and most of the 'internal' CPD they were offered. The chance to gain new specialist arts knowledge was vital to what the teachers were doing. One interviewee referred to this as *bonding through content*. He went on to explain the impact this had on teaching and learning in his school:

> *You get, like, adverts to become a teacher where they sort of wave at each other and then talk about the football results. And that's fine, to have those good relationships with young people and be able to engage with them around that stuff. But the meaningful relationship is through the content that you are studying and the struggle you are having with it in the classroom. We do readings every week in our SLT [senior leadership team] meetings and we share content and talk about it, and that actually deepens our relationship with one another. And, from that, we are now thinking about a kind of stretch project in Year 7 where we will introduce students to more difficult readings, because ... we think it would be great to do difficult content with them and relate as a*

group over content. I think the rehearsal room is a really good metaphor for these things and, through content, you can have a meaningful relationship with young people. So that is where my thinking is at.

One way to understand what the teachers learned from these CPD engagements is in terms of personal and professional identities. We develop this discussion in the next section.

Personal and professional identities

We know from the rich autobiographical accounts in our interview data that engagement in the arts – as practitioners, as audience, as critics and admirers – was a highly valued element in almost all of the teachers' personal identities. They had been interested, excited and moved by art works of various kinds throughout their lives; this was almost invariably the basis of their personal decisions to become students, and then teachers, of arts subjects. The arts were integral to their primary habitus. Meaningful engagement with cultural organisations played an important part in maintaining this element of their identities: they were interested in the work that was going on, wanted to keep abreast of new developments, saw arts and cultural engagement as important to their social lives and the enjoyment of their leisure and family time. For some, the commitments of busy professional and family lives had reduced time and opportunities to express this aspect of their personal identity. These teachers particularly welcomed the opportunity to immerse themselves in the arts again and to re-connect with some of their earlier creative experiences. They were already highly disposed to engage with the CPD on offer.

Our particular concern here, though, is with the effectiveness of the development of teachers' professional identities. This begs the question of what is meant by 'professional', a topic on which there is an extensive literature and debate in the field. The literature proposes and contests different ideas about professionalism and professional identity, but generally agrees that notions about teacher professionalism are changing.

Work by Evetts (2008, 2011) and Sachs (2003, 2016) has been useful to us in developing our analysis. Both commentators identify two broad definitions of professionalism. The first, which Sachs calls "democratic professionalism" and Evetts calls "occupational professionalism", values collegiality and collaboration. Evetts (2008) describes this kind of professionalism as "a discourse constructed within professional occupational groups; it incorporates collegial authority. It involves relations of practitioner trust from both employers and clients. It is based on autonomy and discretionary judgement and assessment by practitioners in complex cases."

Sachs (2003) argues that the rise of managerialism in schools has led to a reframing of ideas about professionalism, shifting the focus to performance and accountability, compliance rather than autonomy. Evetts (2008), however, sees this as "organizational professionalism", which she defines as a discourse used increasingly by managers in work organizations. It incorporates rational-legal forms of authority and hierarchical structures in decision-making. It involves increased standardization of work procedures and practices and managerial controls. It relies on externalized forms of regulation and account-ability measures such as target setting and performance review.

Sachs (2016) argues that different types of CPD for teachers produce different kinds of teacher professionalism and that accountability regimes position teachers as compliant practitioners rather than autonomous professionals. She accepts that:

> These types of professionalism are ideal types and their application in practice may not necessarily be … clear-cut … Nevertheless, there is a chasm between the desires and expectations of teachers and governments to the extent that governments are drawn to and endorse organizational/manage-rial professionalism, while teachers are likely to favour occupational/democratic professionalism.

The literature on what counts as 'good' professional development suggests that four key factors are important: the CPD helps teachers gain new insights, pursue new goal-directed behaviours, acquire new skills or techniques, and embed these changes in their practice (Sims et al., 2021). The design of CPD then aligns CPD with student learning outcomes, is prolonged rather than short term or one-off and has follow-up activities to support teachers to develop new pedagogical practices (Cordingley et al., 2015). It is helpful to note the synergy between this evidence and the CPD offered through the RSC and Tate, although these effectiveness characteristics can also easily be made amenable to the organisational professionalism that Sachs critiques.

Despite its focus, proponents of organisational professionalism often pay scant attention to the teachers' needs to keep up-to-date in their subject areas. Initial teacher education generally focuses in depth on how to teach a subject – how, in Shulman's (1986) terms, to develop "pedagogical content knowledge" alongside "content knowledge" (or subject knowledge – what to teach). But the content of subject disciplines changes over time and, unless teachers have the opportunity to regularly update their knowledge and understanding, the subject – and the peda-gogical content knowledge that gives students access to it – becomes ossified and teachers become deskilled.

These distinctions were very clearly articulated – though not precisely in these terms – by the teachers in the TALE study. Increasingly, because of national policy changes, the professional learning opportunities on offer to the teachers were about developing their organisational professionalism: courses explaining the examination requirements, or generic in-house training about school or trust-level policy implementation. These courses, however important to the day-to-day running of the school, were fundamentally about decisions that had already been made, about managerial control, external regulation and standardisation. CPD with the arts organisations stood in stark contrast to this managerial model. Premised on occupational/democratic professionalism, the CPD offer relied upon the co-construction of meanings, the authority of the group and the teacher's discretionary judgement. The teachers recognised its value to them as individuals and to their identity as subject teachers, and they generally responded to the mode of working and to the underpinning philosophy by engaging wholeheartedly.

We have pointed out, in identifying the four CPD principles listed above, the similarities between the ways in which the RSC and Tate approached teacher learning. Both organisations provided immersive arts experiences for groups of teachers, who were expected to collaborate with one another. The teachers were given access to the resources of the venue, the art works and the staff who worked there. There was a warm welcome, an expectation of ongoing dialogue and attention to nurturing the relationship. There was recognition of what we might now call occupational or democratic professionalism: attention to building collegiality and trust, valuing of the individual and the complementary areas of expertise of group members. All of these elements are mentioned in Lucy's reflection at the start of this chapter.

There were also opportunities for aesthetic experiences. As Maxine Greene (1995, p. 378) indicates, an aesthetic experience involves more than just being exposed to a work of art. She argues that "there must be conscious participation in a work, a going out of energy, an ability to notice what is there to be noticed" – all of which were features of the CPD sessions we observed and the teachers reported on. Greene goes on to point out the crucial balance between being able to "pay heed" – appreciate, name and know about the features of an artwork – and being able to fully engage with it aesthetically. "Knowing about", even in the most formal academic manner, is entirely different from creating a world imaginatively and entering it perceptually, affectively and cognitively.

To introduce people to such engagement is to strike a delicate balance between helping learners to pay heed – to attend to shapes, patterns, sounds, rhythms, figures of speech, contours, lines, and so on – and freeing them to perceive particular works as meaningful. The teachers told us that this aesthetic sense – of being freed up to perceive works as meaningful – was a notable feature of both the RSC and Tate professional development models. Both models encouraged 'conscious participation' in the art-making; they were energetic and highly attentive to what there was 'to be noticed'. They achieved, in Greene's terms, the delicate balance between paying heed to the detail and freeing individuals and the group to create new interpretations and personal meanings from the works. The principles that underpinned the design of both programmes (immersion, attention to the specificity of place, exposure to the norms of the arts discipline, respect for democratic/ occupational professionalism, relationship-building) engaged the teachers perceptually, affectively and cognitively.

Bourdieu is also helpful in understanding this CPD practice, the term 'immersion', the notion of professional identity and how these relate to the arts-world dispositions of the arts-broker teachers discussed in Chapter 3. We can think of the

CPD as operating at an intersection of the field of arts and education, at the borders of schooling. The artists brought with them arts-field practices, logics, ways of relating, talking and acting, ways of thinking and naming. Because the arts organisations initially ran the CPD sessions, as Lucy suggests, it was their practices which dominated activities. It was their practices which formed new, or strengthened existing, teacher dispositions.

Bourdieu argues that dispositions develop through being enmeshed in a field over time (Bourdieu, 1977, 1990). Through engagement with core field practices, agents acquire ways of thinking, talking, acting and relating; they develop a 'sense of the game' of the field which, over time, becomes natural to them. Often without consciously thinking about what they are doing, they adopt the mannerisms, bodily stance, tone of voice and expression, tastes and opinions that are common in the field. Bourdieu argues that dispositions work as lived reflexes; we are disposed to act in particular ways – we have learnt to do this. Just as expert tennis players move to the ball and position their bodies without consciously thinking, any agent immersed in a field over time comes also to act in ways that feel, natural and 'right'. Bourdieu famously describes this as being a "fish in water".

We can see the formation of dispositions in our RSC and Tate data. The time and intensity of teachers' interactions with the artists and arts organisations were significant in supporting the growth of a visual or performing arts disposition. The immersive and affective CPD called for teachers to do, walk, make, read aloud, feel, observe, interact and enact as practising artists and performers, and this was crucial in supporting embodied and embedded dispositional development. And teachers acquired this arts-field disposition without necessarily realising, at first, that this was happening. Teachers in Tate activities who were art and design trained often referred to the activity as "taking them back to art school".

The arts-discipline disposition then became a resource for pedagogical work. The teachers literally carried their arts-field engagement back into the classroom in their minds and bodies. Exactly how they translated this engagement into classroom pedagogies depended, in part, on the students and the contexts of the schools in which the teachers worked. Generally, though, from our observations, we could see that the same principles operated in the teachers' classrooms as in their CPD programmes. The lessons were designed to immerse students in their work, to be attentive to place, to build relationships and to help students understand disciplinary norms and acquire disciplinary skills. As we report in Chapter 7, students overwhelmingly told us that their arts lessons were different from other lessons. The lessons gave them a sense of freedom and a chance to make decisions and judgements that increased their belief in themselves, made them feel good and encouraged them to work hard. This, we think, is in part the aesthetic freedom Greene alludes to: the space to make meanings and connect ideas to your own life and interests. The pedagogies the teachers employed, which in many ways reflected the pedagogies of the CPD engagements with the arts organisations, generated in students the same sense that the teachers experienced on their courses – that there was freedom to explore and create, and that there were no 'right answers'. The sense of being a valued individual within a collegial group of peers was common to both.

As we have already mentioned, the students also told us that their arts teachers were different. In Chapter 3 we explained our analysis of this distinctiveness in terms of the arts-brokerage role that was an important aspect of the pedagogy of so many of the teachers we studied. These were culturally engaged teachers who modelled and shared that engagement with their students. In Maxine Greene's terms, they were teachers who consciously participated, were energetic about making connections and creating opportunities and were committed to noticing. Through sharing their own enthusiasms and ways of looking at the world, they allowed students a glimpse of what arts and culture meant to them. Students appreciated this and told us they learned a lot from it.

What we observed, then, were professional development sessions with cultural organisations that helped to sustain and further develop the arts teachers' personal identities and interests, their disposition, but they were also congruent with the pedagogical values and approaches they operated with in their professional lives – values and approaches that are in danger of being marginalised within the system and, sometimes, in the schools the teachers worked in. This work was sustained through institutional partnerships which, at their best, worked very effectively to the mutual benefit of all concerned. But sustaining these partnerships, as Lucy points out at the start of the chapter, was not always plain sailing.

The erosion of CPD opportunities

Research suggests that subject-specific CPD is less commonly available to teachers in the UK than generic CPD. Generic CPD is apparently easier to provide. As one review puts it, "Financial constraints, teacher workload, the need to prioritise external accountability requirements and the move to school-led improvement all contribute to a culture in which subject-specific CPD is rarely prioritised despite widespread recognition of its value" (Cordingley et al., 2018). It is thus not surprising that a 2022 Teacher Tapp survey (12 May 2022, 7377 responses) reported that only 15% of teachers reported that their last INSET day was 'very useful', while 35% found it 'somewhat useful', 20% 'slightly useful' and 26% 'not particularly useful'. Our research adds further to this picture.

Over the course of the three years of the TALE research project there were marked changes in the amount and type of continuing professional development available to teachers in the case study schools. *In the past but not now – I haven't got the time for it at the moment because things are so full-on, so I've not done anything outside the school.* Opportunities for teachers to engage in professional learning out of school were being reduced by pressures on budgets, which also had an adverse effect on levels of staffing and therefore on the available time. *CPD now is almost non-existent within school just because of financial difficulties.* These pressures, combined in some schools with agendas arising from inspections, academisation or reorganisation into new trusts, led to an increase in 'in-house' CPDL: *my CPD just has to fit in with whatever the school's agenda is for its teaching and learning.* For many of the teachers, recent professional development had consisted largely of being briefed about the changes to the examination system: *for the past couple of years, we've had to do exam moderation courses because GCSE and A Level courses are changing.*

Generally, the teachers we interviewed drew a distinction between professional learning related closely to their discipline and more generic professional development sessions. They recognised the necessity, but also the limitations of what was currently on offer to them. *If I could choose between going for professional development at the Tate over professional development for my specification for the exam board, I would choose the Tate. Unfortunately, I have to know about the exam boards and that's the problem.* Some recognised the impact this was having on their teaching. *I'm increasingly frustrated by CPD and I don't think it is unreasonable to say that I would like to do some CPD that I think would make my teaching or art better than it is by exposing me to some practitioner who may be able to give me a way of working.* One teacher said: *My least concern, when it comes to teaching and learning, is what is on the Ofsted list of things you have to do. I know the way I want to teach and I know what works although I am open to new ideas, but not just for the sake of it. But SLT are preoccupied with this list and, when it comes to CPD, my CPD just has to fit in with whatever the school's agenda is for its teaching and learning. But I think that when you teach something really well and you do it with a passion, then I think kids get that and that is what they want. I don't think they need to have all those tick-box ideas that are driving education.* Another teacher expressed the tension this way: *If you are a full-time teacher in a school it is such a tight system and you get really focused on trying to get the grades and you tend to forget that there are other ways of thinking about art.* We discussed these tensions between the art and education fields in the previous chapter and we pick up this discussion again in Chapter 6.

With regard to CPD, arts-broker teachers tended to resolve these pulls in different directions by using their own time and resources to make sure they maintained the kinds of professional development they valued most:

- *we can't go for an arts-based professional development course during the day, we have to do that in our own time.*
- *I do a lot of professional development, but I tend to do it on my practice.*
- *For me, as a teacher, it's a chance to go to a gallery or do professional development and it's opening a lot more doors than me going to a professional development for [the examination board]. For example, seeing the work of young artists and meeting practitioners who would possibly have something to offer the school.*

Because of the blurring of what is work and what is personal participation, arts-broker teachers may be particularly prone to paying for their own professional learning. The use of personal time for professional development is largely undocumented and not discussed. However, a recent survey of art and design teachers conducted by the UK All Party Parliamentary Group for Art, Craft and Design Education (2023) showed that nearly one in ten secondary teachers had not attended any subject specific professional development since their initial teacher education, and that two-thirds of art and design teachers in both primary and secondary schools routinely pay for their own CPD, which is conducted in their own time (not in school time). The RSC professional development offer notably expects a large proportion of the CPD that they offer to occur during school time. Tate also offers some in-school time professional learning, and bursaries for teachers whose schools would not pay for their attendance at Summer School.

It is fair to say that, in the arts, the subject-specific professional development available to teachers is largely provided by subject associations and by arts organisations, rather than their schools. This is one reason why arts-rich schools have prioritised making and sustaining partnerships with arts organisations. Their CPD offer is thus able to be made bespoke as well as secure.

School arts education partnerships

School partnerships are invoked for a variety of purposes, including to create or cement notions of community, to promote academic achievement, to fill gaps and meet students' basic needs, to improve the flow of financial or other resources and to contribute to righting social wrongs (Perkins, 2015). They are also used to influence, to promote reform and sometimes to exert control (Burgos, 2004; Popkewitz, 2004). This range of purposes is evident in the activities of schools' arts education partnerships. Some, for example, are focussed primarily on access to theatres, galleries, etc. and on civic engagement. Others involve projects related to specific subjects and sometimes exam syllabuses, or to more generalised encouragement of creativity, or to filling gaps in the school's curriculum where arts provision is squeezed. One-off performances and events create opportunities for creative sector workers to be employed in school, contribute to audience building for the arts and are often argued for in terms of enhancing the cultural capital of particular groups of pupils. Often, of course, the partnerships aim to meet several or all of these purposes, and to add others.

These are valuable initiatives. However, as schools' arts education partnerships have proliferated, commentaries on how they function have drawn attention to potential – and actual – drawbacks inherent in some partnership models. In an article about arts partnerships in Canadian elementary schools, Hanley (2003) argues that, in the long term, partnerships can be deleterious to the quality of arts education. The possible damage, she argues, comes from the channelling of resources into the partnerships rather than investing them in specialist arts teaching and teachers. She worries about generalist primary school teachers losing confidence in teaching the arts, specialist arts teachers becoming isolated, arts education associations losing their power to influence. She points out that exposure to the arts does not in itself promote meaningful learning; that high-quality arts education needs to be continuous, sequential and focussed on skill development and process. Partnership initiatives, on the other hand, are often one-off or short term and therefore fragmented, focused on performances or exhibitions as the main outcomes. The danger, Hanley says, is that these partnerships pass for arts education on the grounds that specialist teachers cannot be afforded, there are no qualified teachers available, or the staff does not include teachers competent to teach the arts. This is possible she argues because of the depreciation of the role of arts educators and a general willingness to denigrate teachers and teacher preparation programmes and accord them lower social status than artists and fine art education.

In an article about the Norwegian Cultural Rucksack programme, Christophersen (2013) analyses some of the ways in which this marginalisation and devaluing of teachers' work occurs, even in the context of a widely supported and admired national school arts programme. She observes a competent and experienced music teacher who had been told by a visiting professional musician not to interfere in the musical processes, but who nevertheless subtly facilitated the event to prevent the visiting musician's lack of experience with school children from becoming a real problem. When asked about this, the teacher said, "I offered to help him in the music room, but he said he didn't need it. But I help him anyway; I have to" (p. 5). Because of what Christophersen calls "a perceived twosomeness between artists and students", the teachers sometimes feel redundant, or reduced to acting either as assistants to the visiting experts ("helpers") or as disciplinarians who keep order and intervene to ensure good manners ("guards").

The issue highlighted here is not, then, simply about a devaluing and underutilising of the teacher's expertise but also a lack of clarity about the nature of the partnership. Who are the partners? As Christophersen puts it: "A dyadic relation between artists and students may leave little room for teachers" (p. 8), an exclusion which diminishes the potential educational gains of the partnership and also weakens its sustainability. Kenny et al., in a more recent study of six artist–teacher pairs in Ireland, also highlight the negative connotations of the teachers', in comparison to the artists', role (Kenny & Morrissey, 2021). However, in this case the response was to "disrupt the negative–positive binaries embedded in these categories" by using the partnership to encourage dialogic relationships that "enabled the blurring of boundaries between the identity categories of teacher and artist" (p. 5). So the aim of these partnerships was, in part, to disturb and then blend aspects of the different partners' roles.

These studies raise important questions about the distinctiveness of the roles and the relative positions of the teachers and artists in schools' arts education partnerships. They also beg the question of how – and perhaps whether - the partnerships offer direct educational benefit to students.

The case studies of the RSC and Tate partnerships throw light on these problems. Fundamentally, the TALE schools' arts education partnerships worked well because they took proper account of the importance of teachers' work. They were pedagogical partnerships; enhancing teaching and disciplinary knowledge were at their heart and defined their purpose. They avoided the pitfalls identified by Hanley, Christophersen et al., recognising instead the pivotal role that arts teachers can play in brokering cultural opportunities and ideas to the young people they teach.

Although some teachers also have identities as artists, and some artists are also teachers, the roles are distinct. An arts teacher's role is to introduce students to a range of forms and genres and technologies; to help them develop skills and creativity, find meaningful forms of self-expression and debate ideas and different points of view. But it is also to help students make cultural connections out from and back into their homes and, more widely, to help them become active cultural citizens. Effective schools arts education partnerships, like the two we have considered here, explicitly support and enhance this brokerage element of arts teachers' role. They give teachers – and through them, students – privileged access to arts venues, skilled professionals and high quality resources.

The teachers we saw in the Tate and RSC programmes were immersed in arts learning at their own level. Immersion is a powerful tool to promote professional learning but it involves trust, and an investment of time and energy that teachers often initially feel wary about expending. We contend that the teachers were ready to make this investment because the terms of the partnership were clear: the partnership was between the teachers and the arts organisation. The purpose was clear: to enhance pedagogy. The relationships were open and dialogical, built over time, based on respect for one another's work and an understanding that the professional spheres and identities were distinct but complementary. There was no attempt to blur roles; it was assumed that each group had something to learn from the other. Arts professionals recognised the teachers' pedagogical expertise; they built trust by acknowledging the professional requirements of teachers' day-to-day work, skills and knowledge and the specificity of teachers' commitments to the communities they served. Lucy's comment reminds us of the importance of this: *I think they've learnt to appreciate us and to understand how much time and resources we've put in. For me I think that has been the biggest thing and it seems that we are now being seen as an equal partner.*

In the next chapter, we look more closely at teaching and learning in arts classrooms.

References

All Party Parliamentary Group on Art Craft and Design Education. (2023). *Art now; Report on the teacher workforce.* London: APPG on Art Craft and Design Education.

Bourdieu, P. (1977). *Outline of a theory of practice.* Cambridge: Cambridge University Press.

Bourdieu, P. (1990). *The logic of practice* (R. Nice, trans.). Stanford, CA: Stanford University Press.

Burgos, R. B. (2004). Partnership as a floating and empty signifier within educational policies. In B. M. Franklin, M. N. Bloch, & T. Popkewitz (eds), *Educational partnerships and the state: The paradoxes of governing schools, children, and families.* New York: Palgrave Macmillan.

Christophersen, C. (2013). Helper, guard or mediator? Teachers' space for action in The Cultural Rucksack, a Norwegian National Program for arts and culture in schools. *International Journal of Education and the Arts,* 14(1), 1–17.

Cordingley, P., Greany, T., Crisp, B., Seleznyov, S., Bradbury, M., & Perry, T. (2018). *Developing great subject teaching – Rapid Evidence Review of subject-specific Continuing Professional Development in the UK.* London: CUREE.

Cordingley, P., Higgins, S., Greany, T., Buckler, N., Coles-Jordan, D., Crisp, B., … Coe, R. (2015). *Developing great teaching: Lessons from the international reviews into effective professional development*. London: Teacher Development Trust.

Evetts, J. (2008). Introduction: Professional work in Europe. *European Societies*, 10(4), 525–544.

Evetts, J. (2011). A new professionalism? Challenges and opportunities. *Current Sociology*, 59(4), 406–422.

Greene, M. (1995). Art and imagination: Reclaiming the sense of possibility. *Phi Delta Kappan*, 76(5), 378–382.

Hanley, B. (2003). The good, the bad, and the ugly – Arts partnerships in Canadian elementary schools. *Arts Education Policy Review*, 104(6), 11–20.

Kenny, A., & Morrissey, D. (2021). Negotiating teacher–artist identities: "Disturbance" through partnership. *Arts Education Policy Review*, 122(2), 93–100.

Perkins, T. (2015). School–community partnerships, friend or foe? The doublespeak of community with educational partnerships. *Educational Studies*, 51(4), 317–336.

Popkewitz, T. (2004). Partnerships, the social pact and changing systems of reason in a comparative perspective. In B. M. Franklin, M. N. Bloch, & T. Popkewitz (eds), *Educational partnerships and the state: The paradoxes of governing schools, children, and families*. New York: Palgrave Macmillan.

Sachs, J. (2003). *The activist teaching profession*. Buckingham: Open University Press.

Sachs, J. (2016). Teacher professionalism: Why are we still talking about it? *Teachers and Teaching: Theory and Practice*, 22(4), 413–425.

Shulman, L. (1986). Those who understand: Knowledge growth in teaching. *Educational Researcher*, 15(2), 4–14.

Sims, S., Fletcher-Wood, H., O'Mara-Eves, A., Cottingham, S., Stansfield, C., Van Herwegen, Anders, J., Brien-Pallas, L. (2021). *What are the characteristics of teacher professional development that increase pupil achievement? A systematic review and meta-analysis*. London: Education Endowment Foundation.

Warburton, E. C. (2022). TikTok challenge: Dance education futures in the creator economy. *Arts Education Policy Review*, https://www.tandfonline.com/doi/abs/10.1080/10632913.2022.2095068.

5

SIGNATURE ARTS PEDAGOGIES

Art teachers are entirely different to the other teachers I've had. Most teachers stand at the front while you sit down and talk to you. In art even if we are talking before studio time, it's always more of a discussion.

It's a different teaching style. Miss won't stand up at the front. She comes around and talks to you one to one. It's like you're in a class on your own.

They're there if we need them. They come round and give us advice.

She's more of a guide.

She helps us develop skills and styles.

If you are stuck and you don't know what to do next, Sir will give you guidance and that keeps you going for a while and then you might get stuck again and so on until your exam ... so it's like a build-up of course work.

You are left to do what you want to do and then they come around and see if you are on track and you can ask what you need to improve and they'll come and tell you.

She gives you an interpretation.

The teacher is just there to guide you. You don't rely on the teacher – you are motivated and organised.

Teachers inspire and help you come up with ideas.

We're independent but the teachers help shape our visions.

They don't tell you exactly what to do. They just give you a nudge if you are going off course.

The teacher has to be aware of each student individually. And be one step ahead of them so can advise them what's best for them.

The teachers are there to back us up but we are on our own learning curve right now.

If you need help, Miss will come to you rather than the teacher speaking to the whole class.

Early on it's more teacher led, teaching skills. Later it's more making connections, facilitating – someone to voice ideas to and get something back, rather than being told what to do.

DOI: 10.4324/9781003093084-5

If you go to an arts teacher and say, "I'm thinking of doing this but I don't know how to do it", they'll try to accommodate you rather than say, "You can't do that because that is not part of what we should be doing."

If it doesn't go well, they'll help you change it to what it should be but still fit with your original plan.

When you are studying in a classroom you don't really have that connection with the teacher in a way. They [arts teachers] are less of a teacher and, this might sound weird, more of a friend.

These comments, direct quotations from some of the 14–19-year-old students interviewed as part of the TALE research, introduce the key points we discuss in this chapter. The young people we talked to were generally very perceptive about the arts teaching they experienced: they had a clear idea of the roles their teachers adopted – usually described by the students as a guide or a facilitator – and of the ways in which their teachers worked – through personalised encouragement and feedback, listening to and building on students' own ideas, offering resources and interpretations. There was a remarkable degree of unanimity in what they said about their arts lessons. And one very strong message leapt out at us from the data: they said that arts lessons felt different to lessons in other subject areas and that they made the students themselves feel different too.

We were intrigued by what the students told us; the arts lessons felt different to us too. The first and last quotations above, in particular, pick up some of the ways students talked about these differences and the feelings they generated: the types of talk were different, the teachers' movement around the room was often different, the students felt a different sense of connection to the places where the lessons were taught.

We wanted to understand more about *why* arts lessons felt different and the impact this had on students. Our analytic tools were chosen to help us answer these questions. We set out to identify patterns and suggest ways of understanding processes and outcomes across the TALE schools. Our hope, of course, is that the analytical framework and key concepts we have identified will provide a degree of analytic generalisability – that they will prove useful for the analysis and understanding of other classrooms in other schools in different contexts.

In this chapter, we focus on the 'why they felt different' question; in Chapter 6 we discuss the impact of this teaching on students' personal development and sense of identity. We begin, though, by reviewing some ideas about how feelings, atmosphere and mood are produced and might be understood, before moving on to apply these to the arts classrooms we studied. The key concepts in this chapter are mood and atmosphere, and signature pedagogies.

Atmosphere, mood and cultural feelings

Thinking about feelings took us to the literature on affect. Affect theory focuses on the ways in which non-linguistic effects – feelings, mood, atmosphere – help to shape day-to-day realities. Affects can, in some respects, seem nebulous and elusive: they are not necessarily within our conscious control, or even our immediate awareness; they are difficult to capture in words. But as social beings we all have experience of the importance of atmosphere and mood and their relationship to the creation and expression of feelings. So, we dim or turn up the lights, choose the right music, dress appropriately to the occasion, slow down or speed up the rhythm, smile or look serious, make coffee or light a scented candle ...

For teachers, understanding the power of affect is essential to their professional practice. Teachers need to know how to create moods and atmospheres that support learning. They need to know how to respond to and work with the affect of their classes: moods and feelings that might stem from particularities – the time of the day or week, the weather, what happened in the last lesson, individual pupils' misfortunes or fallings-out or excitement – or, more likely, from a combination of factors, some of which the teacher won't directly know about. Good teachers become skilled at reading and responding to the moods of their classes, making in-the-moment judgements about the tone of their talk, the rhythm and sequence of the teaching, who needs individual attention, etc., and adjusting their teaching as they go along. Sometimes moods and atmospheres might be predictable and therefore able to be planned for – last lesson on a Friday, for instance (though what exactly the mood and atmosphere will be will depend on the circumstances in that particular school and community). Generally, though, mood and atmosphere can be difficult to put into words, and teachers are probably more likely to comment on it in summative ways after a lesson (what went well, what didn't) than to engage in detailed analysis of the elements that generated particular affects and shifted the gears of what was happening.

In our research we were struck not only by the strength of the students' feelings that their arts lessons were different but also by the ways they struggled to find language that articulated exactly what they were trying to express. For example, they spoke about how arts lessons were 'relaxing' but at the same time required them to work very hard and make a serious time commitment. Affect theory (Ahmed, 2004; Gregg & Seigworth, 2010; Sedgwick, 2003) offers insights into how we might understand the complexity and ambiguousness of these feelings that sometimes seem contradictory. It shows us that while 'affect' can refer to an individual's emotional state, moods and feelings are social and, at some points, they are collective. The etymology of the word (from the Latin *affectus*, to be acted upon) points both to the importance of the impact on the person and to the importance of things outside the person. Affect in this latter sense is social, shared and beyond the human body.

Thinking and writing about affect has a long history, but its popularity in contemporary work stems from the mid-1990s. Gregg and Seigworth, editors of *The Affect Theory Reader* (2010), attribute recent interest to two key essays published in 1995, one by Eve Kokofsky Sedgwick and Adam Frank (1995) and one by Brian Massumi (1995). Sedgwick and Frank's essay is about the work of the psychologist Silvan Tomkins, who died in 1991. Tomkins argued that there are nine discrete, biologically based 'affects'. Some are positive (interest–excitement, enjoyment–joy); some negative (distress–anguish, anger–rage, fear–terror) and one neutral (surprise–startle). The coupling of the emotions indicates a scale of intensity. Massumi's essay is also concerned with intensity, by which he means the strength or duration of an affect. Drawing on examples as diverse as children's responses to a short wordless film about a snowman and a story told by Oliver Sacks (1985) about hospital patients' reception of a speech by Ronald Reagan, Massumi illustrates the ways in which "an image's effect is not logically connected to the content in any straightforward way" (p. 84) – often, he argues, there is a notable gap between the content and the effect. The relationship between them is not one of "conformity or correspondence, but of resonance or interference, amplification or dampening" (p. 86). These ideas – about the sometimes unpredictable relationship between content and effect, and the intensity with which effects can be amplified or dampened – are interesting to consider in relation to what happens in classrooms.

Post-critical scholars Sedgwick, Frank and Massumi are interested in the opportunities an affect-oriented theoretical approach offers to focus on the non-linguistic elements of a text, alongside the linguistic and narratological ones. Despite a degree of wariness about Tomkins' attempt to categorise and typify the different dimensions of affects, Sedgwick and Frank are drawn to the ways in which his theory "offers a wealth of sites of productive opacity". Whereas they see cognitive psychology as trying "to render the mind's processes thoroughly transparent from the point of view of cognition" and behaviourist psychology as trying to do the same thing by focusing on behavioural outcomes, Tonkins' affect theory encourages a focus on the messiness of feelings, moods and atmosphere. This approach had resonance for us as we began to probe into what the students meant about their art lessons feeling different. We wanted to 'read' some of the non-linguistic, less immediately visible elements of the classrooms alongside the very visible, material ones that are easily overlooked, often because they are normalised. We wanted to think about the impact of these elements on young people's experience, how far they are integral to the nature of particular curriculum subjects or disciplinary areas and, ultimately, what they contribute to a balanced education in school.

The approach also appeals because it opens up connections with other fields: social psychology, obviously, and anthropology but also political and economic theory (part of the argument in Massumi's essay) and, in Sedgwick and Frank's work, cybernetics, systems theory and neuroscience. The work of the cultural theorist Ben Highmore, who draws on affect theory alongside the earlier work of the cultural critic Raymond Williams, has been important to our own approach. In his book, *Cultural Feelings: Mood, mediation and cultural politics* (2017), Highmore develops an analysis of what he calls 'cultural feelings'; that is, the "sustained and maintained" moods and feelings that characterise a social milieu at a particular historical point. His interest is primarily in moods and feelings expressed at a collective, sometimes national, level rather than at the level of the personal and biographical although, of course, individual responses play into the broader picture. Highmore's historical analyses – for example, of morale building work in Britain during the Second World War – exemplify his contention that

> cultural feelings are neither internal, subjective states of affairs, nor are they ethereal atmospheres that exist outside of history … feelings and moods are

embodied and embedded in practices and habits, in routines and procedures that often have both a linguistic and a material support ...

(Highmore, 2017, p. 37)

At the start of his book, Highmore identifies four axioms which, he argues, are always and simultaneously at play in the arena of cultural feelings. His four axioms are, firstly, that moods and feelings are material – that is, they are embedded in cultural forms through which they are sustained. Secondly, moods and feelings are a form of labour – that is, they are produced, they don't just happen, they are maintained. Thirdly, they are historical – that is, they are related to a particular time. And fourthly, moods and feelings are social – that is, they are collective, though not uniform: "it is the quality of being both generally felt and specifically articulated that is mood's domain" (p. 3).

These four axioms – and the desire to specifically articulate what students told us was generally felt – underpin our analysis in this chapter. We understand mood and atmosphere as being expressed and created through material forms in particular times and places. In school, these are pedagogical forms and places. Highmore illustrates this with the example of a secondary school science laboratory. Bourdieu might call this a habitat, the location where habitus is formed. However, Bourdieu is notably silent on how habitat and habitus are connected, whereas theories of mood and atmosphere are not.

School science labs, Highmore argues, have their own atmosphere and this helps to focus learning in particular ways:

> To enter a science lab for a chemistry or physics lesson ... is to anticipate conducting an experiment (or to watch one being conducted). Such expectations are embedded in the furnishings, in the gas taps, in the large, deep sinks, in the vast cabinets of test tubes, beakers, tongs, pipettes ... In a science lesson we know that there are going to be flat periods of copying down equations, or listening to the uninspired voice of the science teacher explaining some chemical process or other, before anything approaching special effects (which could turn out to be a damp squib) will take place.
>
> *(Highmore, 2017, p. 7)*

In passing, we can probably conclude from this passage that Ben Highmore didn't especially enjoy his science lessons, but his key point is an important one: that the science lab, "like any other classroom, is specifically a machine for orchestrating attention" (p. 7). Attention is focused through the way the room is set out, the wall displays, the furniture. And this organisation is underpinned by a textual genre: the write-up of the experiment, with its very specific requirements (to hypothesise, to demonstrate the method, to detail the results, etc.). So Highmore's contention is that this signature text – alongside the workbenches, charts, etc. – is another material element of the school lab, a cultural form which has been deliberately and painstakingly shaped and produced (an outcome of labour, rather than a matter of chance). These elements "organise in advance how we orient ourselves to the situation we are experiencing" (p. 8); they create a mood that is shared and so part of a collective experience, though of course individual responses to being in the science lesson will vary.

These are some of the ideas we have applied to analysing the art and drama teaching we observed in the TALE research.

The classrooms

Secondary school art teaching generally takes place in spaces that are not called classrooms but art rooms or art studios. Of course, the rooms are not all the same. In the 30 secondary schools we examined we saw a wide range: new-build art blocks, Victorian art rooms no longer fit for purpose and post-war art rooms with well-worn plumbing, ill-fitting windows and inadequate heating. Each art room bore the mark of the individual teacher or teachers who worked in it, and sometimes evidence of the decisions or enthusiasms of earlier incumbents. Nevertheless, there were material, organisational and relational family resemblances between these various spaces.

The secondary school art room is generally not a singleton but a cluster of rooms, positioned together and set apart from general teaching rooms. Art rooms are larger than the average classroom and have their own specialist provision: sinks, storeroom for materials, numerous blackboards or whiteboards or walls that can be used for display. The furniture is most often large, shared tables, with stools rather than chairs. There is generally a teacher's desk, with a computer and associated digital projector. There is often a specialist room or rooms: ceramics, textiles, photography, design and three-dimensional construction all have their own distinctive sets of equipment and materials.

The transition from other parts of the school to the art room is usually a matter of a short walk, but it is a transition which is marked sensorially. Art rooms are often accessed by double doors which close art off from the rest of the school, and vice versa. Pushing the door open, the student/teacher/visitor encounters new smells – paint, clay, detergent, turps – and new sounds – sometimes hammering, cutting, the whirring of sewing machines and, at other times, soft chattering or deep silence. There is also a dramatic change in what's on view. Art rooms are typically visually rich, with carefully curated and often colourful displays of work completed by past and present students, reproductions of established artists' work and a lot of student work in progress. There are interesting objects, as well as orderly stacks of pots, brushes, scissors, boards, rulers and so on, many of which show tangible evidence of previous use. Tabletops, depending on their material, may be palimpsests of the drips, scars and pen markings of previous students' work. Sometimes the art teacher also has work on show, completed or in progress. So this is a hand-made, artisanal aesthetic. It sits, usually, in stark contrast to the aesthetic of front offices and public corridors, where the focus is generally on displaying certificates and trophies, rules and announcements, professionally produced inspirational quotations and badges of partnership and 'kitemarks' designed to 'sell' the school (Thomson, Jones, & Hall, 2009). But it is also very different from the standard classrooms provided by the school.

IMAGE 5.1 Art-room door

IMAGE 5.2 Art-room curated corner

IMAGE 5.3 Art room equipment

IMAGE 5.4 Creative project past

Secondary school drama teaching also takes place in spaces that are not called classrooms but drama rooms or studios. Again, the drama rooms in the 30 schools we studied varied according to the age, size and priorities of the particular schools, but the resemblances between them were marked. Like the art rooms, they tended to be on the periphery rather than central to the school building and they were larger than standard classrooms. Most had a computer with a screen or whiteboard and some specialist lighting and sound equipment, often stored in a walk-in cupboard or small room adjacent to the teaching area. In stark contrast to the art rooms, though, the aesthetic of the drama studios was minimalist: no clutter, little or no natural light, black walls and ceilings, long black curtains, staging blocks and a few metal-and-plastic chairs stacked and pushed to the corners of the room. If there were display boards in the room they tended to be functionally used for notices and reminders.

IMAGE 5.5 Creative project in progress

IMAGE 5.6 Art room as repository

IMAGE 5.7 Drama room 1

IMAGE 5.8 Drama room 2

Pushing open the doors of the empty drama studio, the sensory changes that confront students are about darkness, artificial light and the silence of entering a sound-proofed box. The environment is stripped back: students generally put away their coats, bags and school equipment and remove their shoes as they come in; when they sit, it is usually on the floor rather than on chairs. As they enter, there are no obvious visual or auditory stimuli; the acoustics of the relatively empty space differ from the acoustics of other classrooms; the sound proofing muffles sounds from elsewhere in the school. The paraphernalia of performance – scenery, props, velvet curtains, costumes etc. – is stored elsewhere, in the hall, on the stage, in the theatre, if the school is lucky enough to have one. In the drama studio the emphasis is on bodies in a space large enough to allow them to move freely and blank enough to be a canvas for the imagination.

While the physical features of the environment are important, the teachers' actions in curating the spaces are crucial. Generally, in our research we did not directly ask teachers about their teaching rooms. However, the topic often came up, as we usually interviewed teachers and students in situ. Both art and drama teachers very often explained that they wanted to create a break between the main school and the art or drama studio. They wanted students to enter the space thinking of themselves differently, as performers or artists and not students. One art teacher commented: *I mean, they are sort of becoming artists, aren't they? If they can think of themselves as becoming artists, that's as much as we can hope for.* To support this aim, the teachers often arranged the material space so that there were physical resonances with studios in art schools or professional rehearsal rooms. They wanted to create arts rooms that felt different – and were different – to other classrooms in the school.

Signature texts

Just as in Ben Highmore's example, quoted earlier, the write-up of the science experiment acted as a synecdoche for laboratory life, the art and drama rooms we researched were also distinguished by signature texts. In art, this text was *the creative project*: a work that takes sustained effort and time and is big in ambition and complexity. The massed displays of these creative projects – past, present and in progress – played an important part of creating the art rooms' particular aesthetic. When students entered the art room, their attention was particularly attuned not to essays, tests, exams or curriculum levels and daily targets, but to works which made visible multiple creative possibilities, representations, interpretations and expressions.

The formal assessment of attainment in art is generally based on the portfolio, in which there is at least one significant creative project; the project is mandatory in curriculum qualifications such as the General Certificate for Secondary Education (GCSE). In order to complete a creative project, students have to arrive at a workable idea; research it and bring it into conversation with relevant art traditions; develop, test out and evaluate possibilities and approaches; refine or learn new technical skills; produce the work and defend their artistic choices and decisions through documentation and/or conversation. The idea for the creative project may be in response to a teacher prompt, which is usually the case in lower secondary years, but over time the choice of topic, form, medium, genre and platform is increasingly left to the student.

The following box contains an extract from one teacher's interview about how the creative projects were organised for Year 9 and Year 12 students in her school.

In Year 9, we introduce more mixed media. They have a holiday homework to do and that will involve artist research and producing an artefact. This year it was a textile collage based on the [work of a local] artist ... They develop that into a pencil drawing and then a painting and then a mixed media where they combine their photocopies and different techniques.

At the end of Year 9 the students who have opted to take art at GCSE will be given a project and that will involve a gallery visit or more than one visit and we'll give them summer holiday homework. Last year we asked them to take 30 photographs to represent past, present and future. They had to go and explore [an art festival taking place in their city]. They explored the website and chose a gallery that interested them and documented the work that they liked. They had to talk about the artists and then they had to take photographs which also represented past, present and future, whether it was architecture or places. They had to interpret the theme and then they had to do an A3 drawing and an A3 painting and an A3 mixed media all on the theme. When they came back into school in September they presented their work to the class ... They talked about the artists they like and what they liked most about their work and then they showed what they'd achieved over the summer, which is usually half a sketchbook of work.

[In Year 12] it is the same structure. So the students will be given a theme for the project and it's just the scale of things that increases. They'll have a more in-depth holiday homework and they'll come back with half a sketchbook of work and we'll take it from there. All of the work that they've done in the summer they will bring into school and we'll do another pencil study and a painting and, in the past, we've used their photos and we've created Photoshop compositions. We did one a few years ago based on architecture and we used Photoshop and we layered the students' photographs and they produced a really lovely composition and then they painted it. All of the holiday homework and all of the research will culminate in the final piece.

In drama the signature text is also a creative project, in this case *devised drama*. In the lower school, the curriculum is usually organised to systematically teach drama skills, techniques and terminology. In a typical lesson, the teacher will introduce the new concept or skill to the whole class, then the students will divide into small groups to deploy the new idea in a scene or tableau they devise together. The emphasis is on working collaboratively to demonstrate practical, embodied understanding of what has been taught. The initial stimulus might come from the teacher or a text, but the practical exploration of the new knowledge takes place within the group so, if the lesson is working well, there is an immediate pooling of ideas and shared understandings. The first audience for this devised drama is the teacher and the rest of the class.

By GCSE level (aged 16), students are required to carry out research, develop their own ideas, collaborate with others, rehearse, refine and amend their work in progress, and then analyse and evaluate their own processes of creating devised drama. They must learn how to contribute to devised drama, as either a performer or a designer, in a live theatre context for an audience. They must perform or create realised designs for a devised duologue or group piece. For assessment, they must produce an individual log documenting their devising process and an analysis and evaluation of their contribution. This same emphasis on practical creativity, alongside research and the development of theoretical understanding, continues at A Level (aged 18), where students are encouraged to explore plays practically, devise and work on performances, interpret extracts and create their own original drama while documenting their methodology and the influences on their work.

The following box contains two extracts from interviews with one of the drama teachers in the TALE project. In the first extract he describes how he and a colleague set up a sequence of Year 10 lessons about devising drama. In the second extract he describes the process of documenting drama work for assessment purposes.

S. [the other teacher] and I went away and looked at some stimuli over the Easter period. In their first lesson back we had ten different pieces of stimuli around the room. They had to go around and make notes on each one and they chose one that really sang to them. They created bits of drama around them in small group. Just to introduce them to the different stuff out there, there was a song and a newspaper article, a painting and a piece of costume. And there was a prop which some of them really liked, which was a map of London with a few random places circled. They found that quite interesting to create characters from – thinking about why people would be there and what would they be doing. There was a really cool photo that S. found of a statue where it is like the outline of a woman with a sheet over her face. They created some really nice drama out of that. And there was a picture which I found online which said, 'Take a selfie; fake a life', and a lot of them chose that as well, about how a lot of people live through social media. So I think they will end up choosing stuff along those lines: things about social media; things about pressures to perform a certain way. They are really bright and outspoken so I think they will go down that route …

We tend to get them to write weekly logs. It's getting them into the habit of describing what they did; analysing which skills they used and then evaluating how successfully they used those skills. Initially they do that in log books and then those skills are applied to their coursework. In GCSE Drama they write a devising log which is the one that they can purely write or they can add annotations or they can do it as a presentation but, essentially, they have to do the same thing: they have to describe the stimulus they are working from; they have to analyse the dramatic potential and what they found interesting; and then they have to evaluate the quality of the work that they've produced. It is getting them into the habit of being able to do those three things … I'm always amazed by the pride that they take in their work. Their log books will be a real range of styles and approaches. So you might have a diary entry and next to that a drawing of a character that they played, which is annotated with the skills that they used. Or you might have a script which is annotated in terms of what lines they said and the tone of voice that they said it in. It is a real mixture of things and you might have a mood board of images that they've found to do with a theme that they are exploring.

For students, working on these signature creative projects was an important part of what made art and drama feel distinctive. *Art is different to other subjects*, one Year 11 boy told us. *[The teacher] is open about letting you choose what you want to do. He just guides you, steering about the choice of project.* This recognition of being simultaneously steered and also being free to choose, often expressed (as here and in the comments at the start of this chapter) as a view of the teacher as an expert guide, is typical of many hundreds of comments from students in our sample.

The balance of compulsion and choice helps set the mood and atmosphere of any classroom, but it has a distinctive flavour in the art- and drama-room environments and in the context of schoolwork that, particularly as the students get older, takes longer than usual to produce. The time frames for creative projects, and the fact that the projects – or elements of them – are often portable between school and home, open up space for gathering opinions from other people, changing direction and reworking and repositioning bits of what is being worked on. *You are getting the work done but you are able to express yourself more*, a Year 11 student told us. The project lives with the maker over the period of creating it and, in that sense, it has the chance of becoming something more than just part of a lesson. One Year 12 student put it like this: *In other classes the role of the teacher is almost to limit … so they are constantly trying to make sure everyone is sticking to this exact thing. In arts subjects, though, they might say, hey, look at this maybe really different thing. And you can look at it and try to tie it in, instead of limiting it to just that subject. It's more exploring …* This was a very common feeling about art and drama as subjects across our sample of students. It was expressed sometimes as a sense of freedom; sometimes as being more connected to real life; sometimes as a sense of relief at encountering a degree of expansiveness in what otherwise felt like being caught within tight constraints.

These signature texts – the creative art project and devised drama – share some important features. Both encourage students to make connections that extend beyond the school walls. Both shape and are shaped by the material environments in which they are taught: art and drama studios that are unlike standard classrooms, but which look very different from one another.

These texts are seminal to the signature pedagogies of art and drama as school subjects.

Signature pedagogies

Signature pedagogies are the styles of teaching that are common to particular disciplines, areas of study or professions. The notion of a signature pedagogy and text comes from Lee Shulman (2000, 2005) who coined the term in relation to higher education, saying that it is "teaching that organise[s] the fundamental ways in which future practitioners are educated for their new professions" (Shulman, 2005). Shulman argued that discipline-specific practices (such as the field trip in geography or working with archival sources in history) are the key to understanding what it means to teach and learn specific knowledge of a discipline. These practices are important, Shulman argues, because they "implicitly define what counts as knowledge in a field and how things become known. They define how knowledge is analysed, criticized, accepted or discarded. They define the functions of expertise in a field, the locus of authority ..." While there are some common pedagogical approaches across clusters of disciplines, there are also practices that are distinctive to the particular discipline. These distinctive practices inculcate knowledge but they also set out deliberately to teach 'habits of mind'; that is, the ways in which practitioners are educated to think, perform and act. Learning these habits is part of inducting students into the traditions, conventions and mores of a profession or a disciplinary area (Golde, 2007; Guring, Chick, & Haynie, 2009).

In a previous research project, we studied the signature pedagogies of artists who teach in schools (Thomson, Hall, Jones, & Sefton Green, 2012). In that work, we applied Shulman's concept of signature pedagogies to the school rather than the university context. This allowed us to identify what seemed to us to be distinctive about the artists' pedagogical approaches which, in turn, enabled us to draw some conclusions about the complementarity of the artists' and teachers' roles, about what teachers might learn from artists, and about how partnership working might benefit young people's learning (Hall & Thomson, 2017, 2021). The TALE project gave us the opportunity to learn more about the other side of the equation, the signature pedagogies of the arts teachers themselves.

According to Shulman, signature pedagogies have three interconnected dimensions: surface structure (related to observable, organisational matters), deep structure (related to underlying assumptions about knowledge and beliefs about teaching within the discipline) and implicit structure (related to moral underpinnings, beliefs about values, attitudes and dispositions). These structures connect the ways in which a discipline produces knowledge and inducts new members into the disciplinary community; they help students, as the teacher quoted earlier said, "think of themselves as becoming artists". Looked at through these lenses, we can build a picture of how the students in our study experienced the pedagogy of their art and drama lessons.

In terms of observable surface features, we have already commented on the position, size and look of art and drama rooms (see Images 5.1–8). The contrast between the way the spaces are designed and maintained is significant. The art rooms we visited all bore witness to creative projects, past and present, finished and in process. Materials tended to be stored openly, in ways that allowed them to be accessed easily, usually by the students themselves rather than via the teacher. In these ways the environment signalled the centrality of the ambitious creative project and the materiality of the making process.

In contrast, the drama rooms we visited were stripped back, relatively empty. The design and curation of the environment focused attention on the present moment. The focus was on performance: stimulus might come from a single object or from a text, but primarily it came from the people in the room, the teacher and the group. Past ideas and performances might be remembered and drawn upon, future performances imagined and planned for. But the principal emphasis was on presence, the making of something in the moment, something ephemeral, which could be captured – but never fully experienced – through recordings of various kinds (logs, videos, evaluations, reviews, etc.). The material differences between the teaching rooms for art and drama reflect the material differences in the art forms the students are learning.

Another immediately observable and significant feature of the lessons is the way they tend to start. Art lessons for older (and sometimes younger) students often begin with students entering the room, getting the project they are working on out of storage, finding the materials they need in the room or store cupboard and settling down to work. Sketchbooks, notes, mobile phones and laptops are removed from school bags and arranged according to the student's personal pre-ferences. This lesson-beginning practice is, we think, indicative of the tuning of students' attention and behaviour that is developed in art: the model of working instilled as a habit (disposition) of getting-on-with-it. The calm and focused atmosphere produced by this usually relatively stress-free beginning contrasted with other lessons where protracted disruptive 'settling down' could become challenging for some staff (Thomson, Hall, & Jones, 2010) and wearisome for students. It is notable too that autonomous getting-on-with-the-work-when-you-come-into-the-room is not only what routinely happens in art schools but is also what prac-tising artists do in their studios. School students were thus, through these practices, moving closer towards becoming the artists that their teachers wanted them to be.

The organisational structure that underpins the individual creative project requires art teachers to focus on the systematic teaching of techniques, supporting students to engage with a range of tools, materials and artistic traditions, and helping them evaluate their own and others' work. A combination of the affor-dances of the art-room space, and the specific pedagogy of the discipline, produce this self-managed and self-motivated behaviour. Over time, students become dis-posed to this way of being and doing; it becomes habitual and feels normal to behave in this way in this subject. (In other words, the pedagogic practice was forming the students' artist habitus.)

As with art, the organisational structure that underpins devised drama requires teachers to focus on the systematic teaching of techniques and traditions and to help students to evaluate their own and others' work. But drama lessons, in con-trast to art lessons, almost always start with the group as a whole: often with some teacher-talk and discussion of the project in hand, usually also with some physical warm-up activities, games or exercises to get the students moving together and attending to one another. Once the collective mood, atmosphere and sense of purpose have been established, smaller groups are generally encouraged to work independently. The drama teacher – like the art teacher – teaches by circulating, offering ideas and support, or just keeping people on track.

In art, the scale of the project work often means that it extends over a series of lessons, so the conclusion of the lesson often marks a pause rather than a more definitive end point. The sharing of individuals' work with other members of the class, through mini-plenaries or more formal reviews, can occur at any point in the lesson. In contrast to this, drama sessions tend to work towards an imposed deadline internal to the lesson, a point at which the teacher brings the whole class back together again to share performances and reflect on process and progress, to re-emphasise the social rather than individual nature of the work. So the rhythms of the lessons tend to be different, shaped in drama by the deadlines for sharing process work or for acting as an audience for other students' work. The combination of the drama studio environment and the specific pedagogy of the discipline produces behaviours, habits and norms that emphasise the collectivity of the social group, the ensemble from whom the artwork – the performance – will emerge. The parallels with the rehearsal and devising practices of professional companies are clear.

Students sometimes remarked on the rhythm of their lessons; more often they noticed and commented on what the teachers did to achieve these rhythms. Both art and drama students commented positively on the way their teachers *come round and give us advice* as they worked on their projects. This form of teaching felt personalised, embodied, *more individual – one to one, like you're in a class of your own.* The proxemics, like the routines, were important in generating the atmosphere and mood in the room. A Year 11 student put it like this: *It's a different, bigger, more open space. Your teacher knows more what it feels like.* Or we could refer again to the comment quoted at the start of the chapter: *When you are studying in a classroom you don't really have that connection with the teacher in a way. They [arts teachers] are less of a teacher and, this might sound weird, more of a friend.* For these students the space helps generate feelings that they think their teachers share. This changes the nature of teacher–student interactions and underpins the sense of arts teachers being different.

When things are going to plan, then, the mood of the lessons is set by this combination of feelings: that the teaching is personalised, that the teacher *knows more what it feels like,* that there's space and freedom of movement in the room and that the purpose of the work is to produce creative projects that are meaningful to the students and can be explained and interpreted by them. The teacher talk is filtered through the lens of this mood – *it's more of a discussion.* Feelings of trust, recognition, respect and support are amplified in this atmosphere: *Teachers are helpful. They give us more independence to develop our own ideas. They trust us more, they trust us to rely on ourselves, they see how we work. She is very involved with the class and she knows us very well. Not like some teachers, where they just teach you and literally don't care. She helps us a lot.*

Our evidence shows that, overwhelmingly, students feel positive about learning in these ways; they think their arts lessons add variety and breadth to their experience of school and help them express themselves in ways that they find meaningful (see Chapter 7). Using Shulman's framing, we see here the interconnection between the observable, organisational patterns of the surface level of the signature pedagogies of these two arts subjects (the teachers' movement, the material spaces, the starts and finishes of lessons, when the plenaries occur and what they're about) and how the students are understanding the deeper structures, the underlying assumptions about how knowledge is generated and how teaching and learning should proceed. The signature pedagogies of both disciplines encourage teachers to develop strong and sustained relationships with students as the basis for ongoing negotiation of their students' creative projects. Their support for taking on challenging projects helps students develop a sense of agency and self-belief and encourages them to develop their voices, explore and express new ideas and different aspects of their identities. The implicit values here connect students to the more fundamental case for the arts in general: that the arts are integral to human life, an entitlement for all young people, a means of engaging actively with the world.

In the next chapter, we explore some of the risks and challenges that accompany these pedagogies.

References

Ahmed, S. (2004). Affective economies. *Social Text, 79*, 22(117–139).

Golde, C. (2007). Signature pedagogies in doctoral education: Are they adaptable to the preparation of education researchers? *Educational Researcher*, 36(6), 344–351.

Gregg, M., & Seigworth, G. (2010). *The affect theory reader*. Durham, NC: Duke University Press.

Guring, R., Chick, N., & Haynie, A. (eds) (2009). *Exploring signature pedagogies. Approaches to teaching disciplinary habits of mind*. Sterling, VA: Stylus.

Hall, C., & Thomson, P. (2017). Creativity in teaching: What can teachers learn from artists? *Research Papers in Education*, 32(1), 106–120.

Hall, C., & Thomson, P. (2021). Making the most of arts education partnerships in schools. *Curriculum Perspectives*, 41(1), 101–106.

Highmore, B. (2017). *Cultural feelings: Mood, mediation and cultural politics*. London: Routledge.

Massumi, B. (1995). The autonomy of affect. *Cultural Critique*, 31, 83–109.

Sacks, O. (1985). *The man who mistook his wife for a hat*. London: Picador.

Sedgwick, E. K. (2003). *Touching feeling: Affect, pedagogy, performativity*. Durham, DC: Duke University Press.

Sedgwick, E. K., & Frank, A. (1995). Shame in the cybernetic fold: Reading Silvan Tomkins. *Critical Inquiry*, 21(2), 496–522.

Shulman, L. (2000). Teacher development: Roles of domain expertise and pedagogical knowledge. *Journal of Applied Developmental Psychology*, 21(1), 129–135.

Shulman, L. (2005). Signature pedagogies in the professions. *Daedalus*, 134(Summer), 52–59.

Thomson, P., Hall, C., & Jones, K. (2010). Maggie's day: A small scale analysis of English education policy. *Journal of Education Policy*, 25(5), 639–656.

Thomson, P., Hall, C., Jones, K., & Sefton Green, J. (2012). *Signature pedagogies*. London: Creativity, Culture and Education.

Thomson, P., Jones, K., & Hall, C. (2009). *Creative whole school change: Final report*. London: Creativity, Culture and Education; Arts Council England.

6

THE ART OF MEDIATION

I had arrived at an awkward time. Not only had the school recently been told it was in special measures and was to academise, it was the day when Bob was scheduled to talk with Year 11s about their projected grades and current progress. He was apologetic that I couldn't see him teach a more creative lesson. I reassured him that this was actually really interesting and central to the TALE research and if he and the students didn't mind, I'd like to sit in.

Bob's task for the day, as he explained to me and to each student, was to see if each projected mark could be improved and what that would entail. Students were seated at the somewhat dilapidated art-room tables working on their 'documentation', the record of their processes of exploration and decision-making integral to the summative portfolio-based assessment. Bob called the students up one by one. They sat next to him, looking at the computer on his desk, placed on the far front wall of the room, usually out of mind if not out of sight. The screen showed the students' current gradings, and the projected mark that these would lead to.

Each conversation was carried out in public. Not only I, a stranger, but also all of the seated students could hear what was said. The unwritten rule seemed to be to make it appear as if each discussion was private, as if each student's progress was their own individual concern no matter how potentially humiliating or exhilarating it might be.

Bob clearly had a format for these conversations. He began by asking the student what they were doing and how well, and what challenges and problems they were dealing with. He then went on to look at the current grade and asked if this was what the student wanted and expected. He then either talked about how to make sure the projected grade was to be achieved (if it was good) or how to make the grade better (if it was low or not what the student wanted). The latter part of the conversation involved a discussion of the students' interests, be it an artist, a technique, a tool or a question, and how this interest might be used and developed to achieve the desired grade. "This isn't just about grades," Bob repeated. "It's about using the exam process to help you grow as an artist."

DOI: 10.4324/9781003093084-6

One of the young women who came up to the desk began by saying that she was stuck. She didn't want to do art any more. She didn't want to be at school. Yes, she used to be interested in a particular topic but she was no longer at all motivated. She just couldn't get going, she just couldn't see the point. Bob did not get to grades at all. He spent some time gently trying to find out why art was no longer interesting and made a series of suggestions about artists that the student might find interesting. He put the grades window aside and began to show the student various artists' webpages. He took a book from his shelf and suggested the student look at it and they would talk again. I am sure I was not the only one in the room who was uncomfortable listening to what was at times a teary conversation.

Bob told me later that he hated these grading conversations. They required him to switch focus away from students' art learning. He had to take a highly instrumental view of each student's work. He tried as best he could, he said, to make the students' work the focus but it was, he said, really depressing to suggest that the main point of making art was to get a grade. He was also, he confessed, at his wits' end about the young woman who was stuck. She was very talented but depressed and there were reasons why she was so. He so wanted her to get back to the lively creative spirit she had been a few months before.

Although I was supposed to be a dispassionate observer, I told Bob I could see him struggle with how to not let his deep knowledge of the students and commitment to their art overtake the necessary conversation about grades. "No one could have done it better," I said. "You clearly can't ignore the grades and you made the discussion as positive and productive as was possible." I thanked him for his willingness to let me observe. He thanked me for recognising his ambivalence and efforts. I left wondering about the privatised nature of significant professional work, teachers attempting to shift the reproductive workings of education logics in their students' favour. (Pat, field–note memo)

This anecdote from one of our TALE school visits introduces our sixth key concept – artful mediation. In Chapter 3 we discussed the ways in which, in Bourdieusian terms, arts-broker teachers have to contend with the logics of two overlapping fields, the field of education and the field of art. The logics of those fields sometimes pull in different directions. Bob's teaching, described here, exemplifies the tensions created for teachers in the classroom and with an individual student. Bob's (not his real name) pedagogical practice was simultaneously designed to support all students to become artists and to draw what was productive from the education field, while also negotiating its selective and hierarchising practices. Such artful pedagogy requires teachers to mediate the practices, values, languages and dispositions of the arts and education fields but within the frame of the prevailing logics of the education field.

Mediation is a word in common use. It is often applied to legal situations where a third person manages a negotiation between two or more different parties: neighbours in dispute over a property line, a buyer and a seller with different interpretations of a contract, a family in disarray over a will. In these circumstances the job of the mediator is to find a compromise solution which will not please everyone but is something that they can agree to. In education, mediation is sometimes used in this sense, as in peer mediation, when one student acts as a neutral party to help solve a disagreement between others.

Mediation also has another specific meaning in education. Vygotsky's theory of learning (Vygotsky, 1978) centres on the ways in which learning is mediated by the adult. The teacher is situated between the learner and the learning environment. By manipulating activities, tasks, tools, symbols, interactions and processes the teacher optimises learning for each student. Fuerstein et al (Fuerstein, Falk, & Fuerstein, 2015) also discusses teachers' mediation, arguing that while children who are unfamiliar with a learning environment and its resources need more direct support from the teacher, the teacher's goal is often to move them to self-managed (or indirect, self-mediated) learning. We described just such teaching in the last chapter, explaining that students often experienced this pedagogy as teachers being guides. The reality is much more complex – teachers simultaneously diagnose a student's weaknesses, recognise their interests and strengths, focus on the overall learning goals, determine the next steps the student needs to take and organise the environment accordingly.

Our own use of mediation takes something from both Vygotskian pedagogy and from formal mediation practices. We take from the former a more legalistic definition, the notion of negotiation and compromise. We take from the latter the notion of the highly skilled teacher managing the environment to maximise learning for each student. We can see something of this in the opening field memo, where Bob seeks a pathway between the exam requirements and his goal of developing artists and artistic practice. Other verbs that are useful to consider in relation to the kind of pedagogical mediation that we are referring to are: to reduce/manage the influence of, to balance, make bespoke, to ignore and add, to minimise and prioritise.

Another way of describing the practice of pedagogical mediation is to see it as policy enactment (Ball, Maguire, & Braun, 2012). The theory that sits behind the notion of enactment is that while policy is made at one level, let's say central government, it is interpreted differently at different levels, say a regional office and then the school. Each time the policy is re-read it is combined with other priorities, histories and existing practices. By the time a policy reaches a teacher, it may have been read, re-read and rewritten several times. This refraction, or iterative translation, causes what policy-makers understand as an implementation problem. The policy is not enacted as it was imagined. No matter what the policy says, what happens on the ground in classrooms may not be what was intended. In order to mitigate the implementation problem, policy-makers often introduce regulatory measures which make it much more likely that those on the ground will comply with their intentions. They also tighten gate-keeping procedures such as exams. These regulatory measures create new permutations of the basic sorting and selecting logics of the education field.

Such selective logics are problematic for arts teachers who hold that the purpose of their subject is to support students to become artists, and who also subscribe to the view that everyone can be an artist. But there is significant pressure attached to tests and exams and there are two reasons why teachers cannot ignore them. First, teachers do not wish to see their students fail to get results that are important to their life chances. They thus ensure that the mandated curriculum is covered and that they do whatever is possible to help students get their best results. Just like Bob. But secondly, in England where the TALE research was conducted, additional school performance measures and inspections also work to ensure policy compliance. Both teachers and schools can suffer adverse consequences if policy-directed goals, such as attainment targets, are not delivered. A strong and punitive regulatory framing limits the ways in which teachers are able to move away from the curriculum that counts, as both students and the school could suffer from failure to comply.

Nevertheless, nearly all schools are involved in some form of vernacular modification of policy agendas (Hall & Thomson, 2017), and nearly all teachers are engaged in forms of policy adaptation (Hayes et al., 2018) and curriculum mediation. The TALE research showed that teachers modified and adapted their pedagogical practices to meet specified curriculum goals while also teaching additional knowledge, skills, behaviours and values that they and their school held to be important. This pedagogical mediating work varied from teacher to teacher, but also from subject to subject. Our concern in this chapter is with the artful mediation designed to support the achievement of the mandated curriculum and desired qualification, but also to support students to develop an artist habitus.

We examine the ways in which the TALE arts teachers integrated the arts field into their teaching, and then address the compromises they had to make, and the artful mediation that this required. We begin with the notion of an artist habitus.

Creating an artist habitus

In the Chapter 3 we noted that arts-broker teachers wanted students to become and be artists. We suggested that this desire, combined with the knowledges, values and beliefs that teachers brought from the art field, profoundly shaped their pedagogical approach. Here, we provide more detail about this approach, again in conversation with the teachers. We will hear, in Chapter 7, the students' views of what this meant for them.

We use the Bourdieusian term 'habitus' here to indicate that the teachers' goal was to support the development of persons (agents) who not only thought, acted, felt and spoke like artists but felt at home with the arts, understood the art world, wanted what was on offer in the art world and wanted to be part of it. Habitus is not individualised, but is socially formed; Bourdieu suggested that habitus was the way in which society becomes "deposited in persons" as "long-lasting dispositions, propensities to think, feel and act in particular ways" (Wacquant, 2005, p. 316). These patterns of behaviour are carried throughout life but are not static; they change depending on context (the various fields in which people are located). Dispositions to act in particular ways are a negotiation between conscious reflexive thinking, structure, past and present. Arts-broker teachers had artist dispositions themselves, both as audiences and producers, and this grounded and guided the ways in which they approached their teaching.

Because they were interested in nurturing an artist habitus, TALE teachers had clear priorities:

(1) They were keen to differentiate their work from what they saw as a 'schoolified' art

In the visual arts this meant teachers wanted to see students making art as if they were contemporary artists. Rather than offer template projects and encounters with a few well-known artists and a limited number of techniques, art teachers stressed the importance of process. They prioritised the individual perspectives that students should bring to conceive, develop and carry out a project:

> Something that we really strive for here is that the kids are not making school art. So the things I am NOT going to do is like an African mask project or Australian dot painting project. I'd rather die than tell kids that that's all there is. So our work is more about interviewing interesting people and making political statements. We are going to express what we think about things and we are going to really think about who we are as people and what is important to us. And we are going to express that through the art that we make.

Drama teachers were keen to expose students to a range of dramatic forms, from the canon of Shakespeare to challenging contemporary forms – *there's more to life than panto* as one teacher put it. Arts teachers wanted their students to become familiar with a wide range of arts forms and to appreciate and understand the ways in which the arts not only reflect but also shape the world. They wanted students to engage with arts as artists might, to appreciate the skills involved, understand the processes and engage with the ideas being pursued.

(2) TALE teachers wanted students to deeply engage with core aspects of their arts discipline

Visual art teachers valued students showing that they did not know. Teachers wanted students to value un-learning (Baldecchino, 2019) and un-knowing (Fisher & Fortnum, 2014). They expected students to be thoughtful and reflective. They wanted students to challenge their taken-for-granted ways of thinking and feeling; these were starting points rather than endings:

> It is about ... exposing them to as much contemporary art practice as possible. They don't have to do a still life of a vase of flowers for A Level if they don't want to. We want to help them make whatever work they want. I don't think any of them worry about what art looks like.

They are making things that say something rather than making things that look nice. From Year 7 that is something that we are trying to instil in the kids – the notion of being creative and taking risks and doing projects that give them some independence. So I've brought in projects for homework where the kids take ownership and they work through it themselves.

Drama teachers wanted their students to move towards a performance practice that was geared to exploring self and society:

I think it's asking particular questions but then facilitating a space for them to be able to answer it in their own way. Sometimes they can tackle a question very quickly through a discussion and sometimes they've got the space for it to become an entire project. But to have the freedom to let things evolve, depending on the question and the students.

Some drama teachers saw performance as strongly tied to the development of persons. Persons able to empathise and understand others. Persons who are self-aware and responsive:

It [drama] is about the discovery of self, so I am always struck by the self-esteem that goes with acting and performing. In acting, I sometimes see therapy in the escape of taking on a role and the ability to be someone else and to explore their nature. As long as there are as many kinds of opportunities for that kind of spiritual experience and that kind of self-discovery, then the more the curriculum can do that the better.

Drama teachers wanted students to use and build haptic knowledges – the partially codified practices of communicating through body posture, gesture, facial expression, tone and so on. They wanted students to give up their sense of self to work as one with others, to produce collective affect. They wanted students to have time to explore how to use their bodies to engage with ideas. This did not always sit well with making sure that students could meet exam requirements:

We've had to adapt to new specifications at A Level and GCSE and what we've recognised is that the students need to be much more skilled by the time they hit GCSE and so we've had a rethink about what the skills are that we are trying to teach at Key Stage 3. Now more and more schools are going for earlier GCSEs so the curriculum time for Key Stage 3 has been reduced so they don't get a chance to explore as much as they used to. So I look for a mixture of script and devised work and things that are going to engage. But I've also raised the challenge and I am working with Year 8 on schemes of work that almost would have been GCSE some years ago and I think it is paying off.

All arts teachers wanted to curate the learning environment so that when they entered the arts or drama room, the students 'felt' like artists (the topic we explored in the previous chapter). While they could not change all of their physical environments, the provision of high-quality resources and materials were important components of signalling that this space was not simply a classroom but a place where artistic work was done.

IMAGE 6.1 Art room equipped as a studio

(3) The key to becoming an artist was a curriculum that fostered independence

All of the teachers spoke about the importance of independence:

> *Working independently and solving problems and being given responsibility — because ulti-mately that is what life is about: you're not going to get spoon-fed all your life; you are given a job and you get a full list of what you have to do and the actions you have to do and you have to get on with it. I do think there is too much spoon-feeding in education and I don't think it does the kids any favours whatsoever. And although they find it very difficult and they might begrudge it at first, ultimately the penny drops and then they can apply it to everything. They've got to take responsibility for their own work. So doing something wrong and having failures is fine and it might feel that they don't know what they are doing and it's a bit hap-hazard. But I think they will learn the ways in which they work best. I think that if all children are taught in the same way, then they don't find the ways in which they learn. I think that is why the arts and project work is really important.*

Progress in the arts was not simply about the acquisition of knowledge or building a repertoire of techniques or self-evaluative strategies or having a sure grip on tools, techniques, genres, histories, texts, language and artefacts. It was all this and more.

Meta-cognition was important – learning how to learn – as was growing aesthetic appreciation and critical understanding. Building the concepts, language and understandings of arts disciplines was crucial. But these were important because they were integral to an artist habitus.

Arts teachers were clear that developing arts projects and the artist-self, or artist habitus with its particular arts field dispositions, happened together and that this was core to their subjects, and a point of difference with other subjects:

> *The importance of A Level Art is that it is a subject where you have to think for yourself completely and to be independent. Because you are just given a title and then it is entirely up to you what you do. There aren't that many subjects where that will happen because most other subjects are about task-setting and task-completion.*

TALE teachers were aware that other teachers were less able to foster independence than they were:

> *I think students very much enjoy the independent way of working and the self-motivation that comes with that. So the teacher acts as a guide and a sign-poster and the children will work by themselves and only discuss things with the teacher when they are unsure of how to go on. I don't think this sense of independent learning is going on in lots of other subject areas.*

The desire for independence as a key practice for developing artist habitus sits at the conjunction of the education and the art fields. Independent work allows both fields to come together in mutually compatible and complementary ways. The art-field notion of the autonomous artist corresponds with the long-standing education narrative of the child as artist. In England, the advocacy of the idea of children as artists in their own right, rather than apprentices or learners with deficit skills and ideas, can be traced back to pioneering educators such as Christian Schiller HMI, Robin Tanner HMI and Sir Alec Clegg, long-term Chief Education Officer of the West Riding authority in Yorkshire (Burke, Cunningham, & Hoare, 2021). It can also be seen in present-day manifestations such as Room 13, where children run their own art studio (Souness & Fairley, 2005). However, it also appears as the 'spine' of the school arts curriculum, which, more than any other subject area, supports the development of independent work. The structure of arts subjects moves the students from a more teacher-directed curriculum in junior secondary school to a senior school curriculum where students' autonomy, choices and decision-making are paramount.

In the early years of secondary school, students in TALE schools were exposed to a foundational repertoire of tools and techniques and to core disciplinary knowledges and traditions. The teachers carefully steered students' learning, providing leads to relevant intellectual and material resources, setting milestones, challenging students to take risks and make mistakes from which they could learn. They used whole-class instruction and skills-oriented and practice exercises to support the development of understanding, knowledge, expertise and craft. Teachers used a disciplinary lexicon, introducing norms and expectations derived not only from the education curriculum frameworks, but also from professional theatre and visual arts fields.

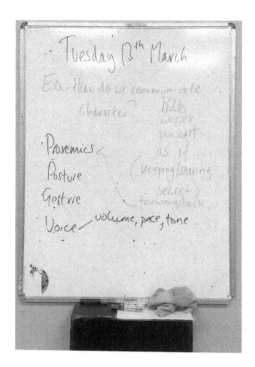

IMAGE 6.2 Introducing disciplinary terms and concepts

Students also began to do their own project work. Some, of course, might have already experienced solo and group project work in primary school, particularly if they had attended a school where there were specialist arts teachers. Independent project work was carefully supervised and scaffolded by arts teachers. For TALE teachers, productions, performances and exhibitions in the junior years were not only about summative assessment or a public relations exercise for the subject and school. Events created a space and time where students could demonstrate their capacity for independent work. But crucially, they were also the vehicle for the development of independent thinking, acting, interacting and making.

When the students reached the final years of school, the time devoted to independent projects increased dramatically. The final-year award in arts subjects is dependent on the production of a portfolio of artistic work. Senior students in TALE schools were thus expected to be self-motivated, show initiative and get on with their work, albeit with continuous checking and sometimes nagging. They had to conducted extensive research and to document, explain and defend their artistic choices in writing and via 'notes' (drama) and 'crits' (visual art).

The focus on building an autonomous artist habitus can be mistaken for an empty-headed child-centredness, but it is far from that. TALE arts teachers saw their responsibility as building and nurturing an artist habitus particularly through supporting students to:

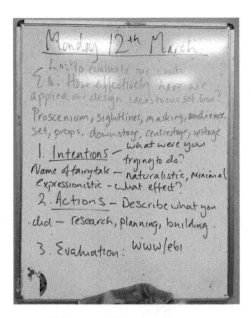

IMAGE 6.3 Building an evaluative artist habitus

1. Take risks. Learning to make mistakes, to be discomforted and to unlearn the familiar was inherent to the arts. Learning from mistakes, using them productively is important. *The arts offer students opportunities to take risks, because if we are having a discussion about something in drama there is never a wrong answer.* It is also important to teachers that students do not focus on what they can't do, but what they might do in order to learn. *It is definitely important that the students have a mixed experience and exposure to stuff so they can make decisions. Because they might feel that they are not good at drawing and for me it's not really about being able to copy something beautifully but it's about being independent and trying new approaches.* TALE teachers were keen that students developed their own particular interests and strengths but not if this meant staying in their comfort zones.

2. Become persistent and patient. *It is about a commitment to doing something – to starting something and sticking to it.* The arts demand continued practice as well as experimentation; artistic skills and techniques are not developed quickly. All of the arts depend on disciplined bodies and many also rely on memorisation. The artisanal aspects of the arts are not about knowledge-free techniques, but about understanding and the acquisition of the proficiencies necessary to pursue ideas.

3. See themselves in the company of a collective of artists. While the performing arts are more obviously about working together, contemporary visual arts highly value collectivity. *It involves working as a team. You have to be a critical friend. It will give you a set of skills that are perhaps obvious but they are transferable*

skills, such as teamwork and organisational skills and working to deadlines. As one drama teacher told us: *The theatre friends that you make will stay with you for life because you go through so much together. You cannot take away from students that camaraderie that they give to each other when they are going to perform together.*

4. Connecting with the world. TALE teachers generally saw the arts as connecting with other areas of knowledge. *We end up teaching the whole range of subjects through art. There is a historical context; it is a science; there is a mathematical side. So I think what is great about art is that there is the potential to really teach, through a visual subject, a lot of other subjects.* All saw the importance of students bringing their neighbourhood and family knowledges and cultural practices into the classroom. They also saw that students were entitled to engage with their art form, and the arts in general, and that this was what we might call a 'right to culture' (see Chapter 9).

However, only some teachers focused on the importance of artists having a social conscience. Studying the arts allowed students to engage with the world:

If you can involve students in the world of the arts it empowers them and it increases their hunger. It enables them to make sense of complicated issues. We've been looking at things around the Stephen Lawrence murder. It's not really in their lifetime but I think it just helps to contextualise their own lives: gang warfare, where does it get you? It's destructive and it destroys lives and families, so let's have nothing to do with it. Be proud of who we are. The power is in our intellect and in our knowledge and our creativity and not in what we own. It's about getting the kids to challenge stereotypes. So we have conversations about racism and bullying and Isis. I think arts teachers are in a brilliant place to make links and to enable conversations to take place and enable kids to question themselves.

TALE teachers were convinced that arts learning was of much wider benefit beyond the subject itself:

The point of studying the performing arts isn't necessarily to become a famous actor or actress but it's about being able to express yourself and about having the confidence to stand up in a room full of people and say 'this is me'; it's about going for a job interview and being able to look somebody in the eye; it's about being a better person I guess, because you have an empathy for other people. I'd love to think that because of the performing arts experience that they get here that it does develop them as individuals.

They also held that the dispositions acquired in the arts were transferable:

We have had generations of medics, dentists and vets and they will come back and say that art was the best subject they did because they were able to fly at university; they can communicate; they can be proactive about sorting out groups and discussions and they have a social network quite quickly. Most kids get a lot out of the experience of doing art and they know that they can transfer some of those skills later on to whatever degree they do.

For this reason, and together with their commitments to access and equity, TALE teachers often told us that the arts were particularly important for students who were not experiencing success in other school subjects:

A lot of the people in that [drama] group are big characters around school but, when you get to know them, they are quite vulnerable and quite alone inside. So it is definitely about giving them more confidence and getting them to work in a real-life situation as well, because they've got to do the sound and the lighting for the performance. So it's about time-management skills and delegation skills and all the skills that they will need when they leave us. They will be a lot more independent as well because having targets all the time means that some lessons are more spoon fed teaching rather than allowing them independence.

TALE teachers in arts-rich special schools emphasised that the arts offered a range of ways to communicate, and their signature pedagogies assumed that all students had ideas and were capable of expressing and realising them. Teachers also told us that the arts offered a repertoire of aesthetic, sensory and emotional experiences that other subjects did not. They were person-centred and afforded holistic teaching and learning.

However TALE teachers, even in arts-rich schools, found that developing the artist habitus and arts dispositions in their students was not straightforward. As indicated in the opening field note, putting the need to (up)grade together with individual interests, work patterns, stages of development and the aspiration to support independent artistic work was not always easy. As we explained earlier, the education field frames the work that schools and teachers are able to do. Changes in funding, examination practices, national curriculum requirements, inspection frameworks, qualification criteria, governance and management systems combine to create particular logics of practice. Improving or maintaining position depends on how well agents and institutions are able to manage these logics.

Most teachers, regardless of where they are, experience some of the tension captured in the opening field note – the necessity of holding together the students' need to acquire qualifications (symbolic capital that they could use in securing further education or work) with their own and the school's view of the purposes of education and thus what learning was important. In TALE arts-rich schools, particular pressures were created by the introduction of the secondary school audit measure the English Baccalaureate, which elevated the importance of some subjects over others (as explained in Chapter 1). The arts were not part of the favoured core.

Arts-rich schools were swimming against the policy tide. However, arts-rich schools may well have been able to attract students on the basis of their arts provision. Stable enrolments make for financial viability and a healthy staffing mix, and these in turn are the basis for a broad curriculum offer which includes a full suite of

IMAGE 6.4 Exams are a constant

arts subjects in the junior years, and a wide range of options in the senior school. A virtuous circle. Nevertheless, exams and audit were a constant presence.

Mediating contextual demands

Because the TALE project lasted for three years, we were able to document how arts-rich schools responded to changes in the education field. The project coincided with changes to the examination system and the introduction of the EBacc performance measures. These brought additional pressures and required additional mediation by both arts-broker teachers and leaders of arts-rich schools.

In the first year of the TALE research, we saw that while senior leaders tried to reduce the negative impact of systemic changes on students and teachers, there were nevertheless signs in some of the arts-rich schools that pressures were mounting. In order to maintain their position in the status hierarchy upon which enrolments depended, and in order to avoid punitive interventions arising from poor results or adverse inspection judgements, some leaders turned their attention to maintaining their field position.

In the second year of the project, two TALE teachers were very concerned about the intensity of their schools' focus on exam results. Others expressed concern about changes to the student options system and the limitations that were being placed on students' curriculum choices. Most teachers were worried about how the changes to the exam system would work out.

By year three, teachers were more attuned to the changes in the exam syllabuses and assessment patterns. Most were less worried than they had been about the new exams, although they remained concerned about the impact of the increase in written rather than practical/performance assessments, especially for certain groups of students. One teacher felt the exams undermined students' chances to reflect deeply on their work and so stopped her doing job properly. Teachers in three schools spoke about increased tracking and scrutiny of exam and progress data and their anxiety about being judged by students' results. Teachers generally were very clear about the privileging of STEM (Science, Technology, Engineering, Mathematics) subjects over the arts which impacted on parents' and students' views of the arts. One teacher spoke about the changing profile of students who were choosing and being encouraged to study arts subjects (those who were seen as less academically capable). Others spoke of the impact of curriculum reorganisation (especially squeezing arts subjects into short slots and then leaving gaps when they weren't available to be studied) on continuity and progression in their subject. By contrast, one school had considered a proposal to encourage students to choose more language options (to improve school EBacc statistics) but had rejected it because they believed implementing the proposal would damage the arts.

Of course, different schools in different positions respond to field logics in different ways. For example, one teacher in an arts-rich special school suggested that their sector was under less pressure to conform to external audit measures, although inspection was still a challenge. The box below, which shows three arts-rich schools, indicates some of the different ways these pressures play out in specific locations.

School A is a London maintained comprehensive with a good reputation. It is highly culturally diverse and has slightly lower than average numbers of students on free school meals. It is associated with the Royal Shakespeare Company (RSC) through the drama department. It has maintained drama as a subject throughout the school despite the changing context. The school also offers music, art and design, and dance.

The pressure is on to achieve, and things like English and maths are double weighted, so we end up being in that third timetable bucket. But the arts are still vital, especially in these days where we are measured all the time but, where we are measuring progress, it is the arts that can move those kids forward. So the school recognises that this is important and I have to say that they've been very good in our school at keeping that breadth of provision. Not many schools offer dance as a discrete subject but the students do enjoy it. We add so much to the life of this school and the senior leaders always recognise this.

School B is an independent school in a regional city. The students are from affluent families. There is considerable parental pressure for the students to gain entrance to elite universities. The school visual art department has strong connections with Tate and the local contemporary arts galleries. While the visual arts have maintained enrolments and their position on the timetable, this has taken more effort each year.

We've had to find other ways to promote the importance of the arts within the school and to parents. We've talked about wellbeing. We've focused more on careers guidance – got more instrumental. We've ramped up the partnership with arts organisations and Arts Mark, organised more placements. I've had the medical practitioners' association talk about how useful the visual arts are for doctors. We've had to push the good marks angle with the senior leaders.

School C is in an outer suburb of a major city. It had a poor inspection rating and was moved out of the local authority and became an academy. It was scheduled to move to a new building but in the interim enrolment fell. The new senior leadership team took some time to be convinced that maintaining their successful arts programme was a good idea.

This year we don't have an A Level textiles class and recruitment to GCSE and A Level generally is a concern. It's about funding and making sure that there are enough bums on seats to allow the courses to be viable, so that's a pressure on us too. It's got to be down to the pressures that come from above from the government. It's all about the EBacc and the so-called academic subjects, so you are getting fewer students who feel that they have the freedom to choose those creative subjects that they may have chosen in the past, because they are not seen as valuable. And that reduces the options down. Drama has gone through the floor. All the creative subjects are having to vie for the numbers. But our subject at Key Stage 4 has gone from six periods a fortnight to five, so there has got to be a commensurate change with the quality of outcomes from that. You've also lost an hour with Key Stage 3. We used to have two hours with Year 7 but now we have one and that does mean that the Year 7 don't have as much attention as they did and we don't have the time to do the same projects as we used to. We used to do a lot of sculpture projects but last year our sculpture project only lasted a couple of weeks instead of half a term or so. We are having to change the curriculum to accommodate that.

In addition to the changes in exams, there were two additional key pressures that arts-broker teachers nominated as potentially undermining their programmes and their mission to have students become artists. These were (1) finances and (2) ethos.

1 Financial pressures

In year two of the TALE project teachers were identifying that the financial pressures on their schools were increasing. One mentioned that they would no longer be able to afford to 'buy in' workshops and other external provision; another mentioned the difficulties of funding the transport for visits to local arts and cultural venues. Several schools were facing reduced curriculum time and the number of arts subject groups was being reduced. One school mentioned working with increased class sizes, others mentioned small group sizes which had led to subjects being cut, particularly in the sixth form. The budget for peripatetic music lessons had been reduced in one school and students were for the first time being asked to pay for their own lessons. One teacher mentioned staff leaving and not being replaced; another mentioned a restructuring which reduced the size (and increased the individual responsibilities) of the senior leadership team. Two people mentioned problems with having the curriculum taught by non-specialist teachers. One school had appointed artists as part-time technicians and developed a technician apprenticeship role.

By year three the perception and realities of these financial pressures had increased:

We've probably lost half of our budget of two years ago … We need to consolidate a really good working practice where students achieve and then we need to think about how we could use outside agencies to furnish us with the diversity of ideas that we will need to grow the department. I'm not actually looking to do anything this year. The other thing is that before we were left alone as a department but now we are not being left alone, we are being very closely monitored. So any decision we make must go through a number of checks.

Teachers in four schools explained how they were being required to do more with the same amount of money. Teachers from four more schools said that lack of money meant that staff had left and had not been replaced. A lot of interviewees spoke of having new roles and titles, often with far wider remits, which were usually adjustments to incorporate the work of staff who had left and not been replaced. By year three, the budget cuts were more obvious at the everyday classroom level: there was a shortage of stationery, including paper, exercise books and red pens; there was a shortage of books including examination set texts. Some schools could no longer afford to allow students to take the books out of the classroom for study at home. One teacher described photocopying the pages of the text the class was studying because the department could not afford to provide books for the class. Others described 'begging and borrowing' resources for school productions. Support staff had been cut back and the cost of cover for professional development had become an issue.

2 Ethos

In year two, one teacher used the image of a balancing act. This sense of uncertainty about how things would go was evident amongst other interviewees. On the one hand, it seemed harder to get students released from lessons to engage in arts activities; on the other hand, schools were encouraging partnerships with local cultural organisations. Three interviewees mentioned the value of the arts to their school's image and branding; one teacher spoke of arts as being central to the school's identity, and this sense was echoed (more faintly) in other interviews. Three interviewees had a sense that things were going to get worse; another spoke about losing her freedom to do her job. Other schools were more positive: two had adopted a new approach to providing professional development, two teachers mentioned enjoying teaching the revised exam syllabuses.

By year three, six of the TALE teachers conveyed a sense that things were settling down; that they were maintaining the status quo – standing still maybe, but not slipping backwards. This was often linked in the interviews to the view that their school was exceptional in maintaining its commitment to the arts in the current educational context; seven teachers expressed this sentiment:

We are doing more with less and things are challenging. But I think we work very hard to make sure that it doesn't affect teaching. That is where the ethos of the school comes in. A lot of our challenges are around covering teachers because we often need to cover large numbers of teachers to go to events or whatever and we have to balance that as carefully as we possibly can. We have an exceptionally competent business manager who deals with those things really well, which helps a huge amount. But I would like to say that that hasn't had an impact on teaching and learning at all. We try to think of what is best for young people in the face of the pressures of exam boards and external scrutiny but also giving them the opportunity to be aspirational. And the RSC has been a talismanic symbol of that. So there is a real commitment to the arts here.

Where teachers felt that senior leaders' support for the arts was somewhat ambivalent, there was a sense that things were likely to get worse rather than better and that the arts were continuing to be relegated in importance. Ofsted inspections had a debilitating effect on two schools where it seemed to the interviewees that they were treading water, waiting for the next judgement to be made (which was different to the sense of managing to maintain the status quo against the odds). In one school a negative Ofsted inspection, in which the arts subjects had barely been considered, had lowered morale and made teachers question the value of the extra commitments they had been making to promoting students' cultural engagement.

By contrast, three schools had reframed their school mission to be clearer about their commitment to the arts. Two had done this in response to negative Ofsted inspections. One of the schools had increased the focus on teaching and learning and rebalanced the curriculum in favour of the arts. The other had expanded the number of arts subjects on offer, increased arts staffing and embedded art history across the arts curriculum. Two other schools had also made a commitment to improving their arts curriculum offer. Two schools had invested significantly in infrastructure projects related to arts provision.

Managing these tensions and challenges was not easy; it took particular kinds of organisational savvy and personal energy and imagination. Continuing to be enthusiastic and upbeat about their arts subject in the face of doubt and increasingly difficult circumstances required arts teachers' continued attention. Teachers were often sustained by their belief that the development of artists is the core of what arts education in school is about. This grounded their continuing arguments and negotiations about the conditions under which the arts were taught. These arts-broker teachers engaged skilfully in the realpolitik of school organisation and culture because of their own embeddedness in both the education and arts fields.

In the next two chapters, we discuss students' perspectives on these issues.

References

Baldecchino, J. (2019). *Art as unlearning: Towards a mannerist pedagogy.* New York: Routledge.

Ball, S., Maguire, M., & Braun, A. (2012). *How schools do policy: Policy enactments in secondary schools.* London: Routledge.

Burke, C., Cunningham, P., & Hoare, L. (eds) (2021). *Education through the arts for well-being and community: The vision and legacy of Sir Alec Clegg*. London: Routledge.

Fisher, E., & Fortnum, R. (2014). *On not knowing: How artists think*. London: Black Dog Publishing.

Fuerstein, R., Falk, L., & Fuerstein, R. (2015). *Changing minds and brains: The legacy of Reuven Fuerstein: Higher thinking and cognition through mediated learning*. New York: Teachers College Press.

Hall, C., & Thomson, P. (2017). *Inspiring school change: Transforming education through the creative arts*. London: Routledge.

Hayes, D., Hattam, R., Comber, B., Kerkham, L., Lupton, R., & Thomson, P. (2018). *Literacy, leading and learning: Beyond pedagogies of poverty*. London: Routledge.

Souness, D., & Fairley, R. (2005). Room 13. In D. Atkinson & P. Dash (eds), *Social and critical practices in art education* (pp. 41–50). Stoke: Trentham Books.

Vygotsky, L. (1978). *Mind in society: The development of higher psychological processes*. Cambridge, MA: Harvard University Press.

Wacquant, L. (2005). Habitus. In J. Becket & Z. Milan (Eds.), *International Encyclopedia of Economic Sociology*. London: Routledge.

7

STUDENTS' PERSPECTIVE ON CULTURAL CAPITAL

2.05pm: I join the Year 10 class just for the rest of the period. They are working on solo singing pieces for a school production. Everyone is spread out around the dance studio, which is in the PE/sports block. The studio is quite spacious with mirrors down one wall, and high windows in the other two walls. There is a wall on which there are many display boards on dance. The students are all in PE gear – black tights and t-shirts which say [name of school] Performing Arts on the back.

The teacher is working with one student while the others are spread out around the studio, working on their own songs and pieces. "Use the chair to ground yourself, feel that tension in the character's body. I want to see character. I want to see emotion, connecting with the words of the song," he tells her. She sings with the backing instrumental. Others sing quietly in the background. "Feel it in your voice. Feel how that is, moving to something else."

As the lesson comes to a close, the teacher reminds the girls about their log-book entries and the need for some reflection in them. He continues working with one student until the bell goes. Once everyone else is out of the room he moves her to the centre of the room, where she can see herself in the mirror. She says, "I don't want to let people see me because I'm ashamed of me."

"That's heart-breaking," he says to her. "At the moment, don't worry about the words and the notes. Connect." He talks her through the emotions of the song, step by step. Once she has finished, he gives her feedback. "Root yourself. Feel connection to the ground. Look out more. Connect a lot more. Finding similarities between the character and your own life will help you connect." (Lexi's field notes)

What do students learn from interactions like these? The teacher talked to us about confidence, agency and voice. But what did the young women get from this personal coaching? We couldn't find out. But during the three years of the TALE

DOI: 10.4324/9781003093084-7

research project, we did speak with 323 groups of students, 1447 young people from Years 10, 11 and 12. There was a strong correlation between what they and their teachers said about what happened in art, drama and English classrooms. But students also had their own perspectives, particularly on what they understood as the benefits of their own arts education and arts education more generally.

We are not alone in our interest in what students 'get' from engaging in the arts. Educational researchers interested in the arts have focused on whether working with artists over a sustained period of time produces changes in attitudes and motivation (Bamford, 2009), supports students' wellbeing (McLellan, Galton, Steward, & Page, 2012), develops 'soft skills' through the adoption of creative pedagogies (Thomson, Coles, Hallewell, & Keane, 2014) and enhances inclusion (Sanderson, 2008) often through changes in school climate (Bragg & Manchester, 2011). Researchers have also looked for cognitive development (See & Kokotsaki, 2015), how to achieve disciplinary learnings and what these might be (Winner, Goldstein, & Vincent-Lakrin, 2013), and the transfer of arts learning to other curriculum areas (Martin et al., 2013). There is, however, surprisingly little research which asks young people directly about what they see as the benefits of their arts experiences.

In 1995, the National Foundation for Educational Research (Harland, Kinder, & Hartley, 1995) interviewed 700 young people (aged 14–24) across five regions about arts participation in and out of school. Researchers reported that young people were positive about the arts, with two thirds affirming that the arts had had an effect on them in some way and that they "wanted some involvement in the arts in the future". The researchers were particularly impressed by the "testaments to the personal and social benefits of arts involvement, as well as the view that the arts were a humanising and civilising force" (p. 275.) A recent Swedish study (Furst & Nylander, 2020) also focused on young people's experiences, examining the decision of 62 students in folk high schools to choose an arts subject. The researchers report that reasons for choice were not all instrumental: while some saw choosing the arts as a 'stepping stone' to becoming an artist, students also valued the opportunities their subjects afforded for the development of creativity. Some also saw their arts courses offering them a chance to regain health and general wellbeing. The results of both of these studies overlap with our own, as we explain in this chapter.

This chapter picks up discussion of our seventh key concept, cultural capital. We first of all discuss how cultural capital is used in the English national curriculum and compare this with Bourdieu's explanation, reprising briefly some of the points we raised in the first chapter of this book. We then go on to introduce the students' views and follow this with some discussion about how this cultural capital might be used, and to what ends. We use a lot of students' words in this chapter to communicate their enthusiasm and their interpretations. We note that these words can also be read as evidence of whether arts-broker teachers have achieved their pedagogical goals (see Chapters 3, 5, 6).

Cultural capital and the English national curriculum

Ofsted drew attention to the term 'cultural capital' in a 2019 update to school inspection guidance. Inspectors were to consider

> the extent to which schools are equipping pupils with the knowledge and cultural capital they need to succeed in life. Ofsted's understanding of this knowledge and cultural capital matches the understanding set out in the aims of the national curriculum. It is the essential knowledge that pupils need to be educated citizens, introducing them to the best that has been thought and said, and helping to engender an appreciation of human creativity and achievement.
>
> *(Ofsted, 2019, p. 10)*

The rationale for this focus was that: "So many disadvantaged pupils may not have access to cultural capital, both in the home and then in their school" (p. 8). According to Ofsted, schools should ensure that all children and young people have access to an entitlement which included "great works of art, music and literature" (p. 8).

In response to this guidance, schools understandably moved rapidly to ensure that they could demonstrate that they were 'doing' and 'delivering' cultural capital. Various 'explainers' were developed for teachers which offered interpretations of cultural capital, often citing Bourdieu (Beadle, 2020). There was also critique: essentially that the Ofsted version of cultural capital took a "cultural restorationist" (Apple, 2001) approach to knowledge, promoting elitist art forms while the cultural practices and forms of more marginalised or disadvantaged groups risked stigmatisation or suppression.

Bourdieu argued that the social and cultural capitals prioritised in the education field were built on the capitals of families who were already privileged in cultural and economic terms. This includes elite cultural capitals, 'the best that can be thought and said', as Matthew Arnold had it. Wealthy families can afford to go regularly to opera, ballet and theatre, and these capitals become familiar to their children. Looked at through this lens, Ofsted's interpretation of cultural capital can be seen, in Bourdieusian terms, as a form of symbolic violence, not simply because it ignores marginalised cultural capitals, but rather because it equates a description of curriculum with the processes of the (re)production of inequity that Bourdieu's analysis exposes (Archer et al., 2018).

The TALE project findings offer evidence highly pertinent to these debates, not least because the research was conducted in 30 schools associated with arts institutions which deal in elite cultural capitals. Tate's mission, as a national and international art museum, is to build a collection which includes the 'best' of popular and avant-garde art forms. The core of the work of the Royal Shakespeare Company (RSC) is the preservation and interpretation of Shakespeare's work, the quintessence of canonical English literature. Shakespeare's plays are the only compulsory texts in the English national school curriculum. Taught in all secondary schools in either English or Drama, or both, the Bard is positioned as a synecdoche for British culture and the 'quality' literary texts that the nation's school children must read and appreciate. But Shakespeare also appears in popular art forms (Lanier, 2002) and supports a small global cultural 'industry' (Shellard & Keenan, 2016), as do many of the reproductions of works in the Tate collection.

Both of these prestigious (inter)national arts organisations invest, as we have seen, in substantive programmes of immersive professional learning for teachers, and participatory activities for students. These school programmes can be seen as exemplifying Ofsted's guidance about access to cultural capital. Both arts organisations start from the position that the artwork they nurture and promote belongs to everyone, a view we wholeheartedly endorse. But, crucially, the pedagogies that they promote and develop, in partnership with schools and teachers, encourage both appreciative evaluation and critical socially situated analysis. These practices – built through the work of the individual arts-broker teachers, at the classroom level, and at the institutional level by the ethos, priorities and practices of the arts-rich school – are equally applicable to canonical forms and to vernacular, community and popular arts.

We turn now to evidence from the students themselves to back up this claim and to illustrate their views on the cultural capital they acquired through their studies.

Students' views of their arts education

Our focus groups were with senior secondary students who had chosen to maintain their arts studies. We report here on why they thought the arts in general were important as well as the reasons they gave for their choices of visual or performing arts. We report first on two themes that were common to all the students: (1) personal development, and (2) the cultural value of arts. We then move to one theme which relates specifically to visual arts, (3) creative self-expression, and another which relates to the performing arts, (4) vocational/professional learning and networking. We first of all describe the theme, illustrated by quotations from students that typify the corpus, then comment on cultural capitals.

1 Personal development

Students overwhelmingly told us that being a teenager was difficult and studying an arts subject helped them to address their emotions. The arts allow you to express your feelings: *It helps me to deal with tricky emotions; It's helped me grow as a person; You can literally get it all out; Being able to voice your emotions is so important.* Arts media, genres and platforms, used to explore feelings, afforded a growing sense of identity: *When I express myself better, I know who I am better.*

The students made connections between the pedagogies used in their arts subjects (see Chapter 6) and their personal development. Their arts subjects:

- work with the whole person, recognising and using everyday knowledges and experiences – *You involve your daily life in your drama piece ... with your other subjects you are not so much doing that.*

- offer daunting challenges – *In drama we have had opportunities to stand in a 900-seat auditorium and perform ... once you can do that you can do a lot more.* Achieving ambitious goals in turn builds self-belief – *I know it's a cliché but I didn't think I'd be able to do it.*
- not simply allow, but demand, that students offer their own interpretations – *I didn't like being told what was right and wrong. I know it's only Shakespeare but we came in the room and they said you can read this text and have your own opinions. It was really good.*
- expect students to be independent learners – *You can do what you want to do and not what you are told to do; you find your own way of doing things.* The move to independent learning is carefully scaffolded by teachers – *They give you guidelines of what you have to have completed by a certain point and they let you get on with it, instead of telling you every single step.* Learning independently often requires new approaches to self-management – *It helps you manage time well. Art takes so long. Planning. Trial and error.*
- require students to work collaboratively with others, to negotiate processes and manage conflicts – *You learn how to cope with other people. You are in a close environment for a number of weeks and you might get annoyed with certain people but you learn how not to show it.* Students see this as something potentially transferable to other aspects of their lives – *teamwork skills ... it's about everybody being involved.*
- offer activities which are 'outside' as well as 'inside' school – *In the holidays when there are no classes or anything I play my viola constantly; Most of my hobbies are what I study in school; A lot of what I do outside of school is related to art and that then links back to school.* Many of the students were engaged in arts as a life practice not just a subject.
- teach vocational and social attitudes and competences – *The only subject I can think outside of art that teaches creativity and empathy is history. Inside art you learn how to critique. ... we learn how to sit and you go, "This part of your work, that is amazing, that is a good foundation but you haven't really executed it well." You need those skills in work and board meetings. What other subject do you get that in?*

Arts practices were used to explore, identify, articulate, explain, communicate and take charge of 'selves'. Arts education contributed strongly to the ongoing formation of a disposition to be self-managing and responsible; it created a form of "emotional capital" (Reay, 2001) that helped young people find ways to negotiate new interactions. (See in the box below students reflecting on the personal benefits of drama.)

When I wanted to pick drama for GCSE a lot of friends and family members asked me, "How is it going to help?" And at that time I struggled to give them an answer. Right now I am doing it for A Level. I spoke to Mr H [teacher] and I said that I was going to do child psychology or clinical psychology and I recognise that when you are speaking to someone as a psychologist or as a therapist, your patient is not likely to come in and give you their whole life story and their trust – you have to find ways to get them to speak about it, and to open up. And that is where drama comes in. You can use activities to gain their trust.

I feel like not many people are aware of how helpful drama really is. They just think it is something that is a hobby or something that you can just use to pass your time. But it is really helpful in terms of the other subjects as well. In drama we learn about mannerisms and people's attitudes. You can start to unpick people, the way they're acting, if they are touching their face, or what connotations their mannerisms have. It helps with interviews in you know what you have to do to portray yourself in the best way possible.

Because I was talking to Mr T and I was like, "Oh, I want to do some work experience over half term." He was like, "Okay, with your interviews remember about acting and always ask for this, this and this." And the way that you portray yourself, you know, as an actor, because when you're thinking – in English you learn about the writer's intention and you learn about the actors' intention in drama and you know what effect you are actually going to have on the audience. So it's like psychology. You can pick up some things about the character before they even speak because of the way that they're acting. And you can act in ways that show that you are open and approachable, because you've learnt those skills during drama.

Research (e.g. Deer, 2003) suggests that being disposed to and capable of organising your 'self' is important for progressing through the education field, going from school to further and higher education. Self-managing practices and emotional capitals are also important in the arts field where market logics dominate and where every artist must to some degree engage in competitive and entrepreneurial practices (Becker, 1984; Grenfell & Hardy, 2007). Additionally, teamwork and successful collaboration are linked with building social capital, with finding and becoming part of socio-cultural-economic networks which are significant in advancing positions in all social and economic fields (e.g. Montgomery, Parkin, Chisolm, & Locock, 2020).

2 The cultural value of the arts

In line with their views of their arts subject as having significant personal benefits, students saw the trend for schools to marginalise arts teaching as one which unfairly limited choices. *Try and keep creative arts in schools! Yes. Do not take them out. We need them! I think it is important for kids' development. It is something different. It is not in the mould. It gives people a chance to explore, find who they are.* The capacity of the arts to explore a self was particularly important for students already on the edges of schooling. *A lot of children in the younger years are very reliant on the arts as a form of avoiding getting into the wrong crowd. It's a good form of guidance and an after-school thing that stops them from going down a bad route. It keeps their concentration, focus and it's unfortunate that people don't see it that way. They see it as an unnecessary thing on the side. But really it helps so many people.* At senior secondary level, students asserted that they ought to be able to take the subjects they were interested in, unimpeded by poor career advice, restricted timetabling or lack of school subject funding.

Relatively few students (fewer than 50) offered reasons for valuing the arts that were societal in nature, although we assume that at least some of the benefits that were ascribed as personal might also be seen as collective. Of the societal reasons, the most common was related to the quotidian nature of the arts – *People don't realise how important the arts are in society today. If you removed the arts, you'd have to stop watching TV or reading magazines; Everything we have is a form of art. It has been designed. It reflects everything of the time, politics, everything.* We took the implication of these comments to be that it was important for young people to both study the arts as an everyday human activity, and to prepare them to make the art that enriches everyday life – *Where are you going to get architects and stuff from? It's literally such a big part of everyday life and I think no one realises. It'd be stupid getting rid of the arts!; There are loads of jobs out there that you need art for and a qualification is a good tool to have; It shows that you are creative.*

Other reasons given were:

- The arts entertain – *I get it, we need doctors, we need lawyers. But at the end of the day the doctor is going to watch Coronation Street or is going to the theatre. Your doctors and lawyers need to be entertained.* And the arts can entertain in ways that other activities do not – *No other subject can move people like the arts. When you go to a theatre you can get lost in this incredible world that has been created around you, and you can get fully immersed in it.*
- The arts are educative; they teach us who we are and who we might be – *The arts aren't just about entertainment, they are about education, information, giving political opinions; We've always had the arts. It's not something new. We've had them for hundreds and thousands of years. They provide knowledge of the past as well.*
- The arts create social bonds – *brings people together, engages other people with other people's stuff. One of my favourite things is when I hear something that my friend has done and I really like it. It makes you go, "That's great." It makes you more communal.*
- The arts are essential for wellbeing and mental health – *Art is such a fantastic way to make people engage, to have awareness, especially in this day and age where it is a really hard thing to have. It focuses you on something that is not there but that can be made by you. The fact that it is made by you and you have taken in and then you're putting out again is quite a sense of gratification and achievement, to create and actually make something. To take in and then push out. For mental health it is just because of that one thing alone. That sense of, I've made something.*
- The arts are integral to the development of place – *Our whole society is based on the arts and it's not appreciated. Quite a lot of artists go to a place and the business follows. But then they have to move on again, because it gets too expensive to live there.*

- The arts offer a platform to express points of view, sometimes highly political views – *the arts have always been a way to stick it to the government … I think cutting the arts at state-school level stops students being able to fully express, in a dramatic kind of way, their views on things that are going on. But it doesn't affect private schools such as Eton with their three theatres because they do it themselves. By them cutting funding for the arts in schools like this one, I think it is a way of making sure we don't fully express what we want to express.*

The students we spoke to did not generally engage in "defensive instrumentalism" (Belfiore, 2012): they largely did not reproduce some of the broader public conversations about the social purposes of the arts. Students did not talk about the importance of the creative industries to the economy, for instance, as do arts organisations and artists. Nor did they talk about art and culture as an entitlement, as did their teachers, and, in a more selective way, Ofsted. (See in the box below students reflecting on encountering elite cultural capital through art.)

Last Thursday we went to Rachel Whiteread. The week before we went to the Barbican to see Basquiat. We went to the Jerwood Space to see the Jerwood Drawing Prize. That was really cool. I really liked that.

I feel really lucky because we didn't really have that at my old school. We did go to one exhibition in Year 10 but that was about it, and she did tell us about artists and things that we could go to but there weren't many people that did it. I did do because I was like, "Oh, I want to see exhibitions."

So I was really excited when I first got here and Miss was, 'We're going to be going to loads of exhibitions." It takes me some time to go out and actually try and explore. So it's really good that we're seeing different things, things you might not know about. It is just really important I think to widen your view of what art can be. I think before, when I came here, I wouldn't say I was narrow minded but I would say I didn't know that much about other types of art. I was mostly focused on what I knew before, certain artists. But going to the Basquiat exhibition, I never thought I would like that sort of stuff. It is so abstract. So many brushstrokes you can see. I just didn't think I would like that sort of thing, but it was really cool to open my eyes.

We also learnt about more particular cultural capitals by looking separately at art and drama students' conversations.

3 Individual creative self-expression (visual art)

Whether asked about their reasons for choosing an arts subject, their arts experiences, or the reasons arts were important in the curriculum, the vast majority of visual arts students talked about the crucial importance of individual creative expression (see Chapter 5). Some students enrolled in drama or English spoke of the value of individual interpretation of given texts – *English has been the only subject that's allowed me to be able to interpret different attitudes. All the teachers we've had and all the plays we've studied, they've all prompted us to have our own different attitudes to stuff.* But art students said that *Art helps people to express their own ideas, their own views.* Furthermore, the processes of self-expression were an object of study themselves – *Art is a journey. In physics, it's a bit like coming into a film halfway through, other people have made a lot of discoveries and you are working with some givens ... you are being asked to work something out based on an assumption, and that one thing links to another. But in art I am trying to understand my creative process, my entire way of doing things.*

The students described their art practices as individualised, but this singularity was also understood in democratic terms:

- the arts are not an elite practice; everyone can make art – *Once you start creating your own work, you become an artist.*
- failure to ensure that everyone is able to express themselves has negative consequences – *You have the freedom to express yourself in a positive manner and no other subject lets you do that. And if it's not important for people to express themselves, then you're effectively creating a dictatorship.* It is thus important for those in power to ensure that individuals are free to express themselves through the arts – *I hear stuff like art's not important and I'm like, "Well, it is important to some people, but it may not be important to you."*

Students had different views on why self-expression was connected with democracy. While some saw politics in art as a question of individual expression and rights – *We have a joke that we all have our own thing. Casting, folding paper, miniatures, defying government* – others disagreed. Some students engaged in forms of socially engaged art – *I did identity as my project. I moved house during last year. One thing I did was talking about identity of objects and the identity of them you overlook. So I was looking at a tree in my old house's garden and then I knitted this jumper for a whole tree. When it's windy the trees are still the same, when it's sunny the trees are the same. I was like that means they have a vulnerable identity which we all overlook so I had that and then I went to my new house and developed the work by putting the same knitting on the tree and then because this tree was bigger, this tree was even more exposed so I knitted some more layers for it. I liked that because it was different and it was fun to knit. It's this art called yarn bombing.* Others saw that art offered them the opportunity to become politically well-informed – *My art is very political. I don't want to just spread messages, I want to fully understand.* Other students saw art as a means of answering back, and thus to change power relationships and hierarchies – *The art that is promoted is probably art that comes from middle-class society, where it's art that represents white people in really heroic roles. It's not for mainstream people. I try to do representation, like painting Muslim women who are not depicted in art at all. And I'd like to stamp their place in history to be honest.*

Students most often connected politics, arts and themselves. (See the box below on how social and cultural capitals go together.)

Education was originally invented for the system where you sit in a row, you do something, you ask to do something else. So arts subjects completely threw that out the window and let people be themselves and I think that is really important for actually becoming yourself.

Art is not a lesson you come to and dread, because you can do your own thing. You are sitting there doing your own work. You can put your earphones in, listen to music. It is different to my other classes. When you think about our subject combinations, we've all got intense humanities or maths. Then you've got art. You think, "Oh good, I can just sit there and make something." I don't have to write a 1000-word essay that gets an A*. I can just sit and I can do my screenprint and, wow, that is amazing.

Sometimes it can be quite therapeutic as well. If I am doing something and I have my mind set on it in art, I can literally put my earphones in, just be doing it and it is so relaxing. It gives you time off if you like, time to chill, free your mind. For the rest of time you have to be on it just to live up to everyone else's expectations. When I know what I am doing in art I look forward to it. I can't wait to get in and do it. And you can make it personal. If I am angry about something – my whole project now is what I am angry about! I am angry about the way Trump treats this group of people! Let me make art about that. And then everyone is like, "I'm angry about that too", and that is the way you spread the message.

Because it is more creative, you can really bring out your personality. It is more you in your work and in the environment. So you can bond and build that chemistry with other people. At the beginning of the project I was like, "I have no idea", and then someone else was like, "What do you like to do? Okay, put that into art, how can you address that in art?" And through that you learn about each other further. We always end up having random debates about things in art. There is not one person you listen to for the whole two hours. You can feed off each other, talk to each other. You can sit and do what you like but if someone needs help, or you need help, instead of just having the one person, your teacher, to go to, you can go to anyone.

And if your teacher is not present in the classroom, you don't necessarily need them for that time. You can work with each other and you can learn from each other and actually I feel like some of my better ideas have come from when I've been turning to people I know.

Art as self-expression – expressivism – is doxa in the art field and in school art education. Biesta (2017) offers a critique of this, arguing that expressivism in itself is insufficient to underpin an art curriculum in that it fails to raise the question of whether all forms of self-expression are equally morally justifiable. Because the education field is charged with teaching about ways to be and become, such failure, he argues, is significant. As Biesta puts it, referring to the way in which expressivism could be used to justify racist or sexist art, the educational concern can never be about the expression of voice, creativity and identity as such, but has to engage with the far more important and also far more difficult question of the right voice, the right creativity and the right identity

(p. 14)

A Bourdieusian approach to creative self-expression raises additional questions. As doxa, expressivism misrecognises the workings of the education field. In the case of the subject art, the co-located 'truths' of creativity and self-expression obscure the field's sorting and selecting logics. Rather than merit being the 'ability' and 'effort' required to pass various tests and assessments which measure the (re)production of valued disciplinary and linguistic capitals, merit in art is seen as individual, original, creative expression, as we showed in Chapter 5. Selection occurs via teacher judgements about the deployment of art capitals in questioning and making, materialised in artefacts.

However, the capitals acquired in school art may play out differently for different students. Some teachers in the TALE study told us that higher education art schools appear to select young people who not only possess a portfolio of interesting work, but also particular embodied cultural capitals: young people who can talk about their own art practice (creative self-expression) in relation to other art and artists, those who also "look and sound arty". Paradoxically, artiness may involve questioning the very institution they are being interviewed for – as Bourdieu puts it, "Art Schools expect those who attend them to be interested in an art constituted against Art Schools" (Bourdieu, 2001, p. 8). Working-class and BAME students in particular may not easily be able to suppress their desire to make the next move in the field in order to assume the disinterested philosophical stance necessary for elite higher education (see personal accounts in Bennett, 2004; Rose, 1989).

Many students studying art told us they did not want to go to art school. They were, however, worried about how art might be viewed for university entrance more generally. For a short period, advice from the elite Russell Group of universities was not to use subjects outside of the EBacc for entry to any courses. This advice was changed, in part as a result of our own TALE project data, which included students' reports of the ways in which their schools and families had attempted to dissuade them from choosing arts subjects because of the universities' admission advice. Research in the US (Elpus, 2018) on college entrance suggests that there is no adverse effect of including creative arts subjects among those used to gain admittance, but also no positive effect. The same may be true in the UK, although there is no substantive research on this particular topic. Bourdieusian logic leads us to suspect that in the most elite universities and courses, where entry is not only by marks but also by interview, the cultural capitals from studying an arts subject may be an advantage. And as elite universities and courses are disproportionately taken up by students from privileged schools and families (Reay, 2017; The Sutton Trust & Social Mobility Commission, 2019), we have a strong hunch that, in this particular context, arts capitals may play out to further advantage the already advantaged.

Arts dispositions and capitals can of course be used in different ways. While they signify a 'cultured person', they also support contestation of relations of power. The "unknowing" and questioning disposition that is highly valued in the art field (Fisher & Fortnum, 2014) may support art students to resist the dominant pedagogies of the national curriculum but may also support oppositional practices beyond education. The artist habitus may play in other fields.

4 Professional and vocational learning (performing arts)

Unlike the Tate programme which offers immersive professional development to teachers, the RSC works with schools, teachers and students. The RSC bring tools and techniques used in the professional company into schools, advocating and teaching the use of rehearsal room pedagogies (Neelands, 2009; Winston, 2015). All of the students who had been involved in the RSC programme told us about personal benefits (see the first box above), and the particular advantages of the ensemble performance-based approach (as explained in Chapter 5). Students reported the benefits of this pedagogy for their comprehension of plot and language – *It's the language everybody finds a bit hard. When you read a part and you have no idea what they are saying unless you go through it and you'll be like, "Oh yeah, it makes sense now"; It's much more understandable to me and whereas I used to hate it, now I don't because I understand the text, I understand what he is trying to get across. It's taught me quite a lot about Shakespeare.* The rehearsal room's full-bodied engagement with text brings additional insights into character, theme and dramaturgy – *When you act something out, you can put your own interpretation and you can see what kind of feelings that character is feeling; It opens up your eyes – ah, Shakespeare in this scene is trying to depict, let's say, Iago as malicious. But when you're not really acting it out it is hard to picture where that character is coming from.* Being an audience for RSC productions brought students additional insights into the play's potential meanings (c.f. Yandell, Coles, & Bryer, 2020).

These capitals were of benefit to the students in their subject learning, but the benefits differed according to which subject. The RSC secondary school offer is to drama and English literature students, both subjects where Shakespeare is likely to be studied. Students generally had a very clear perception of the hierarchy of subjects within which they were located – *I was having a conversation with my uncle and I was talking about university and what course I'm going to do and he said to me, "Oh, but you're going to take drama at A-Level aren't you?" I said, "Yeah." He said, "You want to be careful of that because some universities don't accept it when they look at your entry requirements." And I just think that's silly. That's how you can tell drama isn't seen as a serious subject. It's seen as something fun that doesn't take much.*

While the capitals and practice offered by the RSC were the primary object of study in drama, they were only part of what was required in English. The subject English requires additional learning: close analytic reading of the text leads to understandings about literary composition and aesthetic qualities; exploration of Shakespeare as theatre-maker in Elizabethan society leads to understandings about the role of the arts and the artist in their own and future society/ies (Olive, 2015). The RSC programme thus offered core drama capitals while English teachers had to do more to cover those required for subject success – *We learn a lot about Shakespeare's context and his influences in the text and how they are shown in the way he writes. Whereas poetry is a bit more, a lot is unseen extracts so you just do it first, annotating, and then we find out a bit more about it ... she [teacher] gave us the questions to help us annotate it and we used those for both Shakespeare and poetry. There are a lot of similar things regarding structure, narrative voice.* Additionally, since drama-associated capitals were not directly assessed in English exams, prioritising acquisition of the exam symbolic capital may have meant that the RSC engagement was time-limited (Schupak, 2018).

Visiting Stratford-upon-Avon to see the home of an elite national theatre company always impressed students – *We went on to Stratford-upon-Avon, the actual theatre itself. We went up there. We saw their version of Romeo and Juliet. To see that stage, that was insane. The special effects, the stage, the cracked floor. I was like wow. Even my technical theatre teacher was like, "I've never seen this before. How are they even doing it?"; I was taking moments out where I just like sat back, just looked around at everyone, saw how many people were engaged with it, were enjoying and it was just a beautiful moment.* Such magical moments create theatre audiences and reinforce the value of this form of cultural capital, precisely as the current national curriculum advocates. Inevitably, of course, such opportunities will be available only to a small minority of students.

Some students got to be more than audience members with backstage passes; they had prolonged access to the company. For those selected to be part of this inner circle the Stratford experience offered additional capitals. Some got very close to their desired future – *I want to be an actor when I am older so being the ambassador, getting to meet other people that have done what I want to do, being with people that want what I want ... the fact that I'm able to talk to these actors that have done the experience that I really want to have, and they give me so many pointers, it is just so great for me.* Not all students wanted to be actors, and the Stratford experience offered insights into associated arts occupations – *We learnt how theatre works as one collaborative machine because there are so many different components and they are all important. So you immediately think the actors are the most important thing but without other parts it wouldn't work at all. 90% isn't acting; Me, L and M went to Stratford-upon-Avon for the RSC. L did marketing, M did costumes and I did stage management. We went for five days. We got to learn the roles that we chose. We got to meet professionals.* The company's ambassador programme offered additional social as well as cultural capital – *We got to meet other people from around the country* and this new network could bring additional personal benefits – *a sense of belonging, that we should be here.*

The RSC programme, which deliberately ensures a wide spread of schools and school mixes in its programme, and of students in its various selective programmes, may not translate into cultural capitals that count equally for all students. Success in drama might variously be of advantage in general university study. Drama and performing arts are offered, as they are in schools, as separate degree subjects and also as part of the subject English. Drama languishes near the bottom of the higher education disciplinary hierarchy, together with media studies, while English is much closer to the top because of its associations with canonical literature (Ladwig, 1996). Drama is more likely, although not exclusively, to be offered as an award in higher education institutions lower in the prestige league tables. The capitals gained through RSC school partnership programmes are likely to be advantageous in all of these instances, but it is the other symbolic capitals – general entry scores combined with class, gender and race – that are likely to carry most weight, particularly with the more prestigious courses and institutions (Barker & Hoskins, 2015; Brooks, 2003).

Most of the students we spoke to had little sense that successful acquisition of the cultural capitals from the school subject drama might not translate into access to further or higher education or to elite drama schools, or that the road to acting via reading English at university is far from straightforward. The students who wanted to work either as actors or in associated occupations seemed to have little idea that the performing arts are dominated by white middle-class alumni of a narrow range of high-fee independent schools (Brook, O'Brien, & Taylor, 2020). Recent scholarship on the creative industries suggests there is no meritocratic pathway leading from schools to further and higher arts education (O'Brien, Laurison, Friedman, & Miles, 2016). Careers in the performing arts in particular are, as Freidman et al. evocatively put it, "like skydiving without a parachute" (Friedman, O'Brien, & Laurison, 2016).

Of course, as the students told us, acting is not the only option in the performing arts and the RSC, like other arts organisation, may be able to offer a selected few students access to other kinds of jobs. (See the box below about vocational capitals and drama.)

We are linked with the RSC as a college. Initially we were given the choice of what we would prefer to do, so whether you'd prefer to do stage management or lighting or props, and you were given your most wanted pick, then your next if you didn't manage to get your choice. Props was a nice combination of my design and technology side of making things and also theatre studies.

We were making the props for a small piece, the first scene from Twelfth Night. There was a shipwreck. There were various different ones you could've gone in, lighting, sound, costume, set design, props. We all worked together to create this piece and they had two professional actors who were acting. It was quite cool at the end of the week to see what everyone had been working on. So the set design people had made the wooden structures. The lighting crew had all these different effects. Sound obviously, the waves and things like that. It was really nice working with the professionals because it was nice to be in that sort of environment. Rather than being sort of kids, doing this because oh you need to be able to get a grade, you're actually doing this because you actually want to create something.

> *I've actually been asked to go back again. They had apprentices up there that we talked to about it, so it's a possible apprenticeship. It is something that I never considered before doing it. It was always more the local wood joineries I was more looking at working for, so it is nice to go a bit further afield to something more creative.*

While Ofsted may understand all of the above as students' access to valued cultural capital, students understood their experiences in more nuanced terms. They saw a range of benefits and applications arising from the acquisition of visual and performing arts cultural capitals. We saw that these capitals might benefit different students differently depending on their social positioning and their life trajectories. Nevertheless, there is much more to cultural capital than being selected for success in school examinations or being able to acquire a place in highly competitive higher education or job market. It is this more general use of cultural capitals that we examine in the next chapter.

References

Apple, M. (2001). *Educating the "right" way: Markets, standards, God and inequality*. New York: RoutledgeFalmer.

Archer, L., Francis, B., Miller, S., Taylor, B., Tereshchenko, A., Mazenod, A., ... Travers, M.-C. (2018). The symbolic violence of setting: A Bourdieusian analysis of mixed methods data on secondary students' views about setting. *British Educational Research Journal*, 44(1), 119–140.

Bamford, A. (2009). *The WOW factor: Global research compendium on the impact of the arts in education*. New York: Waxmann Munster.

Barker, B., & Hoskins, K. (2015). Can high-performing academies overcome family background and improve social mobility? *British Journal of Sociology of Education*, 38(2), 221–240.

Beadle, P. (2020). *The fascist painting: What is cultural capital?* Woodbridge: John Catt.

Becker, H. (1984). *Art worlds*. Berkeley, CA: University of California Press.

Belfiore, E. (2012). "Defensive instrumentalism" and the legacy of New Labour's cultural policies. *Cultural Trends*, 21(2), 103–111.

Bennett, A. (2004). The history boy. *London Review of Books*, 26(11), https://www.lrb.co.uk/the-paper/v26/n11/alan-bennett/the-history-boy.

Biesta, G. (2017) What if? Art education beyond expression and creativity. In C. Naughton, G. Biesta, & D. Cole (eds), *Art, artists and pedagogy: Philosophy and the arts in education* (pp. 11–20). London: Routledge,.

Bourdieu, P. (2001). *Thinking about Art – at Art School* (M. Grenfell, trans.). http://www.michaelgrenfell.co.uk/wp-content/uploads/2016/08/ThinkingAboutArtSchoolPDF.pdf.

Bragg, S., & Manchester, H. (2011). *Creativity, school ethos and the Creative Partnerships Programme*. London: Creativity, Culture and Education.

Brook, O., O'Brien, D., & Taylor, M. (2020). *Culture is bad for you: Inequality in the cultural and creative industries*. Manchester: Manchester University Press.

Brooks, R. (2003). Young people's higher education choices: The role of family and friends. *British Journal of Sociology of Education*, 24(3), 283–297.

Deer, C. (2003). Bourdieu on higher education: The meaning of the growing integration of educational systems and self-reflective practice. *British Journal of Sociology of Education*, 24(2), 195–206.

Elpus, K. (2018). Estimating the effects of music and arts coursework on college admissions outcomes. *Arts Education Policy Review*, 119(3), 111–123.

Fisher, E., & Fortnum, R. (2014). *On not knowing: How artists think*. London: Black Dog Publishing.

Friedman, S., O'Brien, D., & Laurison, D. (2016). 'Like skydiving without a parachute": How class origin shapes occupational trajectories in British acting. *Sociology*, 51(7), 992–1010.

Furst, H., & Nylander, E. (2020). The worth of arts education: Students' justification of a contestable educational choice. *Acta Sociologica*, 62(4), 422–435.

Grenfell, M., & Hardy, C. (2007). *Art rules: Pierre Bourdieu and the visual arts*. Oxford: Berg.

Harland, J., Kinder, K., & Hartley, K. (1995). *Arts in their view: A study of youth participation in the arts*. Slough: NFER.

Ladwig, J. (1996). *Academic distinctions: Theory and methodology in the sociology of school knowledge*. New York: Routledge.

Lanier, D. (2002). *Shakespeare and modern popular culture*. Oxford: Oxford University Press.

Martin, A. J., Mansour, M., Anderson, M., Gibson, R., Liem, G. A. D., & Sudmalis, D. (2013). The role of arts participation in students' academic and non-academic outcomes: A longitudinal study of school, home, and community factors. *Journal of Educational Psychology*, 105(3), 709–727.

McLellan, R., Galton, M., Steward, S., & Page, C. (2012). *The impact of Creative Partnerships on the wellbeing of children and young people*. Newcastle: Creativity, Culture and Education.

Montgomery, C., Parkin, S., Chisolm, A., & Locock, L. (2020). 'Team capital" in quality improvement teams: Findings from an ethnographic study of front-line quality improvement in the NHS. *BMJ OPen Qual.*, 9(2), e000948. 000910.001136/bmjoq-002020–000948.

Neelands, J. (2009). Acting together: Ensemble as a democratic process in art and life. *Research in Drama Education*, 14(2), 173–189.

O'Brien, D., Laurison, D., Friedman, S., & Miles, A. (2016). Are the creative industries meritocratic? *Cultural Trends*, 25(2), 116–131.

Ofsted. (2019). School inspection update. https://assets.publishing.service.gov.uk/government/uploads/system/uploads/attachment_data/file/772056/School_inspection_update_-_January_2019_Special_Edition_180119.pdf.

Olive, S. E. (2015). *Shakespeare valued: Education policy and pedagogy 1989–2009*. Bristol: Intellect Books.

Reay, D. (2001). A useful extension of Bourdieu's conceptual framework? Emotional capital as a way of understanding mother's involvement in their children's education? *The Sociological Review*, 48(4), 568–585.

Reay, D. (2017). *Miseducation: Inequality, education and the working classes*. Bristol: Policy Press.

Rose, M. (1989). *Lives on the boundary: A moving account of the struggles and achievements of America's educational underclass*. New York: Penguin.

Sanderson, P. (2008). The arts, social inclusion and social class: the case of dance. *British Educational Research Journal*, 34(4), 467–490.

Schupak, E. B. (2018). Shakespeare and performance pedagogy: Overcoming the challenges. *Changing English*, 25(2), 163–179.

See, B. H., & Kokotsaki, D. (2015). Impact of arts education on the cognitive and non-cognitive outcomes of school-aged children. https://educationendowmentfoundation.org.uk/uploads/pdf/Arts_Education_Review.pdf.

Shellard, D. & Keenan, S. (ed.) (2016). *Shakespeare's cultural capital: His economic impact from the sixteenth to the twenty-first century*. London: Palgrave Macmillan.

The Sutton Trust, & Social Mobility Commission. (2019). Elitist Britain: The educational backgrounds of Britain's leading people. https://www.suttontrust.com/wp-content/uploads/2019/12/Elitist-Britain-2019.pdf.

Thomson, P., Coles, R., Hallewell, M., & Keane, J. (2014). *A critical review of the Creative Partnerships archive: How was cultural value understood, researched and evidenced?*Swindon: Arts and Humanities Research Council.

Winner, E., Goldstein, T., & Vincent-Lakrin, S. (2013). *Art for art's sake? The impact of arts education*. Paris: Educational Research and Innovation, OECD.

Winston, J. (2015). *Transforming the teaching of Shakespeare with the Royal Shakespeare Company*. London: Bloomsbury.

Yandell, J., Coles, J., & Bryer, T. (2020). Shakespeare for all? Some reflections on the Globe Theatre's Playing Shakespeare with Deutsche Bank Project. *Changing English*, 27(2), 208–228.

8

THE SCHOOL ARTS EFFECT

Everybody in every single school across the country, and any good school anywhere, is going to do the exact same subjects. They're going to do the main language that they study, they're going to do maths, they're going to do science. What sets you out as an individual is all your creative things. Because now, with the technology developing, you can put an equation into a computer and it will spit it out and it will be perfect. Whereas you can't get a computer to create something because it just follows instructions so it's not creative.

I've come from a different sixth form so the art department here is different from my previous school. There's more stuff to do. More materials. Different types of work that we can focus on. That's a different experience for me. I'm being exposed to more things compared to my old school because we didn't really have facilities to do the things we're doing now. So a bit of a difference. Last year in my old school there was more of a focus on just general painting and drawing but now the teachers are trying to make us think further about art and how they expand our ideas of what art is. It's much more broadening our horizons in art.

It's different to other schools locally because a lot of people don't get the opportunities that this school gives you. Though it's not expected, there is a chance for you to do something in the arts here. Even if you're not an artsy type of person you can go and try something and you won't be judged, whereas with other schools, they focus on core subjects like science and maths and English. Whereas here, every time, we have a production and the whole school watches what you've been spending hard work on and everyone applauds you for what you've done. It makes this school different to [names other local schools].

This used to be a technology college. Although DT [design and technology] is pretty solid, science has always been pretty strong, they've always had good teachers. Maths is starting to come back because they've got some great teachers coming in now. But yeah, performing arts has always had strong teachers. It lacked the facilities behind it and our previous headteacher had no intention of expanding performing arts but since the new headteacher came in a few years ago there has been a huge initiative on that. The partnership with the RSC [Royal Shakespeare Company] came in. They built this new building. They try and actively progress it year after year of doing things.

DOI: 10.4324/9781003093084-8

They're helping the teachers who are good at this. I wouldn't have got the grades I got in GCSE and I don't think I would've got the grades I've got now if it weren't for support that the teachers have given me. But the facilities have helped that and the support from the school has helped that. So I think that, yeah, the school does value the arts and they are on the same level as maths and science.

Students in TALE schools had a strong sense of the distinctiveness of their school and how it stood in relation to others. Their assessment of the value of their school's particularity, its vernacular practices and local connections, was comparative. However, while they made normative judgements about their school, students did not always agree with official priorities and evaluations.

Following the lead offered by senior students in arts-rich secondary schools, this chapter begins to examine additional/alternative criteria against which arts-rich schools might be seen. We focus in particular on the benefits to students of their arts education, one of our core research questions. We begin by briefly recapping the current policy context in England before moving to look at the question of 'outcomes'.

English school policy

In England, successive governments have set targets for improvements in school attainment, generally measured through standardised tests and exams. Improvements in education are part of public policy agendas whose details and names change – social inclusion, social mobility, social justice, closing the gap, levelling up – but which are all claimed to offer chances to those at the bottom of the social hierarchy. Successive governments in the UK, where this study is based, have claimed positive changes in educational outcomes as a result of their efforts. However, at the same time, social mobility is stagnant, poverty has increased, the gap between rich and poor has widened, a situation made worse during the Covid-19 pandemic (Pierson, 2022). This apparent paradox suggests that while schools can make some differences, these are unlikely to change wider social inequalities. Schools do not create work beyond their own immediate staffing establishment, for example, even though they can educate young people so that they are ready for work, should jobs be available. Schools can educate more young people so they are ready to go on to further and higher education but cannot guarantee that they will have affordable choices available to them to 'be anything they want to be'.

For the last 50 years, educational researchers have focused on the persistent nexus between family income, family levels of education, school practices and children's educational attainment. Educational researchers have asked how much improvement schools can realistically make. And, if they can make some difference, what that difference is and how it is made. Researchers do not agree about these questions (Slee, Weiner, & Tomlinson, 1998; Thrupp, 2005), and there are various calculations on offer about how much headway schools can make against the odds. There is also considerable discussion about the possible nature of changes in classrooms, schools and the wider school system.

The TALE research sits within this research field. We wanted to know what engaging with an arts-rich curriculum did for students. We were not interested in transferability of arts learning to other subject areas, where there is conflicted evidence. Our interest was on the core arts disciplinary learnings. Expressed more formally, one of our interests in the TALE research was in whether attending an arts-rich schools made a difference to the arts and cultural education and engagement of students, and if so, what kind of difference.

In this chapter, we focus on what we call a school arts effect, our penultimate key concept. We begin by saying a little more about our survey and the TALE arts-rich schools. We then discuss our survey results in relation to two key questions. Firstly, does being in an arts-rich school make young people more interested in the arts? And secondly, from this evidence, what other effects do arts-rich schools have? We also consider how our findings stack up against evidence from other research.

The TALE survey

The TALE survey was designed to assess whether and how the school had influenced students' general interests in the arts. It was administered during the second and third years of the TALE research project. It was originally conceived as an online survey to be conducted at the end of year two, but many of the schools found this difficult. Only one was able to distribute the survey by email to individual students, a situation that has probably now changed because of the pandemic. We therefore offered hard copy surveys to schools early in year three. In total 4477 surveys were completed.

The survey was distributed to all senior secondary students, regardless of whether they were still doing an arts subject or not. Because they were in arts-rich schools, all of them had had at least three years in junior secondary of a rich arts curriculum, and they undertook their particular courses of study in schools where the arts were integral to the school culture. The arts were celebrated publicly through displays and exhibitions, performances, media and school assemblies and events (Chapter 2). We thought that these experiences were likely to be important and wanted to know if this was the case. Students had also been taught by arts-broker teachers who embodied and advocated arts participation outside school (Chapter 3) and whose signature pedagogies were designed to support the development of an artist habitus (Chapter 5) despite the difficulties presented by current examination and audit measures (Chapter 6). Students who studied arts subjects were clear about a wide range of benefits that accrued from the arts learning (Chapter 7). But what about the rest of the students? And how did students in arts-rich schools compare with their peers elsewhere in 'arts-poor' schools?

We start with the question that we suspect many people are most interested in.

Does being in an arts-rich schools make a difference to overall learning outcomes?

The arts-rich schools in the TALE study were not all of a piece. Nearly all of them were in an Ofsted 'good' or 'outstanding' category but two were judged as requiring improvements. However, heads and teachers told us that the overall exam results that senior secondary students obtained in arts subjects were either very good or outstanding and that many students who struggled in other subjects got their highest marks in their arts subject or subjects. Because of the 'success' of the arts, it was hard to consider reducing or cutting them. Even schools under pressure to improve their core academic offer found it difficult to remove or diminish a subject that was both popular and doing well for students. The success of students in arts subjects worked to affirm its importance for students and for the school more generally.

We were able to examine TALE school's results against the national average. Not surprisingly, these results reflected the socio-economic composition of the school's population. (See Table 8.1 for an indication how the socio-economic status of the school population makes a difference in arts-rich schools with quite similar curriculum and teaching practices.)

The six schools in the table above are generally indicative of our data. We can see that in the majority of cases that arts-rich schools did as well as or better than the national average. Some did a little worse overall.

It is important to see what can and cannot be deduced from this data – for example, we can't assume that higher ethnic diversity correlates with lower results. We might conclude that the TALE data suggests that the lower academic results of schools with above-average numbers of pupils in receipt of free school meals (Schools F and C) shows the correlation between socio-economic status and educational outcomes that researchers have been documenting for a very long time. Schools A and B, conversely, indicate class advantage.

We did not have funding or time in the TALE research to carry out a systematic comparison of subject marks in arts-rich schools with comparator schools, so we could not see if an arts-rich school serving an economically prosperous population was the same or different from an arts-poor school with the same kind of population. Nor did we have the time to look specifically at comparator school arts subject results, although in all cases we were told that arts subject marks were high,

TABLE 8.1 Six TALE schools' academic results, free school meals and ethnicity data.

School	Number of pupils	Free School Meals	BAME (as measured on school census)	Ofsted grade	Attainment 8 score	Grade 5 or above in English & Maths GCSEs	Staying in education or entering employment
A	1023	10.4%	19.3%	Outstanding	64.3%	72%	99%
B	1493	15.9%	65.5%	Outstanding	50.3%	46.7%	94%
C	1843	21.3%	25.1%	Good	46.3%	34%	88%
D	1827	21.2%	70.7%	Good	45.6%	48%	96%
E	674	46.7%	74.4%	Good	44.1%	40.2%	89%
F	908	26.6%	1.9%	Good	44.2%	28%	89%
National average		20.8%	32.1%		44.6%	39.6%	94%

and above average. There are, however, pointers we might take from the research literatures which chime with our study.

It may be that the benefits of arts education are to be found in both arts learning and attitudes to school. Researchers suggest that students studying arts subjects have a more positive attitude to and experience of schooling (Bowen & Kisida, 2019) and our research affirms this. Researchers also argue that the arts reduces dropout rates (see Thomas, Singh, & Klopfenstein, 2015 – a five-year large-scale long-itudinal study in Texas) and impact on what some psychologists call 'academic resilience'. Swedish researchers (Thorsen, Hansen, & Johansson, 2021) have strongly associated academic resilience with interest in the arts and perseverance in acquiring arts practices. The general conclusion in the research literatures is that students studying the arts are often highly engaged and motivated to do well in their arts subjects and to continue with them. They thus continue in other subjects as well. Heads, teachers and students in arts-rich schools certainly told us that this was the case.

Closer to home, a recent suite of randomised control trials of arts interventions in England examined whether the arts made a difference to literacy learning (Anders et al., 2021). The meta-analysis, conducted at the end of the intervention, showed that there was no significant difference in literacy between students who had participated in the arts programmes and those who had not. The researchers concluded that this showed that studying the arts neither negatively nor positively affected literacy learning. The researchers note that the results might be different if they were to test students later or if the interventions had been for a longer time.

A three-year longitudinal study of an arts intervention programme in Canada supports the view that the English studies were too short and testing was premature. Similar to the English study, Smithrim and Upitis (2005) showed that involve-ment in the arts did not come at the expense of achievement in mathematics and language. However, they reported a modest but statistically significant effect on student achievement in maths computation and estimation. The researchers note that this difference did not occur until three years of arts programming had taken place.

US researcher Elpus similarly concludes no 'transfer effect' but interprets his results more positively. Elpus's longitudinal studies of high school students studying music suggests that

- well-meaning guidance counsellors and parents can mistakenly assume that studying the arts puts students at a disadvantage. But music students were more likely to apply to college and to attend college than their non-arts peers (Elpus, 2018).
- arts students and non-arts students did not differ in terms of the selectivity of the colleges to which they applied or to which they were admitted. Arts stu-dents were not at a disadvantage in terms of college selectivity when compared to peers who had elected to take more STEM or English courses instead of arts courses in high school (Elpus, 2014).

- music and non-music students dropped out of high school, applied to college, attended college, received college scholarships and grants, and majored in STEM fields at statistically similar rates. These results suggest that school music study does not disadvantage students in the transition to college even when compared with peers who elected additional 'academic' subjects in lieu of music (Elpus, 2022, p. 402).

Elpus notes that studying one art form often meant engagement with arts more generally. In this study, music students were considerably more likely to major in a broader visual or performing arts field than non-music students. Many students were interested in more than one arts field and the blurring of arts disciplines into multi-modal performance forms supported a multi-arts disciplinary focus. Arts-rich schools, where students do well in their arts exams, can take cheer from Elpus's conclusion that there is no 'opportunity cost' in students choosing to specialise in arts subjects. He concludes that

> arts students are served well by their arts study when compared to non-arts students on outcomes related to college admission and attainment. Arts students were more likely than non-arts students to participate in the college admissions process—a necessary step on the pathway toward the attainment of a college degree and the attendant social and financial benefits that accrue to college graduates in American society—and applied to more schools than their non-arts peers.
>
> *(Elpus, 2014, p. 5)*

There is other even more encouraging research about the outcomes of arts learning at school. Catterall's large-scale panel studies are often cited and his claims of a school arts effect go much further than most others. Catterall demonstrated substantial and significant positive differences in academic achievement between students highly involved in the arts and those with little or no arts engagement; this difference held true for economically disadvantaged students. Catterall shows that consistent involvement in the arts equated to increased advantages over time (high school through college to post college destinations) which he argues shows that the arts can go further than any other educational programme in breaking the connections between socio-economic status and education outcomes.

Early evaluations of recent initiatives in the US also show some impact on academic outcomes. The Boston Public Schools Arts Expansion programme uses a range of data sets and data over 11 years to

> estimate changes within, rather than across, students, relative to their own changes in arts education participation. In other words, rather than simply comparing students who take arts courses to students who don't, this student fixed effects approach implicitly compares students to themselves at different points in time
>
> *(Bowen & Kisida, 2021, p. 2)*

75% of the student population in the Boston study was classed as disadvantaged. The study found consistent positive effects on attendance, higher levels of parents' and students' school engagement but mixed effects on test scores. The most positive impacts appeared in middle schooling rather than the early years. However, the goal of the Boston programme was to increase access to arts education per se, not look for the impact on other subjects. This is also the goal of the Seattle Creative Advantage programme where the major focus is on improving arts learning in elementary schools and what the city calls 'Twenty First Century Skills' – critical thinking, creative thinking, communication, collaboration and perseverance. Pre-pandemic evaluations over the life of the programme show consistent improvement in both access to the arts and in the target skills (Baker, Mehlberg, Chighizola, & Patel, 2019).

However, some researchers (see, for example, Xu, Diket, & Brewer, 2018 secondary analysis of NAEP data) strongly disagree that the arts can overcome the impact of the socio-economic (family and neighbourhood) on learning outcomes. The logics of Bourdieusian analysis would also suggest that this is the case. Bourdieu, concerned to explain how schools produced and reproduced the status quo (Bourdieu & Passeron, 1977, 1979), argued as we have discussed that schools favoured particular capitals – those already generally possessed by wealthier families – and ignored the capitals of the working class and immigrants. An example of 'ignoring' can be found in school literacy practices. Schools favour students who already know 'book behaviour': that text and illustrations are related, that the writing goes from left to right, that pages are turned after they are read, that in a formal setting a person being read to waits for an invitation to join in – rather than students who are steeped, for example, in rich oral storytelling traditions (Comber, 2016; Hayes et al., 2018). Bourdieu, as we discussed earlier, called this an "inheritance effect" which, he said, families, educators and policy-makers alike saw as a meritocratic inevitability, rather than as a systematic logic of selection (Bourdieu & Passeron, 1979). Absence and deficit of valued capitals and practices, rather than difference, were noticed and catalogued. Stigmatising rhetoric accompanied pedagogies and testing regimes which rewarded selected children and young people for acquiring elite capitals (Reay, 2017).

Following Bourdieu, we might expect that schools would use only some arts-related cultural capitals which would advantage students who come from homes where they are everyday currency. This is indeed the direction that the national curriculum in England, supported by Ofsted advice, wants schools to take. But, as we have already shown in Chapters 3 and 4, visual and performing arts pedagogies mobilise the capitals that students already possess, including those from family, church, neighbourhood and popular cultures, through processes of idea-generation, improvisation and self-expression. Visual and performing arts do offer elite cultural capitals but also use processes which bring the two capitals together in ways that students find very meaningful and can explain (see Chapter 7). It is not entirely beyond possibility that the arts do, as Catterall's studies suggest, make headway against what often appears to be the inexorable reproduction of educational and social hierarchies.

At the very least, the presence of very large-scale longitudinal research which suggests that arts education may be a sound strategy for what UK policy-makers currently call 'levelling up' should be a reason for much more research to be undertaken on the learning outcomes and life trajectories of students in arts-rich and arts-poor schools. TALE schools suggest that there could be similar positive results.

Does being in an arts-rich school make young people more interested in the arts?

The short answer is yes. Regardless of whether they were still doing an arts subject or not, just over half of the surveyed TALE students reported that their school made a difference to their involvement in and attitude to the arts. The TALE survey showed the importance to young people of encouragement for their engagement with the arts. It also showed the importance of school support and what we call a positive school effect:

1. **School was the place where a significant number of students became interested in the arts.** We might assume that all the students in arts-rich schools had chosen the school for its arts programme. But two out of every ten (22%) of students, and a quarter of students with disabilities, said that their school started off their interest in the arts. They were not interested in the arts before they came to the school.

2. **School had a significant impact on students' engagement with the arts.** Overall, nearly half (45%) of the students thought that their school supported their interest in the arts. Females were more likely than males to think this (51% v. 34%).

3. **Families were also important in encouraging young people's engagement in the arts.** Overall, 38% of students thought their family supported their interest in the arts. *However, about a quarter of the students (26%) did not receive encouragement from their families,* and a further 15% were not sure about family support. Females (45%) were more likely than males (26%) to be encouraged to participate in the arts.

4. **Schools were vital for students whose families did not encourage their arts interest.** Roughly one in ten students (9%) reported that support for their arts interests came only from their school.

5. **For about a third of students (36%), school was where almost all their arts engagement took place.** This is the case for more females (39%) than males (31%), and for more younger than older students (37% Year 10s and 11s, 32% Year 12s and 13s). Two-thirds of the students engaged with the arts outside of school: we discuss this further later.

6. **A small but significant proportion (17%) of students thought that an arts organisation had helped them develop their interest in the arts.** More females (21%) than males (9%) felt this way, and older students were more likely to think it than younger ones.

7.   **The arts featured strongly in students' plans for the future.** More than a third (36%) planned to continue to participate in the arts in their own time. Over a quarter of the students (27%) had plans to study an arts subject; another quarter hoped to get a job in the arts. There were clear gender differences in these plans: 31% females and 19% males planned to study the arts; 28% females and 20% males planned to get a job in the arts; 43% females and 23% males planned to participate in the arts in their own time.

8.   **Many students (43%) would have liked to do more arts activities.** More than half of the females (52%) and just over quarter of the males (27%) felt this way. 38% of students thought that they did not have time to take part in arts activities because of school work. More females (42%) than males (31%) felt this way. 44% of students thought they participated in more arts activities when they were younger. However, students with physical disabilities or learning difficulties were less likely to feel that their participation in the arts has declined as they got older.

9.   **Support and encouragement made a difference to students' engagement in the arts.** When we considered the three types of encouragement to participate in the arts that we asked students about – encouragement from school, their family and from arts organisations – as one variable, we found that:

     •   42% of students did *not* feel encouraged to participate in the arts (by their school, family or an arts organisation)
     •   9% received encouragement only from school
     •   15% received encouragement only from family
     •   2% received encouragement only from an arts organisation
     •   16% received encouragement from school and family
     •   3% received encouragement from school and an arts organisation
     •   3% received encouragement from family and an arts organisation
     •   Only 9% of students received full support (from school, family and an arts organisation).

22% of the students who received full support, (from school, family and an arts association) were highly involved in the arts. Of the students who received no support or encouragement, only 4% were in the 'highly involved' group and 81% were in the 'least involved' group.

There was a marked gender bias towards girls in the degree of support and encouragement received. About a quarter (26%) of females perceived that they were encouraged by two of the three sources of support, while only 15% of males felt this way.

These data could be read negatively. However, it is unrealistic to expect that all students are interested in the arts. It is also possible that some of them did not accept the support that was on offer. We see two things in this data that are highly significant.

Firstly, it is clear that schools do have an effect. Schools introduce students to the arts, students who had not engaged before. To reiterate, in TALE arts-rich schools this was two out of every ten students.

Secondly, the support that schools offer to students interested in the arts makes a difference to their levels of involvement. As we said, one in ten students reported that the only support they got for their arts involvement came from the school. Given the current lack of policy support for arts education, this data is important. It suggests that simply expecting families to do the work of introducing children and young people to the arts and supporting their involvement equates to a recipe for inequity. Schools play an important role in ensuring both arts access and participation.

What other effects does the arts-rich school have?

There were two other areas where the TALE survey showed significant benefits for students. The first was wellbeing and the second the high levels of arts engagement outside of school.

Wellbeing

There is no agreed definition for wellbeing. Research into wellbeing usually refers to two broad types of wellbeing – eudaimonic, the subjective experience of flourishing in a meaningful life, and hedonic, which focuses on happiness and pain-avoidance (Ryan & Deci, 2001). The term wellbeing is often used in association with self-actualisation, realising one's potential, being satisfied with life, being full of vitality and enthusiasm. It can also refer to the absence of pain, not feeling out of control, coping well with problems, being resilient in the face of challenges. Social and economic conditions, cultural norms and individual histories contribute to wellbeing (Diener, 2009). Low levels of wellbeing are strongly associated with inequality (Wilkinson & Pickett, 2010). Wellbeing can be researched through the use of statistical measures such as longevity, physical and mental health, and productivity. It is also researched through self-report – people are asked about their quality of life, levels of stress, happiness and so on. This is what we did in the TALE survey.

The TALE survey showed that *engagement in the arts promoted a sense of personal wellbeing for students*. Nearly half (45%) said that engagement in the arts helped them relax and reduce stress. This was particularly the case for females (53%) and for sixth-form students (49%). Only 22% of students actively disagreed with the idea that engagement with the arts had a positive effect on wellbeing.

This is perhaps to be expected. The arts are often connected with wellbeing. An extensive Systematic Review of over 900 items of published research, commissioned by the World Health Organization (Fancourt & Finn, 2019), examined the beneficial role of the arts in promoting health and wellbeing. Covering a wide range of art forms, the report examined how the arts could prevent, promote, manage and treat a series of factors that affect health and wellbeing. These included:

- affecting the social determinants of health (inequality)
- supporting child development (speech, language, education, etc.)

- encouraging health-promoting behaviours
- helping to prevent ill health (enhancing wellbeing and mental health, reducing the impact of trauma, etc.)
- helping people with mental illness
- supporting people with neurodevelopmental and neurological disorders including autistic spectrum disorder (ASD)

A follow-up report (Fancourt, Warran, & Aughterson, 2020) considered the quality, consistency and impact of over 3500 studies. It found 'strong' support for the ability of the arts to improve wellbeing and mental health in adults and concluded that there was 'some' evidence for the arts to support the child's social development and wellbeing in most policy situations.

Unlike programmes in health and care settings where wellbeing is clearly a major goal, there is some debate about how much wellbeing should be the goal of subjects outside of PSHE, even though it might be a beneficial 'side-effect'. But the connection of arts education with wellbeing features in the education research literatures:

- Elpus, mentioned earlier in this chapter, tracked US students from the earliest years of high school into adulthood (2013). He claimed that students of the arts at school and college had better mental health and were more optimistic about their future study and adult lives.
- A UK-based Systematic Review which focused on the health and wellbeing benefits of the arts (All Party Parliamentary Group on Arts, 2017) briefly covered the benefits of arts education noting increased self-esteem and confidence through music, drama and movement.
- Another narrative review analysed around 2500 pieces of evidence which covered the therapeutic use of the arts for factors of wellbeing and physical health (McLellan & Galton, 2014). In addition to the extensive literature review, the report built on previous research (McLellan, Galton, Stewart, & Page, 2012) by the authors that looked at inspirational arts practitioners in schools and how they fostered a positive 'classroom climate' that promoted eudemonic aspects of wellbeing, as well as the hedonic aspects that tended to be promoted by the control schools.

In education, wellbeing is often associated with an inclusive school climate, the quality of pastoral care, character education, teaching methods and assessment regimes. There is research which connects creative curriculum programmes with a positive school ethos and student wellbeing.

But researchers vary in the ways that they name aspects of wellbeing. A three-year Danish mixed-methods study (Chemi, 2015) of an arts intervention in 35 schools in one municipality (1600 teachers and 12,000 students) concluded that 'positive emotions and cognitive intensity' were the most significant outcomes. Other researchers suggest that the arts can be a 'healing avenue' for students to work through difficult knowledges and historical traumas (Hickman & Sinha Fuller, 2020); the arts offer students the opportunity to build 'positive feelings' by allowing them to interact with peers and younger students (Hickman, 2006); the arts allow students to 'regain health' after a difficult period in their lives (Furst & Nylander, 2020). Some students told us about these in the focus groups. The emerging research on arts education during the Covid pandemic also suggests that arts education may be crucial for both a recovery curriculum and rethinking schooling, because of its impact on wellbeing (Kraehe, 2020; Tam, 2020).

Wellbeing is often connected with autonomy and self-efficacy (Bonneville-Roussy, Hruska, & Trower, 2020; Woodson, Quirogi, Underiner, & Karimi, 2017) and inclusive environments (Roseth, 2019) and these connections resonate strongly with our analysis of the dominant independence- and agency-focused pedagogies and curriculum structures of the visual and performing arts. The sizeable proportion of TALE students who agreed with the statement that their arts activities alleviate stress sits very comfortably with this particular body of research.

Engagement and participation

The TALE survey results showed that young people overall were highly engaged with the arts. Regardless of whether they were studying an arts subject or not:

1. **Students' interests in the arts ranged across a variety of forms.** Nearly all of those surveyed (91%) listened to music daily; about three-quarters of them (74%) sometimes painted or drew; over half (53%) read books or comics outside school at least once a month.
2. **Students were enthusiastic audience members.** 79% of those surveyed had attended a live performance in the previous year. Almost all students were interested in films: 43% visited cinemas at least once a month and 60% watched a film at least once a week. 36% of students had attended a dance performance and more than half (52%) had visited an art museum in the previous year.
3. **Students used digital media to explore, share and discuss their interests in the arts.** Half of the students (51%) used websites to research the arts; more than a quarter (26%) used them to share and discuss arts. 16% of students had created their own arts related blog, website or podcast.

If policy-makers are interested in audience creation, then is it clear that arts-rich schools can play a significant role. The expansive arts curriculum on offer, the work of arts-broker teachers and the partnerships with arts organisations work together to encourage students to participate in the arts outside of school as well as inside.

Participation also means students moving beyond being an audience member to becoming arts producers in their own right.

1. **Students were creative in their spare time.** 40% had created stories, plays or poems on their own at least once or twice in the past year; 31% were involved in producing, writing or creating music. 34% had created computer games. A third of students engaged in photography, drawing or painting at least once a week. Over a third (35%) made models or sculptures once a year or more often. Over a quarter of the students (27%) regularly worked with textiles or engaged in craft work such as jewellery making, wood or metal work (26%). 13% of students created their own films at least once a month. 28% had created new dance routines in the previous year.

2. **For a significant minority of students, engagement in out-of-school arts activities was a daily event.** 20% read, 11% painted or drew and 16% took photographs every day. 26% of students played a musical instrument very regularly. About a third (32%) of students worked part-time outside school and doing paid or voluntary work was not a barrier to arts engagement. In fact, students who worked out of school were more involved in arts activities than those who did not.

3. **Students were interested in arts learning out of school.** Many joined arts groups and enjoyed performing. Nearly one third (32%) took part in out-of-school music lessons or projects and 60% played a musical instrument or device. 29% sang as part of a band or choir. About a quarter (23%) belonged to drama or theatre groups out of school. 28% were in dance clubs and 25% took dance lessons. 13% had performed poetry in the previous year and 12% were part of a book group or club.

One of the most interesting survey results came from the comparison between the TALE students and the national picture. Our survey was designed to allow comparisons to be drawn between the cultural engagement of students in the sample schools and a representative national sample who had responded to the DCMS/Arts Council's annual *Taking Part* survey. To account for the technical differences between the two surveys, we created a matched sub-sample of findings from the responses of 14- and 15-year-olds. Figures 8.1 and 8.2 shows the percentage of this sub-sample of TALE respondents (final column) who were engaged in different arts activities, compared to the national picture (the other columns) in previous years. Although there were differences depending on the arts activity/venue, the survey data show levels of cultural participation amongst students from the TALE arts-rich schools that are often significantly greater than the national average and arrest what looks like a slow decline over the years.

We also compared levels of engagement with everyday creative activities. Figure 8.2 shows that students in the TALE schools were significantly more engaged in these creative activities.

However, it was also clear in the data that there was not a level playing field: some TALE students experienced more barriers to cultural engagement than

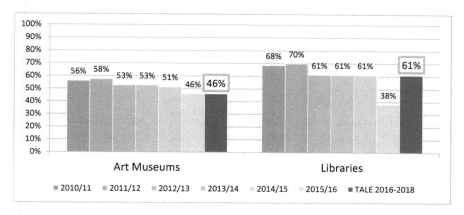

FIGURE 8.1 Student engagement in arts activities.

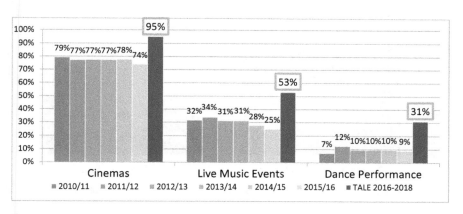

FIGURE 8.2 Student engagement in arts activities.

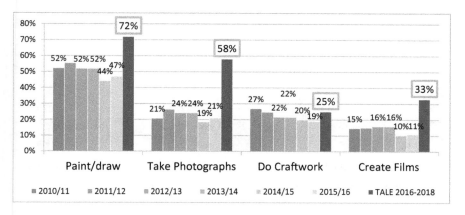

FIGURE 8.3 Student involvement in producing arts.

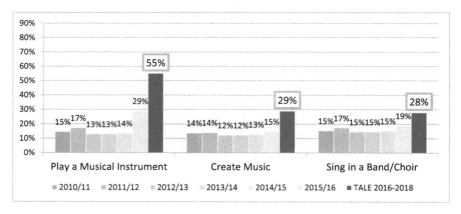

FIGURE 8.4 Student involvement in producing arts.

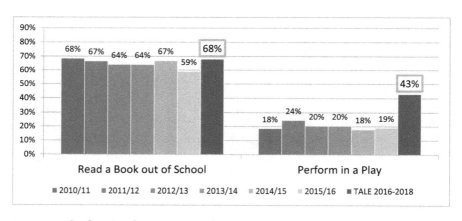

FIGURE 8.5 Student involvement in producing arts.

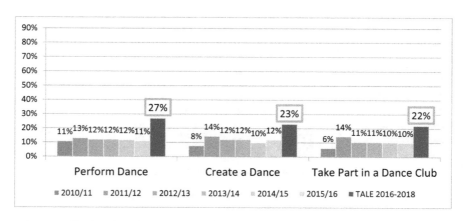

FIGURE 8.6 Student involvement in producing arts.

others. When we divided the students into three groups – highly involved, averagely involved and not very involved – we found that:

- Students who were highly engaged in one arts activity were more likely to participate in other forms of arts activity as well (c.f. Elpus, discussed earlier)
- The highly involved group particularly engaged with music, drama and dance
- Students who were least involved with arts were most likely to be involved with film, music, visual art or craft
- There were slightly more females (6%) than males (4%) in the highly involved group. 28% of the 112 students who identified as non-binary were in this group
- Males made up 78% of the least involved group
- White British (66%), Asian British Bangladeshi (77%) and Asian British Pakistani (64%) were the least involved ethnic groups
- Almost a quarter (23%) of students with a physical disability and 14% of students with learning difficulties (compared to 5% of those without physical disabilities or learning difficulties) were in the highly involved group.

These data point strongly to school-level effects in relation to attendance at cultural events and performances. While there is clearly scope for improving understanding about the barriers that inhibit the engagement of some social groups, the implication of the comparative findings is that attending an arts-rich school brings the benefit of supporting a wider group of young people to be active participants in the arts, regardless of whether they choose to continue studying arts subjects. Following both Bourdieu and Catterall's longitudinal studies on the power of the arts to challenge the reproductive effects of schooling, we might assume that many of these students did not have access to these cultural capitals at home.

TALE is not the only research project to produce evidence of significant 'outside school' arts activity which correlates with a school effect. Catterall (2009) and Elpus (2013), whose work was discussed earlier, also found something similar, as did Xu, Diket and Brewer (Xu et al., 2018) who conducted a secondary data analysis of 3912 records of US National Assessment of Educational Progress eighth-grade visual arts data. They found that home environment had the strongest impact on student arts performance, a result congruent with the broader educational research field. They also found that while school arts activities had a lesser impact than families on curriculum performance (test and exam results), they had a strong and significant impact on what the researchers call 'Not-for-School' activities, the activities that we call extra-curricular and out-of-school arts engagement and participation. Here, the school influence was stronger than the home. A school effect. Xu et al. suggest that school performance as measured by the NAEP could be improved if Not-for-School activities were more in tune with formal education. Their recommendations include:

- Make certain that national arts organisations do not over-emphasise, promote and over-fund Not-For School programming that is shown to have questionable school performance results.

- Make certain that cultural and community arts centres and programmes align with the more academic qualities found in school curriculums (Xu et al., 2018, p. 240).

We take a very different view, as we will explain in the next chapter, where we introduce our final key concept, cultural citizenship.

References

Ainscow, M. (2015). *Towards self-improving school systems: Lessons from a city challenge.* London: Routledge.

All Party Parliamentary Group on Arts, Health and Wellbeing. (2017). Creative health: The arts for health and wellbeing. London. https://www.culturehealthandwellbeing.org.uk/appg-inquiry/Publications/Creative_Health_The_Short_Report.pdf.

Anders, J., Shure, N., Wyse, D., Bohling, K., Sutherland, A., Barnard, M., ... Behavioural Insights Team. (2021). *Learning about culture: Overarching evaluators' report.* London.

Baker, D. B., Mehlberg, S. M., Chighizola, B., & Patel, R. (2019). The Creative Advantage. Year 5 Evaluation Report. https://www.creativeadvantageseattle.org/wp-content/uploads/2019/05/CA-Eval-Y5-2017-18.pdf.

Bonneville-Roussy, A., Hruska, E., & Trower, H. (2020). Teaching music to support students: How autonomy-supportive music teachers increase students' well-being. *Journal of research in Music Education,* 68(1), 97–119.

Bourdieu, P., & Passeron, J. C. (1977). *Reproduction in society, education and culture.* London: Sage.

Bourdieu, P., & Passeron, J. C. (1979). *The inheritors, French students and their relation to culture.* Chicago: University of Chicago Press.

Bowen, D. B., & Kisida, B. (2019). Investigating causal effects of arts education experiences. Experimental evidence from Houston's arts access initiative. https://kinder.rice.edu/sites/default/files/documents/Investigating%20Causal%20Effects%20of%20Arts%20Education%20Experiences%20Final_0.pdf.

Bowen, D. H., & Kisida, B. (2021). The arts advantage: Impacts of arts education on Boston students. https://www.edvestors.org/wp-content/uploads/2021/04/The-Arts-Advantage-Impacts-of-Arts-Education-on-Boston- Students.pdf.

Bragg, S., & Manchester, H. (2011). *Creativity, school ethos and the Creative Partnerships Programme.* London: Creativity, Culture and Education.

Bragg, S., & Manchester, H. (2017). Considerate, convivial and capacious? Finding a language to capture ethos in "creative" schools. *Discourse,* 38(6), 864–879.

Bukodi, E., & Goldthorpe, J. H. (2018). *Social mobility and education in Britain: Research, politics and policy.* Cambridge: Cambridge University Press.

Catterall, J. S. (2009). *Doing well and doing good by doing art.* Los Angeles: I-Group Books.

Catterall, J. S., Dumais, S. A., & Hampden-Thompson, G. (2012). *The arts and achievement in at risk youth: Findings: four longitudinal studies.* Washington, DC: National Endowment for the Arts.

Catterall, J. S., & Peppler, K. (2007). Learning in the visual arts and the world views of young children. *Cambridge Journal of Education,* 37(4), 543–560.

Chemi, T. (2015). Learning through the arts in Denmark: A positive psychology qualitative approach. *Journal for Learning through the Arts,* 11(1). http://escholarship.org/uc/item/84q9717f.

Comber, B. (2016). *Literacy, place and pedagogies of possibility.* London: Routledge.

Diener, E. (2009). *Assessing well-being: The collected works of Ed Diener.* New York: Springer.

Earley, P., & Greany, T. (eds). (2017). *School leadership and education system reform.* London: Bloomsbury.

Elpus, K. (2013). *Arts education and positive youth development: Cognitive, behavioral, and social outcomes of adolescents who study the arts.* Washington, DC: National Endowment for the Arts.

Elpus, K. (2014). Arts education as a pathway to college. https://www.arts.gov/sites/default/files/Research-Art-Works-Maryland2-rev.pdf.

Elpus, K. (2018). Estimating the effect of music and arts coursework on college admissions outcomes. *Arts Education Policy Review,* 119(3), 111–123.

Elpus, K. (2022). School music and the transition to college. *Journal of Research in Music Education,* 69(4), 402–424.

Eyles, A., Elliott Major, L., & Machin, S. (2022). *Social mobility – past, present, future.* London: Sutton Trust.

Fancourt, D., & Finn, S. (2019). *What is the evidence of the role of the arts in improving health and well-being? A scoping review.* Copenhagen: World Health Organization.

Fancourt, D., Warran, K., & Aughterson, H. (2020). *Evidence summary for policy. The role of arts in improving health and wellbeing. Report to the Department for Digital, Culture, Media and Sport.* London: UCL Department of Behavioural Science and Health.

Fullan, M., Quinn, J., & McEachern, J. (2018). *Deep learning: Engage the world change the world.* Thousand Oaks, CA: Corwin.

Furst, H., & Nylander, E. (2020). The worth of arts education: Students' justification of a contestable educational choice. *Acta Sociologica,* 62(4), 422–435.

Gorard, S. (2018). *Education policy, equity and effectiveness: Evidence of equity and effectiveness.* Bristol: Policy Press.

Hayes, D., Hattam, R., Comber, B., Kerkham, L., Lupton, R., & Thomson, P. (2018). *Literacy, leading and learning: Beyond pedagogies of poverty.* London: Routledge.

Hickman, R. (2006). Raising pupils' self-esteem through leadership activities in Art. *IJADE,* 25(3), 329–340.

Hickman, R., & Sinha Fuller, K. (2020). Healing trauma with art and the affective turn. *JCRAE,* 37, 90–91.

Hill, B. (1977). *The schools.* London: Penguin.

Joseph Rowntree Foundation. (2022). *UK Poverty 2022: The essential guide to understanding poverty in the UK.* York: Joseph Rowntree Foundation.

Kraehe, A. M. (2020). Dreading, pivoting, and arting: The future of art curriculum in a post-pandemic world. *Art Education,* 73(4), 4–7.

Leithwood, K., Jantzi, D., & McElheron-Hopkins, C. (2006). The development and testing of a school improvement model. *School Effectiveness and School Improvement,* 17(4), 441–464.

McLellan, R., & Galton, M. (2014). *The impact of arts interventions on health outcomes: A survey of young adolescents.* Cambridge: University of Cambridge Press.

McLellan, R., Galton, M., Stewart, S., & Page, C. (2012). *The impact of creative initiatives on wellbeing: A literature review.* Newcastle: Creativity, Culture & Education (CCE).

McLellan, R., Galton, M., Steward, S., & Page, C. (2012). *The impact of Creative Partnerships on the wellbeing of children and young people.* Newcastle: Creativity, Culture and Education.

Pierson, C. (2022). *The next welfare state? UK welfare after Covid-19.* Bristol: Policy Press.

Reay, D. (2017). *Miseducation. Inequality, education and the working classes.* Bristol: Policy Press.

Roseth, N. E. (2019). Features of university environments that support well-being as perceived by lesbian, gay, bisexual and questioning undergraduate Music and Art students. *Journal of Research in Music Education,* 67(2), 171–192.

Rutter, M., Mortimore, P., & Maugham, B. (1979). *Fifteen thousand hours: Secondary schools and their effects*. Boston: Harvard University Press.

Ryan, R. M., & Deci, E. L. (2001). To be happy or to be self-fulfilled: A review of research on hedonic and eudaemonic well-being. *Annual Review of Psychology*, 52(8), 141–166.

Slee, R., Weiner, G., & Tomlinson, S. (eds). (1998). *School effectiveness for whom? Challenges to the school effectiveness and school improvement movements*. London: Falmer.

Smithrim, K., & Upitis, R. (2005). Learning through the arts: Lessons of engagement. *Canadian Journal of Education*, 28(1/2), 109–127.

Social Mobility Commission. (2019). State of the nation 2018–19: Social mobility in Great Britain. https://assets.publishing.service.gov.uk/government/uploads/system/uploads/attachment_data/file/798404/SMC_State_of_the_Nation_Report_2018-19.pdf.

Stoll, L., & Fink, D. (1996). *Changing our schools: Linking school effectiveness and school improvement*. Buckingham: Open University Press.

Tam, P.-C. (2020). Response to COVID-19 'Now I send you rays of the sun': A drama project to rebuild post-COVID-19 resilience for teachers and children in Hong Kong. *Research in Drama Education*, 25(4), 631–637.

Thomas, M. K., Singh, P., & Klopfenstein, K. (2015). Arts education and the high school dropout problem. *Journal of Cultural Economics*, 39, 327–339.

Thorsen, C., Hansen, K. Y., & Johansson, S. (2021). The mechanisms of interest and perseverance in predicting achievement among academically resilient and non-resilient students: Evidence from Swedish longitudinal data. *British Journal of Educational Psychology*, 91(4), 1481–1497.

Thrupp, M. (2005). *School improvement: An unofficial approach*. London: Continuum.

Tomlinson, S. (1997). Diversity, choice and ethnicity: The effects of educational markets on ethnic minorities. *Oxford Review of Education*, 23(1), 63–75.

Townsend, T. (ed.) (2007). *The international handbook of school effectiveness and improvement*. Dordrecht: Springer.

Van de Werfhorst, H., Sullivan, A., & Cheung, S. Y. (2014). Social class, ability and choice of subject in secondary and tertiary education in Britain. *British Educational Research Journal*, 29(1), 41–62.

Walford, G. (1994). *Choice and equity in education*. London: Cassell.

Wilkinson, R., & Pickett, K. (2010). *The spirit level: Why equality is better for everyone*. London: Penguin.

Willis, P. (1977). *Learning to labour: How working class kids get working class jobs*. London: Saxon House.

Woodson, S. E., Quirogi, S. S., Underiner, T., & Karimi, R. F. (2017). Of models and mechanisms: Towards an understanding of how theatre-making works as an 'intervention' in individual health and wellness. *Research in Drama Education*, 22(4), 4465–4481.

Wrigley, T., Thomson, P., & Lingard, B. (eds). (2011). *Changing schools: Alternative approaches to make a world of difference*. London: Routledge.

Xu, L., Diket, R., & Brewer, T. (2018). Predicting student performance via NAEP secondary art analysis using partial least squares SEM. *Arts Education Policy Review*, 119(4), 231–242.

9

CULTURAL CITIZENSHIP

9.45am: [Name] Theatre Company arrive. Teacher 1 explains to the Year 12s what they are doing.

[Theatre Company] are here because they are working on their 'Rambles' project. Local heritage organisations in partnership with [Theatre Company] have organised tea parties where local people share their stories. Some of the stories have been written up by the young people and others have been written by various writers but they are all based on the tea party oral histories. People will be able to download the app and then listen to the stories while they follow a local walk. The idea with the app is that people then share their own stories while doing the walk, take photos and load them up using a set hashtag.

Today the young people are to record the stories that they have helped write. [Theatre Company] are here to record the students' readings (the school has a recording studio) and also do a social media workshop.

Teacher 1 jumps between the [Theatre Company] group, who are based in the music room that is attached to the recording studio, and the drama studio where he has a group of Year 8s this lesson.

I chat to Actor 1 who explains that the project is all about 'place and heritage' – it is about how you talk to the community about their lives and experiences and then also how you talk to the community about what you've made about their community – circular conversations. They are encouraging sharing through the young people. She says that they work with different groups of young people, sometimes through schools but other times through other channels, building on already existing partnerships. The school has a long-standing relationship with the company.

10.10am: The students sit with Actor 2 to review the stories they are going to read. A student is coached through his reading, focusing on the delivery of various lines. "It's like a ghost story," the actor tells him, making him say various words in a scary, ghostly voice.

10.35am: The Year 12 group return and they all gather around the main table. The [Theatre Company] general manager explains to the students that marketing and comms are

DOI: 10.4324/9781003093084-9

hugely important for performers because people need to know and share in your show. If you've rehearsed and have it super-polished but then no one comes, that's it. It is not like fine art where you can put your work up and leave it. The performance happens there and then, in the moment. The [Theatre Company] communications officer then explains how the app marketing will work. He says one of his main jobs is social media and so they are going to focus on how [Theatre Company] use social media. He runs through the various platforms and asks what students use. [Theatre Company] mainly focus on Facebook, Twitter, Instagram and YouTube. He says you should focus on one to three platforms for "engaging with the audiences. Once you have an audience, you have to keep that audience," he explains. He talks about posting, selling, engaging contact and posting stuff for 'friends'. He shows students their marketing plan for the year, with the performance deadlines on. Then he shows them the company social media plan. "To keep the audience engaged, you don't want to keep posting the same things. It is really important to plan what to put on social media," he says. He talks about knowing the Facebook algorithm and understanding what is being championed at a particular moment. He says he doesn't look for likes on Instagram. Rather, he is looking at what people are saying and the comments.

10.45am: They all talk about things that don't work on social media, drawing on students' examples – blurry pictures; not posting enough. They want to keep people interested in the app. They move on to an activity. They start building an audience profile for the app and talk about creating a person who they all think might download it. (Lexi field notes)

We have seen in the TALE study that, in the arts-rich schools, the arts are expansive. They exceed curriculum guidelines. The curriculum is covered, and then more is added. In their arts subjects, students learn how an art form is professionally practised, and what it means to work as an artist. In our opening example, students working with the theatre company not only learnt how to write and read for broadcast purposes, but also about verbatim theatre traditions, and the practices associated with giving a performance and making and keeping an audience. Story making was not only practical and theoretical but also had the explicit moral purpose of place-making (Parkinson, Buttrick, & Knight, 2020); the arts were fundamental to a process which recognised and recorded local experiences and funds of knowledge in order to build community and local identity. Here, the arts were integral to civic development.

As we saw in the previous chapter, many of the students in arts-rich schools told us that they engaged with out of school audiences and practices. These students were more likely to be more engaged, well-informed and critical audiences than their peers, and also more likely than their peers to be active cultural producers, keen to advance their skills, reach and influence audiences. We use the term cultural citizenship to describe this wider participation in the arts. We suggest in this chapter that TALE arts-rich schools and arts-broker teachers were engaged in supporting students to learn practices associated with cultural citizenship. The students in TALE arts-rich schools were disposed to, and had the knowledge and know-how necessary for, actively participating in a wide range of cultural activities outside of school. Cultural citizenship was integral to their artist habitus.

This chapter explores cultural citizenship. We begin this more theoretically oriented chapter by addressing the terms 'culture' and 'citizenship' and then consider what they mean when put together.

Culture

What do we mean by culture? The term culture is complex and contentious (Williams, 1976). There are entire sections in university libraries devoted to defining, debating and exploring what it means. It is ubiquitous in discussions about the arts. We cannot avoid dealing with it. But we recognise that here we are sign-posting larger and more extensive conversations when we indicate our use of the term.

We understand culture to be centrally concerned with making meanings. The anthropologist Clifford Geertz suggested that culture can be thought of as 'socially established structures of meaning' (Geertz, 1973, p. 12). Culture is produced and situated in specific times/spaces, it is a tangle of practices, narratives and teleologies manifest, inter alia, through the inter and intra actions of materials, bodies, narratives, images, sounds, movements, platforms, genre, media. Using the metaphor of the inseparability of the spider and the web – one cannot exist without the other – Geertz suggested that we live in a cultural context of our own making. Cultural events, behaviours and institutions are not 'caused' by context but can be explained and described contextually. Both individuals and groups are produced by, and also produce, specific cultural contexts, through processes of interpreting, mediating, influencing, creating, making, maintaining and abandoning. Culture is thus not static, it is always in formation.

Within this broad understanding of culture as patterns of meaning that are continually changing, we refer to an additional three common understandings and uses of the term culture. The first relates specifically to the arts in all their forms. The second refers to culture as attached to a particular language and ethnic or racial community, heritage, customs (Kymlicka, 2001). The third refers to wider social practices, in the way that anthropologists might refer to particular societies and their culture. In each of these three meanings, culture is actually plural – cultures. Cultures are elite *and* popular, national *and* international *and* local, everyday *and* institutional, professional *and* amateur, kitsch *and* refined. Culture is also defined in opposition to what it is not – nature, science. And culture has a very wide applicability, so it is not uncommon to read about cultures of science for instance or school cultures. As Highmore (2017) notes, the term culture has an "extraordinary ability to absorb everything in its wake".

To make things even more complicated, the three approaches to culture – as the arts, language and ethnic traditions, and society itself – are not separate or separable, as Geertz suggested. All three forms of cultures exist in specific local forms, and at various scales. They are mutually interactive, productive and reproductive. They are globally connected through digital communications, globalised media and financial markets, commercial practices, environmental risks, voluntary and forced travel across borders and global quangos. Cultures are challenged by flows, mobilities, networks from above and below. And some cultural practices are marginalised in networked contemporary societies. Cultures exist, blur and blend in everyday life (Highmore, 2002). The arts cannot be cut off from questions of language, heritage and society more broadly.

The tangles and complexities of culture are why, as we have already explained, education policy interpretation, and Ofsted promotion, of cultural capital is problematic: because it attempts to separate the first meaning of culture, the arts, from the second – language and ethnic traditions and heritages – and the third, the wider society. Ofsted's definition also fails to grapple with the idea of making meaning, and sees culture as static artefacts, performances, texts and institutions, rather than what it is that they do.

Our interest in this book is primarily in the arts, the first of our meanings of culture, but also in the ways in which they recognise, value and sustain cultural differences, the second meaning, and also offer resources for young people to become participants in the wider culture, our third meaning. We are not alone in seeing this engagement with the arts as a right.

The right to cultural participation is encapsulated in Article 27 of the Universal Declaration of Human Rights, which states that 'Everyone has the right to participate in the cultural life of the community, to enjoy the arts and to share in scientific advancement and its benefits' (http://www.un.org/en/universal-declaration-human-rights/). The right to culture is seen as inseparable from other human rights and vital to the health of democratic societies. As UNESCO puts it, "Accessing and enjoying culture is an important part of being a citizen, a member of a community and, more widely, a member of society." According to Delanty (2002, p. 66) cultural participation is not simply an important part of being a citizen, but one of its *most* important aspects:

> one of the most important dimensions of citizenship concerns the styles and forms of language, cultural models, narratives, discourses that people use to make sense of their society, interpret their place in it, construct courses of action and thereby give rise to new demands for rights, which we may call cultural rights.

Cultural rights are, however, theoretically underdeveloped (Symonides, 1998), and in the UK this lacuna is highly political. The UK has ratified the UN Declaration of Human Rights, but cultural rights have not been incorporated into specific national laws, although this move is under consideration in Scotland (Boyle & Hughes, 2018). The rights addressed by the UK Equalities Commission are generally socio-economic, and often related to discrimination on the grounds of race, gender and disability. These priorities are understandable and perhaps explain why there has been no debate about the risks inherent in addressing the guarantee of cultural rights – for instance, the risks involved in reifying cultures, promoting some cultural practices at the expense of others, maintaining parochial and potentially politically insular groups, and preventing the natural evolution of cultural practices and meaning-making (Reidel, 2010). The absence of this debate about whose culture counts makes the curriculum goal of studying 'the best that has been made and said' both logical and possible.

Portolés and Šešić (2017) suggest that the lack of debate about cultural rights is a more widespread international phenomenon: "economic, social, and cultural rights have generally been less attended to than civil and political rights, cultural rights have been particularly neglected, and sometimes been termed the 'cinderella' of human rights" (p.160).

Understandings about cultural rights and citizenship are situated in a discussion which is emergent, asynchronous and scattered across disciplines and organisations. We have drawn upon some of these scattered existing understandings about cultural rights in order to help us think about arts education.

Rights are of prime concern to legal scholars. Laura Reidel (2010), for instance, sought a definition of culture that ensured that the cultural heritages of minority groups could be legally protected. At the same time, she wanted to prevent cultural heritage from becoming fixed in time and/or narrowly parochial and socially divisive.

Her definition of culture places "the emphasis on shared norms, meaning, and practices", while also stipulating that "those cultures that are eligible for protection by cultural rights are those that express a comprehensive world view". She suggests that this approach limits "cultures worthy of protection and ... bases the distinction on the idea of what culture provides to its members". Culture that is worthy of protection is not merely that which characterises the way people tend to form groups with distinctive characteristics, but those that are valuable to their members and enrich their lives (Reidel, 2010, p. 70).

While Reidel's definition of cultural rights would apply to particular language and heritage groups, it would not apply to youth cultures. There are limitations to legal definitions of rights.

Sen (2004) offers an alternative to the legal perspective, suggesting that rights are primarily ethical demands. Rights arise from and refer to significant human freedoms, such as the right not to be subject to violence. Rights are not intended to describe utilitarian necessities such as access to affordable transport. Sen argues that, because rights are ethical, they depend on reasoned public discussion and advocacy; this may lead to legislation but, equally, may not. The right to culture is one example of an ethical matter that is not subject to specific legislation, although some laws, such as anti-discrimination law, might be relevant to its realisation. The ethical nature of rights, Sen suggests, requires correlative duties; that is, people need to accept that it is their duty to ensure that rights are enacted in everyday life and in institutions. From Sen's perspective, understanding and ensuring cultural rights are entirely dependent on public debate and institutional actions. Neither one is sufficient in itself. Sen's definition would have us see participation in a cultural education as an ethical obligation.

Cultural rights are also central to questions of social justice and social sustainability. Miranda Fricker (2007) argues for the importance of what she calls epistemic justice, the right to have one's testimonies and interpretations of experience not only heard but also acted on. Epistemic justice is, she proposes, a fundamental prerequisite of citizenship. The maintenance of heritage languages, artistic traditions, artefacts and architectures are vital to epistemic justice, but as important is the capacity to be seen to have a credible contribution to make to the processes of social meaning-making and their political, economic and legal enactment. Fricker's perspective suggests that an arts education can be seen as a fundamental foundation for epistemic justice, as it supports students to learn about cultural meaning-making practices as well as to contribute to them.

Paul Willis (Willis, with Jones, Canaan, & Hurd, 1990) argues that the social justice implications of cultural rights support a normative idea of an overarching common culture in which all (sub)cultures are equally valued for their difference. Everyday cultural participation, in which people do what they find valuable, enjoyable and meaningful – from singing in church, knitting, performing in community plays, to making YouTube videos – is as important as any other cultural practice (Miles & Gibson, 2016). Willis's perspective points to a view of arts education that is more than a narrow canon, but is inclusive of multiple practices, perspectives, histories, genres and platforms.

How does this cultural rights perspective compare to the current situation in England? Perhaps in support of the direction of current education policy, the Arts Council (ACE) set out a ten-year strategic framework in 2010 (Arts Council England, 2010) entitled *Great Art and Culture for Everyone* which states: "We believe it is every child's birthright to have the opportunity to experience the arts, to access the knowledge in our libraries, and to see the wonderful objects within our museums and learn about the stories behind them" (p. 35).

The language here is of the right to have an opportunity to experience, rather than the right to participate more fully. The focus is on the possibility of access to particular kinds and forms of arts and culture. The ACE framework also elides culture with the arts, with libraries as places of knowledge and with the 'wonderful objects' and stories in museums. This suggests an institutional and canonical approach to culture. However, contrary to this interpretation, the framework has been taken as a brief to differentially support a range of practices and organisations, from high-status national arts organisations to some community arts. The ACE strategy aims for breadth of engagement, in part through supporting arts and cultural education programmes, many offered via local Cultural Education Partnerships. These partnerships feature on the Arts Council's Cultural Education Portal, through which data on participation at local, regional and national level can be accessed. Arts Council funding is used to ensure that funded cultural provision serves a diverse, but highly segmented and hierarchised, national audience.

Evrard (1997) identifies the modernist logic of this approach, which focuses on culture as a 'thing' that can be distributed, access to which can be measured against specified targets and outcomes (see also Rose, 1991; Strathern, 2000). Cultural capital can also be monetised, and the benefits to communities calculated as 'value for money'. Every public pound is expected to bring a return expressed as contribution to a social measure – of wellbeing, employment, reduction in crime, economic growth and so on (HM Treasury, 2022). Evrard argues that this kind of cultural policy approach predates neoliberal government, though it has been easily laminated into the audit agendas that typically accompany marketised and contractualised modes of governing (Pollitt, 2011). It is not surprising then that Arts Council England's rationale for their youth strategies takes an individualised and economic turn, rather than an elaboration of cultural rights:

> Involvement with arts and culture is crucial to imagination, self-expression and creativity in young people. It also develops the skills that fuel the success of the UK's creative industries, and that will result in the next generation of creative talent across the country.
>
> *(https://www.artscouncil.org.uk/how-we-make-impact/children-and-young-people)*

Access to arts and culture is to be directed towards national economic ends.

This approach – access to culture as a canon, a thing and an economy – stands in contrast to an approach that sees culture as historically situated, social and semiotic (associated with public conversations and shared communication). This latter notion, of a common but diverse culture and cultural practices, foregrounds meaning-making, and the rights of individuals and groups to offer interpretations, narratives and knowledges through a variety of cultural production practices. A 'participation in culture' approach to rights directs attention to agency. An agentic social semiotic approach to culture positions cultural rights as worthwhile and purposeful participation in social meaning-making. The cultural practice orientation directs attention to discourses, narratives and representations, the ways in which these are interpreted and produced, where this consumption and production occurs, under what conditions, and in whose interests these cultural rights are exercised.

And it is in relation to cultural participation that the arts come into their own. The arts offer a wide range of media, platforms, forms and genre for meaning-making, as well as for extending meanings beyond the rational and cognitive to encompass the imaginative, the corporeal and the haptic (McDonnell, 2018). This is the kind of arts practice endorsed by arts-broker teachers. It is at the heart of their visual and performing arts signature pedagogies. It is also the kind of arts education that many of the leaders of arts-rich schools told us about and that students not only discussed but also report as doing.

But why do we marry this with citizenship, another vexed term?

Citizenship

Citizenship, like culture and rights, is a contested term. It can be taken as legal membership of a particular nation-state or be seen as a practice in which an individual assumes the duties, obligations and behaviours of a citizen as laid out in law and in expected, but often inexplicit, norms. The term citizenship is also used in connection with membership of an organisation and often in a moral sense – someone is a good citizen of a school community, for example.

Understandings about citizenship are historically and socially specific, with different kinds of states affording different duties and benefits (Cooper, 2018). Citizenship is often connected with some kind of public political assembly – a polis – and the right to speak, be heard and participate in decision-making (Kivisto, 2015). And, as the history of suffrage attests, participation in the polis has been subject to ongoing contestation along class, gender and race lines (Lister, 2003). There are also varying political views of citizenship, and the role of the state in relation to its citizens (Van Gunsteren, 2018). In Western countries these differences generally polarise around various versions of a liberal individualism where the nation-state acts primarily to support the activities of autonomous and economically oriented citizens (Jessop, 2015). However, the liberal individualist spectrum is further differentiated by the stance taken towards the civic-republican view of citizenship – whether, how much and how citizens are able to take part in democratic debate, the kinds of public forums that are available and their affordances, and the degree of freedom able to be exercised in public life (Balibar, 2015; Bellamy, 2008). If we take a view of citizenship informed by the notion of culture as social and semiotic, and of cultural rights as the moral right and freedom to participate in social meaning-making, we will be particularly concerned with the civic-republican aspects of citizenship. Economic aspects are also important in as much as they enable or restrict democratic participation. We will therefore be interested in how much schools and arts educators support children and young people to participate in citizenly practices of social meaning-making.

Bryan Turner (2007) suggests that societies are faced with two contradictory citizenship principles: of scarcity and solidarity. He argues that where social inequality is intensified by neoliberalist policies, citizenship becomes the major marker and maker of social solidarity. This aptly describes the context in which we write where questions of identity, civic virtue and community are under duress. Perhaps arts education has a particular social role to play in our current context.

Boele van Hensbroek (2010) certainly thinks so. He argues that because cultural citizenship is concerned with social meaning-making, practices must take account of limiting contexts, such as the commercialisation of cultural processes and practices – and with agency. The capacity to take action. Citizenship is something that is lived, and done. Van Hensbroek argues that cultural citizenship is 'the ability to co-author the cultural context in which one lives' (p. 69). Because a citizen exists in relation to other people as well as a polity, he argues that authorship is a collective process. His is a civic-republican view, which has

> citizenship not only as an individual legal entitlement laid down in a vertical relation with the state, but also as a social role, namely the role of co-producer of the political (or cultural) community. ... [This] is basically a horizontal relation with fellow citizens.

(p. 326)

But Van Hensbroek suggests that a focus on the horizontal does not negate the context of vertical relations. Rather,

> it draws attention to a range of societal and socio-psychological preconditions that need to be fulfilled for the actual practice of citizenship roles. It can, in addition, draw attention to the broader historically specific societal dynamics of power and class relations, institutional arrangements, and social, political and economic systems which frame citizens' action.
>
> *(p. 326)*

We are drawn to the agentic and quotidian orientation taken by Van Hensbroek. It chimes strongly with what we have seen in the TALE project where students made meanings in and through their arts subjects with each other, but also spoke with and to wider audiences beyond the school. We can see exactly this in the field note from the theatre company project with which we started this chapter.

We also see value in the approach taken by our colleague Nick Stevenson (2003). He too takes a social semiotic and civic-republican approach to the question of cultural citizenship. He points to the importance of moving beyond nation-statist views, arguing that recognising the continuing importance of democratic notions of a civil society means taking account of globalisation, digitised communications and the politics of difference. He suggests that cultural citizenship, in Willis's (1990) local–global common culture, now demands a cosmopolitan approach, which reconciles the popular and everyday with elite cultural practices. Stevenson (2003) defines cosmopolitan cultural citizenship through three interlinked criteria:

> Cultural citizenship can be said to have been fulfilled to the extent to which society makes commonly available the semiotic material cultures necessary in order to make social life meaningful, critique practices of domination, and to allow for the recognition of difference under conditions of tolerance and mutual respect.

This is a normative notion of cultural citizenship which brings together the work of meaning-making (which we take as cultural participation in production when applied to arts education), with contextual and policy matters (access and opportunity to be audience and producers) and ethical questions (how difference, equity, power relations and critique are afforded and constrained). This trio of practice, context and ethics are integral to our thinking about arts education as cultural citizenship. They were also integral to the thinking of arts-broker teachers, even if they were not expressed in exactly these words.

Citizenship education – the official version

How does this approach to citizenship education stack up against the official curriculum? In short, it's an uneasy fit.

Citizenship education is mandatory in the compulsory years of schooling in English schools. Like many other national systems, the English citizenship curriculum focuses primarily on civics – the study of the rights and duties of citizens – set in a particular time and place. Students are expected to acquire understandings about the UK nation-state and its particular form of democracy, including party politics, elected tiers of government and Houses of Parliament. The other three specified components of the curriculum are volunteering (otherwise known as service-learning), skills in debating political issues and financial know-how (https://www.gov.uk/government/publications/national-curriculum-in-england-citizenship-programmes-of-study).

While cynics might see this as a curriculum designed in part for a politics of austerity – being able to live on precarious wages and volunteering to pick up the slack in the post-welfare state – for the purposes of this chapter, there are four key things to note. We use the term 'curriculum-citizens' here to distinguish the particularity of the formulation of citizenship in this curriculum.

Firstly, the curriculum-citizens are universalised individuals with responsibilities. If they act responsibly, then they are accorded particular rights – freedom of movement and speech, a safety net if they are out of work or ill, and so on. Critics challenge this very contemporary Western view (Bellamy, 2008; Turner, 2007). Political theorist Will Kymlicka (2001), for instance, addresses the connections between the individual and groups, culture(s) and society and the diverse and interconnected nature of modern societies constituted as globalised nation-states. He argues that rights associated with particular identities must be understood as both individual *and* group – the nation-state has the responsibility to recognise the demands of social movements and alternative polities, such as those of First Nations peoples in Canada, Australia and Aotearoa-New Zealand.

A 'recognition and redistribution' (Fraser, 2000) approach to citizenship attends to ways in which the rights – understood as voices, histories, knowledges, social and arts practices and interpretations – of particular raced, classed and gendered population groups have been systemically marginalised and, importantly, how this discrimination might be addressed and redressed. Recognition of the rights of marginalised groups also means attending to the very particular circumstances of peoples whose claims to citizenship are vexed, difficult and often life-threatening – peoples who are historically mobile, peoples who have been made stateless through civil wars, borderline trading, and peoples whose identities are not associated with a nation-state at all (Appadurai, 1996). Citizenship encompasses the rights of marginalised groups to struggle against and change national government/governing practices (Lister, 2003; Taylor, 1994; Van Gunsteren, 2018).

Secondly, curriculum-citizens are sutured firmly to the nation-state. However, citizenship goes beyond the state. We are interconnected through the workings of travel, interlocked economies and businesses, sophisticated information and communication technologies, and by the environmental changes that humans in particular have brought on the living world (Castells, 2000; Harvey, 1996). These mobilities, networks and bondings are part and parcel of everyday life and demand particular sensibilities of us, including a 'cosmopolitan' understanding of diverse cultures and practices (Beck, 2006) and an orientation to the material world which decentres human activities (Cohen & Duckert, 2017). In schools, these beyond-nation sensibilities may be called global citizenship and eco-citizenship. But regardless of whether they are named or not, understanding the nature of our 'runaway world' (Giddens, 1999) demands a curriculum that has strong associational and ontological, as well as epistemological, orientations. Responding to contemporary life demands, as Haraway (2016) puts it, that we 'stay with the trouble' rather than ignore it.

Thirdly, the purpose of citizenship education is preparation. Citizenship education is about learning to be a citizen at a time *in the future*. Students in schools are not seen as *already* citizens of society with current rights and responsibilities. They are to be made ready to be full and active members of society – they cannot/are not able to do this now (c.f. James, Jenks, & Prout, 1998). This view takes little account of the varying ages at which young people are able to drive, parent, take on onerous caring responsibilities, contribute to family income through part time work, and the age at which they can leave home and be declared independent. Nor does it recognise that the school itself is not only a preparatory experience but might also be a public space and a polis in its own right (Kennedy, 1997).

Finally, the framing of the aims of curriculum-citizenship education lend themselves to a discrete subject which an auditor might easily identify. While this might satisfy a tick-box approach to accountability, it takes little account of the reality that the curriculum is not only what is formally taught but also includes all of the informal learning that occurs through extra-curricular activities, school governance practices and organisation and school culture(s) (Marsh, 2009; Priestley, 2013). If the school is concerned with learning, being and doing citizenship, then every teacher and every curriculum subject has a part to play. As Kymlicka (1997, p. 1) puts it:

> Citizenship education is not just a matter of learning the basic facts about the institutions and procedures of political life; it also involves acquiring a range of dispositions, virtues, and loyalties which are intimately bound up with the practice of democratic citizenship. Children acquire these virtues and loyalties not just (or even primarily) in civics classes. Rather, they are inculcated throughout the educational system. The aim of educating citizens affects what subjects are taught, how they are taught, and in what sorts of classrooms. In this sense, education for citizenship is not an isolated subset of the curriculum, but rather is one of the ordering goals or principles which shapes the entire curriculum.

Educator Richard Pring (2016) supports this view and brings to it a more generous notion of citizenship than that articulated as the national curriculum-citizen. He nominates as a key to citizenship education:

- Concern for the public good
- Being able to articulate an oral position in social life

- An understanding of the political context
- Critical engagement with moral and social ideas
- Determination to improve civic society. (p. 7)

Pring argues that literature, history, geography and the arts have a lot to teach about the qualities necessary for citizenship. This is the view which underpins this chapter – all teachers and all subjects play a part in ensuring education for citizenship. While arts education is scarcely included in the official view of what schools must do to teach citizenship, this alternative position values arts education and its very particular role and special affordances.

Education for citizenship – the unofficial version

Critics of the curriculum-citizen framing begin from the pedagogical premise that it is insufficient to learn *about* what citizens do, students must also *practise* in order to understand what is involved and to develop the embodied dispositions and skills of a citizen (Apple & Beane, 1995; Dewey, 1916). In this respect the argument begins in much the same way as driver education – knowing the rules of the road doesn't make you a driver, you also have to get in the car and practise. You have to know and do, together, in order to be (Delors, 1996). This is also education for 'active citizenship' (Crick & Lockyer, 2010; Potter, 2002). Students have to not only know but also do and be citizens.

Education for active citizenship focuses on process and practices which offer an alternative pedagogy to that more usually associated with civics lessons (Cohen, 2005). Active citizenship as pedagogy has at its heart an implicit understanding of citizenship itself. It shifts away from simply understanding how to participate in particular processes associated with governing at various levels, to consider participation itself. And it goes beyond volunteering. Active citizenship pedagogies usually raise questions about who gets to speak and act. Inclusions, exclusions, representation – formal and symbolic – and recognition of particular identities become part of a cognitive, emotional and lived curriculum. This is often challenging for schools. As UNESCO notes:

> One of the major flaws in civics instruction has been that it fails to bring democracy to life in schools, and remains at the stage of merely enunciating principles and describing institutions. When the organization of a school does not lead to a democratic mode of operating in which pupils can give their opinions, children and adolescents lose interest in citizenship and see only the mismatch between what adults say and what they do, between knowledge and action, a mismatch which they usually call 'hypocrisy'.
>
> *(http://www.unesco.org/education/tlsf/mods/theme_b/interact/mod07task03/ appendix.htm)*

Education for active citizenship takes different forms, but usually includes the classroom and the school as polis – as an arena in which diverse young people have both rights and responsibilities and are able, as the Convention on the Rights of the Child (United Nations (UN), 1989) suggests, to have a say in matters that are of concern to them. This happens in three major ways:

1. A focus on student participation in school governance. Formal structures such as elected student councils, and open student forums and school/class town meetings allow for representation in decision-making (Osler, 2000). Such bodies sometimes constrain what students can do – they are confined to raising funds, organising charity drives or perhaps designing their school uniforms – and sometimes only involve selected 'good' students, not all (Bragg, 2007; Fielding, 2001). But there are numerous examples of schools in England and beyond that do encourage students to participate in more general governing decisions about policy, planning and curriculum.

2. Social action programmes which address issues of concern in the school and community. This is not the same as service learning in which students work as volunteers in existing community facilities. Rather, social action programmes take a community development approach which recognises and works with community assets and strengths to find solutions to pressing issues. Students may be engaged in school-based reforms; for example, changing the schools' environmental practices through collective interventions (Thomson, 2006; Thomson, McQuade, & Rochford, 2003). Or students may work with community partners to co-construct and implement community projects (see Holdsworth, Stafford, Stokes, & Tyler, 2001 for examples ranging from building community amenities to changing local by laws). Sometimes social action programmes extend to social 'organising' in which students become part of a wider social movement designed to put pressure on local or national government in order to bring about change (see Cammarota & Fine, 2008 for examples of students working with social movements to address racism; Fine et al., 2004).

3. A classroom focus for active citizenship where teachers adopt pedagogies which ensure that the classroom functions democratically. While there may be a strong element of 'knowledge'-based teaching within and across subject domains, this is complemented by equally important active components where the affordances include co-designed projects with peers and adults inside – and perhaps outside – the school.

Arts subjects lend themselves to democratic practice. In drama rooms, a democratic commitment becomes collaborative improvisation and ensemble-based pedagogies (Neelands, 2009). In art rooms, a *negotiated curriculum* (Boomer, Lester, Onore, & Cook, 1992) allows students and teachers to co-construct a learning activity, an extended project, a single module of work or an entire year's programme. Negotiating the curriculum is not uncommon in art and design classrooms, particularly in the senior secondary years, where it is usual for students to engage in large projects. In order to meet the requirements set by qualifications authorities, teachers engage in ongoing negotiation with students about ideas they want to explore and the work that they have to do in order to bring their ideas to fruition. Contrary to the view that offering agency to students means handing over responsibility for learning to the student, a negotiated curriculum always works with required knowledge outcomes and teacher expertise as well as the vernacular knowledges, interests and everyday practices of students and their communities. However, because the pressure of exam results also tends to individualise students' work, ensuring that students have opportunities to work together requires explicit planning.

Some art and design rooms are set up as collectives. Room 13 – a visual art workspace run by students for students – is one of the best-known examples (Gibb, 2012; Souness & Fairley, 2005). Rooms 13 affords young people regular experience of working together to make choices and decisions, to work as an artistic cooperative in charge of their own studio, its finances and commissions. Room 13 exemplifies the four essential elements of the rights of the child: students manage a *space*, exercise *voice*, have *influence* over what happens in their studio and beyond, and arrange *audiences* for their collaborative work (Lundy, 2007). Room 13 has now become an international movement of artists, art teachers and children (http://room13international.org). In Room 13s, students are not simply learning how to be an artist, they are already engaged in wider artistic practices that engage the whole school and people/organisations outside the school. But much of the online material about Room 13 now emphasises entrepreneurialism. This raises interesting questions about what is and what might be learnt about active citizenship and democratic process in a child-led studio.

The Room 13 example brings us to the crux of our case in this chapter and the book: arts education in *and* beyond the classroom and school.

Arts education and/as cultural citizenship

Community arts and socially engaged practitioners see a strong connection between arts practices and citizenship (Jeffers & Moriarty, 2017). The arts provide opportunities for representations that challenge dominant discourse and create opportunities for ethical praxis and collective reimagining through the provision of counter-spaces and, sometimes, explicit social and political action (Elliott, Silverman, & Bowman, 2016). This is also a position taken by some arts educators. Drama practitioners, for example, have long said that applied, community and participatory theatre and the family of associated ensemble pedagogies create and support active citizenship (Neelands, 2009; Nicholson, 2005). Drama creates empathy, which is key to an equitable politics of difference. The processes of drama also encourage students to develop communication, collaboration, debate and decision-making (Braverman, 2002). However, this is arts as a means of learning and exercising political citizenship, not about cultural citizenship per se.

Robert Kuttner (2016, p. 74) argues that arts education is not simply for cultural citizenship, but actually develops it.

No matter what other outcomes arts educators seek, we are teaching students about their roles and responsibilities in relation to artistic creation and consumption. We are helping to shape students' capacities and orientations towards participating in an important aspect of cultural life.

Kuttner is interested in social action and social justice and in the affordances of arts education. He suggests that the notion of cultural citizenship, understood as agency exercised through meaning-making practices, provides a way to link the everyday, heritage and bedroom cultures of young people with larger political challenges related to globalisation, privatisation and commercialisation (c.f. Dolby & Rizvi, 2008). He argues in particular for an arts education which supports young people to change their worlds – an activist view of citizenship – which uses art media, genres and platforms to express opinions and explore options for change (see Soep, 2010 for an example through youth radio).

Kuttner advocates an expanded notion of arts education with a justice-oriented citizen at its heart, critically and systematically analysing power, advocating for marginalised communities and stories, using art for justice in communities via collective action. He proposes three 'types' of co-authoring cultural citizens formed in and through arts education:

1. an informed cultural citizen who 'has the capacity to understand, appreciate, and critique works of art within a larger social, political, artistic, or cultural context',
2. a participatory cultural citizen who is involved in 'producing, remixing, and sharing original artistic works. She has a strong connection to her own cultural heritage, along with the freedom to explore new forms of expression and to share in cross-cultural exchange', and
3. a justice-oriented cultural citizen who can 'critically analyze the ways that the arts are implicated in processes of oppression and resistance', works to counter dominant oppressive representations and practices and uses art practice to make changes in communities through individual and collection action (2016, p. 76).

The latter two options support an arts education that focuses on a wide range of forms of cultural production and critical audience participation (Gaztambide-Fernandez, 2013), just as TALE students reported in the survey and in interviews.

Kuttner writes from the United States, and his proposition is not intended to be universalised, but his three cultural citizenship possibilities do have some traction in contexts where arts education might support nation-states reconstructing themselves to interrogate and embrace difference and diversity (see Singh, 2012 on the role of arts education in South Africa) and contexts in which traditional arts practices and knowledges can be used to deconstruct and redesign contemporary schooling (e.g. Colin, 2014 on Mexica palimpsest). There is also a strong connection between Kuttner's participatory and justice-oriented citizens and socially engaged art practices where civic engagement and/or social activism are the goal (Thompson, 2015).

This view of arts education for cultural citizenship is inclusive, and thus does not deny young people, especially those who are socially and culturally pushed to the edges, access to the kinds of cultural capitals that are held in highest esteem. As Stevenson (2003, p. 342) argues, an arts education as cultural citizenship "would need to follow an inclusive cultural strategy that offered school children a range of cultural repertoires drawn from across the popular and high cultural divide". Such cultural education would not only "seek to revalue cultural practices and narratives that more traditional forms of education had branded as unworthy" but also support students to develop "a critical appreciation of artistic practices from classical music to performance art".

This is a very good description of much of what we saw in TALE arts-rich schools. To go back briefly to Bourdieu, we can also see this as a description of the kinds of arts education that students with a developing artist habitus might engage with.

Following Stevenson, practices associated with what Kuttner calls informed cultural citizenship would still matter. If every child is to be a cultural omnivore (Friedman, 2012; Peterson & Kern, 1996), possessing more than knowledge of and admiration for the cultural capital that officially counts, then they must be engaged in an arts education that offers them the opportunity to produce meanings using their own funds of knowledge, heritages and teleologies. If every child is to have the competencies to engage critically in the 'creator economy' (Warburton, 2022) of popular media and popular cultures more generally, then they must not only have practical skills, but also critical evaluative understandings. But it is also important that students should not be denied access to the kinds of knowledge and skills that allow them to engage critically with mainstream and elite cultural practices. This is, as Siegesmund (2013) puts it, an arts education which develops 'wide-awakeness' (Freire, 1974) to the world, and supports well-informed citizens to reimagine possibilities for living together. This combination is what we saw and have presented as the signature pedagogies and practices of arts-broker teachers, and which students also reported as their experiences, as valuable cultural capitals.

Maxine Greene argued passionately for an informed and imaginative education. Hers was a highly political vision of teachers working with students to consider and make a fairer future world through changing what happens in the present.

> I still believe that the ground of a critical community can be opened in our teaching and in our schools. It is out of such thinking that public spaces may be regained. The challenge is to make the ground palpable and visible to our students, to make possible the interplay of multiple plurality of consciousnesses and their recalcitrances and their resistances, along with their affirmations, their "songs of love." And, yes, it is to work for responsiveness to principles of equity, principles of equality, and principles of freedom, which still can be named within contexts of caring and concern.
>
> *(Greene, 1995, p. 198)*

One way to conceive of Greene's ideal is as an education for cultural citizenship. We think of this as integral to an artist habitus – curious, questioning, risk-taking, collegial and collaborative, caring and critical. This is, we suggest, an arts education for life, not simply for passing exams. Not simply for being 'someone' in future, but for being an active thoughtful and responsive audience and a creative engaged cultural producer right now.

Of course, it is worth remembering the warning issued by Clare Bishop (2012) about the dangers of collapsing together art and the social, art and pedagogy. She suggests that when artistic practices merge with social and pedagogical fields, it requires us to examine our assumptions about each of the fields of operation and to "ponder the productive overlaps and incompatibilities that might arise from their … conjunction". Learning to think these things together will need us to "devise adequate new languages and criteria for communicating these transversal practices" (p. 274).

Bishop's caution is not negative. It seems to us that it offers an agenda for enquiry and debate which would not only have positive benefits for students, but also strengthen the professional orientations of arts-broker teachers. Asking what kinds of cultural citizens and what kinds of culture(s) we are producing today would be a highly (re)generative conversation, a contribution to making post-pandemic schooling more attuned to the challenging social, economic, environmental world in which we live, a world vociferously clamouring for intelligent care.

The next and final chapter presents, as an Afterword, a heuristic which represents the ecological workings of arts-rich schools and a wide-awake arts education, taught by arts-broker teachers.

References

Appadurai, A. (1996). *Modernity at large: Cultural dimensions of globalisation*. Minneapolis, MN: University of Minnesota Press.

Apple, M., & Beane, J. (1995). *Democratic schools*. Alexandria, VA: Association for Supervision and Curriculum Development.

Arts Council England. (2010). Great art and culture for everyone. https://www.artscouncil.org.uk/sites/default/files/download-file/Great_art_and_culture_for_everyone.pdf.

Balibar, E. (2015). *Citizenship*. Cambridge: Polity Press.

Beck, U. (2006). *Cosmopolitan vision* (C. Cronin, trans.). Cambridge: Polity.

Bellamy, R. (2008). *Citizenship: A very short introduction*. Oxford: Oxford University Press.

Bishop, C. (2012). *Artificial hells: Participatory art and the politics of spectatorship*. London: Verso.

Boele van Hensbroek, P. (2010). Cultural citizenship as a normative notion for activist practices. *Citizenship Studies*, 14(3), 317–330.

Boomer, G., Lester, N., Onore, C., & Cook, J. (eds). (1992). *Negotiating the curriculum: Educating for the twenty first century*. London: Falmer.

Boyle, K., & Hughes, E. (2018). Identifying routes to remedy for violations of economic, social and cultural rights. *The International Journal of Human Rights*, 22(1), 43–69.

Bragg, S. (2007). 'But I listen to children anyway' – teacher perspectives on pupil voice. *Educational Action Research*, 15(4), 505–518.

Braverman, D. (2002). *Playing a part: Drama and citizenship*. Stoke-on-Trent: Trentham Books.

Cammarota, J., & Fine, M. (eds). (2008). *Revolutionising education: Youth participation action research in motion*. New York: Routledge.

Castells, M. (2000). Materials for an exploratory theory of the network society. *British Journal of Sociology*, 51(1), 5–24.

Cohen, E. (2005). Neither seen nor heard: Children's citizenship in contemporary democracies. *Citizenship Studies*, 9(2), 221–240.

Cohen, J. J., & Duckert, L. (2017). *Veer ecology: A companion for environmental thinking*. Minneapolis, MN: University of Minnesota Press.

Colin, E. T. (2014). *Indigenous education through dance and ceremony. A Mexica palimpsest*. New York: Palgrave Macmillan.

Comber, B. (2016). *Literacy, place and pedagogies of possibility*. London: Routledge.

Cooper, F. (2018). *Citizenship, inequality and difference. Historical perspectives*. Princeton, NJ: Princeton University Press.

Crick, B., & Lockyer, A. (2010). *Active citizenship*. Edinburgh: Edinburgh University Press.

Delanty, G. (2002). Two conceptions of cultural citizenship: A review of recent literature on culture and citizenship. *The Global Review of Ethnopolitics*, 1(3), 60–66.

Delors, J. (1996). *Learning: The treasure within*. Paris: UNESCO.

Dewey, J. (1916). *Democracy and education: An introduction to the philosophy of education* (1996 edn). New York: Free Press.

Dolby, N., & Rizvi, F. (eds). (2008). *Youth moves: Identities and education in global perspective*. New York: Routledge.

Elliott, S. J., Silverman, M., & Bowman, W. D. (eds). (2016). *Artistic citizenship: artistry, social responsibility and ethical praxis*. London: Wiley Blackwell.

Evrard, Y. (1997). Democratising culture or cultural democracy? *The Journal of Arts, Management and Law*, 27(3), 167–175.

Fielding, M. (2001). Beyond the rhetoric of student voice: New departures or new constraints in twenty first century schooling? *Forum*, 43(2), 100–110.

Fielding, M., & Moss, P. (2010). *Radical education and the common school: A democratic alternative*. London: Routledge.

Fine, M., Roberts, R. A., Torre, M. E., Bloom, J., Burns, A., Chajet, L., … Payne, Y. A. (2004). *Echoes of Brown: Youth documenting and performing the legacy of Brown v Board of Education*. New York: Teachers College Press.

Fraser, N. (2000). Rethinking recognition. *New Left Review*, 3(May–June), 1–9. http://www.newleftreview.net/NLR23707.shtml.

Freire, P. (1974). *Education: The practice of freedom*. London: Writers and Readers Publishing Cooperative.

Fricker, M. (2007). *Epistemic injustice: Power and the ethics of knowing*. Oxford: Oxford University Press.

Friedman, S. (2012). Cultural omnivores or culturally homeless? Exploring the shifting cultural identities of the upwardly mobile. *Poetics*, 40(5), 467–489.

Gaztambide-Fernandez, R. (2013). Why the arts don't do anything: Toward a new vision for cultural production in education. *Harvard Educational Review*, 83(1), 211–237.

Geertz, C. (1973). *The interpretation of cultures*. New York: Basic Books.

Gibb, C. (2012). Room 13: The movement and international network. *International Journal of Art & Design Education*, 31(3), 237–244.

Giddens, A. (1999). *Runaway world: How globalisation is reshaping our lives*. London: Profile Books.

Gonzales, N., & Moll, L. (2002). Cruzanda el puente: Building bridges to funds of knowledge. *Educational Policy*, 16(4), 623–641.

Greene, M. (1995). *Releasing the imagination: Essays on education, the arts, and social change.* San Francisco, CA: Jossey-Bass.

Haraway, D. (2016). *Staying with the trouble: Making kin in the Chthulucene.* Durham, NC: Duke University Press.

Harvey, D. (1996). *Justice, nature and the geography of difference.* Cambridge: Blackwell.

Highmore, B. (2002). *Everyday life and cultural theory: An introduction.* London: Routledge.

Highmore, B. (2017). *Cultural feelings: Mood, mediation and cultural politics.* London: Routledge.

HM Treasury. (2022). *The green book: Central government guidance on appraisal and evaluation.* https://assets.publishing.service.gov.uk/government/uploads/system/uploads/attachm ent_data/file/1063330/Green_Book_2022.pdf.

Holdsworth, R. (2000). Schools that create real roles of value for young people. *Prospects,* 115(3), 349–362.

Holdsworth, R., Stafford, J., Stokes, H., & Tyler, D. (2001). Student Action Teams – An evaluation: 1999–2000. Working Paper 21. Melbourne: Australian Youth Research Centre.

James, A., Jenks, C., & Prout, A. (1998). *Theorising childhood.* New York: Teachers College Press.

Jeffers, A., & Moriarty, G. (2017). *Culture, democracy and the right to make art: The British community arts movement.* London: Bloomsbury.

Jessop, B. (2015). *The state: Key concepts.* Cambridge: Polity Press.

Kennedy, K. (ed.) (1997). *Citizenship education and the modern state.* London: Falmer Press.

Kivisto, P. (2015). *Citizenship: Discourse, theory and transnational prospects.* Oxford: Wiley-Blackwell.

Kuttner, P. J. (2016). Educating for cultural citizenship: Reframing the goals of arts education. *Curriculum Inquiry,* 45(1), 69–92.

Kymlicka, W. (1997). *Education for citizenship.* Institute for Advanced Studies, Vienna: Institute for Advanced Studies.

Kymlicka, W. (2001). *Politics in the vernacular: Nationalism, multiculturalism and citizenship.* Oxford: Oxford University Press.

Lister, R. (2003). *Citizenship: Feminist perspectives* (2nd edn). New York: Palgrave.

Lundy, L. (2007). 'Voice' is not enough: Conceptualising Article 12 of the United States Convention on the Rights of the Child. *British Educational Research Journal,* 33(6), 927–942.

Marsh, C. (2009). *Key concepts for understanding curriculum* (4th edn). London: Routledge.

McDonnell, J. (2018). Is it 'all about having an opinion'? Challenging the dominance of rationality and cognition in democratic education via research in a gallery setting. *International Journal of Art & Design Education,* 37(2), 233–243.

Miles, A., & Gibson, L. (2016). Everyday participation and cultural value. *Cultural Trends,* 25 (3), 151–157.

Mitra, D. (2008). *Student voice in school reform: Building youth–adult partnerships that strengthen schools and empower youth.* New York: State University of New York Press.

Neelands, J. (2009). Acting together: Ensemble as a democratic process in art and life. *Research in Drama Education,* 14(2), 173–189.

Nicholson, H. (2005). *Appled drama: The gift of theatre.* Basingstoke: Palgrave Macmillan.

Osler, A. (2000). *Citizenship and democracy in schools: Diversity, identity, equality.* Stoke-on-Trent: Trentham.

Parkinson, A., Buttrick, J., & Knight, E. (2020). Arts and place: Evidence review. https://www.artscouncil.org.uk/sites/default/files/download-file/placemaking%20wavehill.pdf.

Peterson, R. A., & Kern, R. M. (1996). Changing "highbrow" taste: From snob to omnivore. *American Sociological Review,* 61(5), 900–907.

Pollitt, C. (2011). *Public management reform: A comparative analysis. New Public Management, governance and the neo-Weberian state* (3rd edn). Oxford: Oxford University Press.

Portolés, J. B., & Šešić, M. D. (2017). Cultural rights and their contribution to sustainable development: Implications for cultural policy. *International Journal of Cultural Policy*, 23(2), 159–173.

Potter, J. (2002). The challenge of education for active citizenship. *Education and Training*, 44 (2), 57–66.

Priestley, M. (ed.) (2013). *Reinventing the curriculum: New trends in curriculum policy and analysis.* London: Routledge.

Pring, R. (2016). Preparing for citizenship: Bring back John Dewey. *Citizenship, Social Economics and Education*, 15(1), 6–14.

Reidel, L. (2010). What are cultural rights? Protecting groups with individual rights. *Journal of Human Rights*, 9(1), 65–80.

Rose, N. (1991). Governing by numbers: Figuring out democracy. *Accounting, Organisations and Society*, 16(7), 673–692.

Sen, A. (2004). Elements of a theory of human rights. *Philosophy and Public Affairs*, 32(4), 315–356.

Siegesmund, R. (2013). Art education and democratic citizenry. *International Journal of Art and Design Education*, 32(3), 300–308.

Singh, L. (2012). Constructing a nation: The role of arts education in South Africa. In J. Lavia & S. Mahlomaholo (eds), *Culture, education and community* (pp. 163–182). New York: Palgrave Macmillan.

Soep, L. (2010). *Drop that knowledge: Youth radio stories.* Berkeley, CA: University of California Press.

Souness, D., & Failrey, R. (2005). Room 13. In D. Atkinson & P. Dash (eds), *Social and critical practices in art education* (pp. 41–50). Stoke: Trentham Books.

Stevenson, N. (2003). Cultural citizenship in the 'cultural society': A cosmopolitan approach. *Citizenship Studies*, 7(3), 331–348.

Strathern, M. (ed.) (2000). *Audit cultures: Anthropological studies in accountability, ethics and the academy.* London: Routledge.

Symonides, J. (1998). Cultural rights: A neglected category of human rights. *International Social Science Journal*, 158, 559–573.

Taylor, C. (1994). *Multiculturalism and "the politics of recognition".* Princeton, NJ: Princeton University Press.

Thompson, N. (2015). *Seeing power: Art and activism in the twenty-first century.* New York: Melville House.

Thomson, P. (2006). Miners, diggers, ferals and showmen: School community projects that unsettle identities? *British Journal of Sociology of Education*, 27(1), 81–96.

Thomson, P. (2007). Making it real: Engaging students in active citizenship projects. In D. Thiessen & A. Cook-Sather (eds), *International handbook of student experience in elementary and secondary school* (pp. 775–804). Dordrecht: Springer.

Thomson, P., McQuade, V., & Rochford, K. (2003,11–14 October). "My little special house": Re-forming the risky geographies of middle school girls at Clifftop College. Paper presented at the British Education Research Association, Herriot-Watt University, Edinburgh.

Turner, B. S. (2007). Citizenship studies: A general theory. *Citizenship Studies*, 1(1), 5–18.

United Nations (UN). (1989). Convention on the rights of the child. UN document A/44/25. Geneva: UN.

Van Gunsteren, H. (2018). *A theory of citizenship: Organising plurality in contemporary democracies.* New York: Routledge.

Warburton, E. C. (2022). TikTok challenge: Dance education futures in the creator economy. *Arts Education Policy Review*. https://www.tandfonline.com/doi/abs/10.1080/10632913.2022.2095068?tab=permissions&scroll=top.

Williams, R. (1976). *Keywords*. Harmondsworth: Penguin Books.

Willis, P., with Jones, S., Canaan, J., & Hurd, G. (1990). *Common culture: Symbolic work at play in the everyday cultures of the young*. Milton Keynes: Open University Press.

AFTERWORD

The arts-rich school ecology

School G Head: *Our job is to make sure that every single child in this school has an opportunity to learn and succeed. Schools are where society looks after its young. In this time we have a responsibility to equip them for the challenges and responsibilities of adult life. The function of the school curriculum is to lay the foundations of a just democracy.*

School G Teacher: *The arts have a set of values that are both in tune with but also separate from the values of the main school. We embrace a contemporary approach that runs right the way through the arts. I think the way we interpret the subject specifications is to take the most open view of what is possible and then it is up to the examiners to argue with us if they don't like it. We feel fairly confident in how we are interpreting it and we feel we have the real spirit of the syllabus in it. We've got the world of contemporary art to use as a model which we are fully engaged in; colleagues are going to exhibitions all the time and recommending exhibitions and we feel plugged into that world. And we have artists come in to remind us of what it is like to be a real artist. That has been a key thing about our practice. We want that to be reflected in the way that we teach and the values that we communicate to the kids.*

School G Student 1: *I'm more interested in art and the history of art and art as something to view than in the creation. My outlook on history is quite heavily based on art. There are so many periods that I love and there are so many artists that I really admire. There is art that I would love to make but I don't think I have the skill to make.*

School G Student 2: *I go the opposite way. Spending your life studying art is like spending your life watching people watch TV. I think the creation is far more interesting than just viewing people's creation of art, although that is intrinsic to art.*

Schools are complex ecological systems (Eggleston, 1977; Goodlad, 1987; Harris and de Bruin, 2018; Matusov, 1999; Snyder and Anderson, 1986; Steketee et al., 2021; Theron, 2016). While they are often represented in organisational charts as simple hierarchies, with layers interlocked like Russian dolls, the reality of schools is much more complex. What happens in one area affects others. The school senior

DOI: 10.4324/9781003093084-10

leadership and governing body sets directions for the school, elaborating its educational purposes. Senior leaders ensure that the management of the school supports both the guiding values and vision. Teachers with different skills, interests, backgrounds, strengths and talents work with individual classes. But faculties work with disciplinary knowledges and through collaborative discussion they adapt the national curriculum and grow their pedagogical expertise and distinctive repertoire of practices. Their work is framed by national and school policies but is also bespoke to the particular school community and population. Teachers focus on their own continuing learning, often with support from external agencies and partners. All these elements work together so that a particular school atmosphere, ethos, set of traditions, expectations and vernacular practices are formed, sustained, changed. Students recognise and can explain what they learn in the classroom and what they learn out of the classroom.

In this Afterword we draw together learnings from the book about the ecology of arts–rich schools, an ecology that supports students to become cultural citizens. We focus here on the key 'actors' whose intertwined work creates the ecology that supports students to become cultural citizens. We offer this summary as a possible starting point for schools, teachers and arts organisations wishing to critically evaluate their own programme.

Values and practices in the arts-rich school

The arts–rich school prioritises the arts. The arts–rich school is dedicated to ensuring all students have access to valued knowledges and the common culture(s). The school philosophy statement makes explicit reference to the importance of cultural education.

The arts–rich school is connected to its community, to cultural organisations and is grounded in the wider everyday life of society.

The arts are embedded in the school; they are part of its educational DNA and its identity. The arts are central to the story school tells about itself – in the foyer and corridor displays, promotional materials (webpages, blogs and newsletters), in assemblies and in the calendar of activities.

The arts–rich school is inclusive. The arts are a significant pathway for inclusion. Students see this and can articulate what it means to belong to this school community.

The arts are integral to ensuring that the school is inclusive, and teachers and students recognise and are respectful of the cultures and cultural practices of individuals and groups. The curriculum supports the development of critical appreciation of a wide range of popular and elite art forms, media, practices and platforms. All students are encouraged to use the meaning making affordances of the arts to explore their own identities, histories, heritages and cultural practices, as well as to engage with diverse others.

Senior leaders

Senior leaders in the arts–rich school understand schooling as a public good. Senior leaders are committed to their school being futures-focused, offering an education for an equitable world. They are strongly people-oriented. They see every student's growth and empowerment as important and thus advocate teaching that combines high expectations, demanding tasks, robust teaching of knowledge and skills and carefully designed support.

Senior leaders are strongly supportive of arts and cultural learning. They enact the right to cultural participation through ensuring that the school offers a wide range of arts subjects at all key stages. They ensure governors and/or trustees understand the importance of the arts and the cultural capitals the school offers. They inform parents about arts education, the school arts programme and arts events. They are a visible presence at arts performances and exhibitions. As educational leaders, they ensure that a range of arts practices are available in both formal and extra-curricular programmes, including contemporary, local and cross-cultural arts. Everyday cultural practices, genres and media are valued equally with dominant art forms.

Senior leaders take responsibility for ensuring that all students can participate in cultural activities and arts learning. A range of additional cultural activities are provided through clubs, lunchtime and after-school activities, elective programmes. All students are actively supported to participate. Partnerships are established with local and national arts and cultural organisations.

Senior leaders make sure that the arts are integrated into school organisational and management structures. They are in regular conversation with arts leads in the school. At least one middle leader is in charge of arts provision. Arts teachers are encouraged to take whole-school leadership responsibilities and are encouraged to collaborate with teachers in other subject areas. Arts teachers are supported to work as 'arts-brokers'. They are supported in both discipline-specific and more general professional development and the extra-curricular activities of arts teachers are recognised and valued through provision of time and esteem. Risk-management procedures for excursions and employment of artists are enabling.

Senior leaders see themselves as stewards of resources and effort. They ensure that the arts have equal worth with other subjects and that there are sufficient resources – money, time, space, specialist teachers – for all of the arts subjects. Students are actively encouraged to take arts subjects; the timetable supports choice-making, work experience and career advice incorporates arts careers. Qualified and experienced arts teachers are employed; arts facilities are well maintained and equipped and budget allocations recognise the actual costs of arts activities. Cultural learning outside of school is well resourced. There is a subsidy for students where necessary, to support regular cultural excursions, visiting artists and performances.

Senior leaders want the arts-rich school to have a situated sense of 'place'. They ensure that it is engaged with its wider communities, including its immediate geographical neighbours. The school supports neighbourhood cultural activities and employs local artists, thus contributing to both the local cultural environment and the local economy. Arts teachers are supported to participate in 'outside-school' subject specific and arts projects. The school engages with the diverse range of heritages, languages and religious traditions of its extended school community.

Senior and middle leaders showcase the benefits of arts learning to wider publics and policymakers.

Arts faculties

The philosophy of the arts faculty/department(s) situates the arts as key to cultural citizenship and integral to a holistic education. It commits the faculty to equity, inclusion and the productive recognition and valuing of diverse cultural capitals – resources, histories and practices.

Faculty curriculum planning is strongly connected with contemporary arts discipline practices and dialogues. The development of collective pedagogical content knowledges is a prime concern, and time is devoted to discussion and exploration of relevant research. The faculty promotes reflection and arts-led practitioner enquiry. Visiting artists are encouraged to run workshops for and engage in discussions with teachers, as well as work with students. The faculty produces artefacts that communicate the key disciplinary concepts and practices to students and visitors, including other staff; these help to create a common language and narrative about what is important about arts learning.

The faculty builds and sustains arts networks through partnerships with national, regional and local arts and cultural organisations. All arts teachers are encouraged and supported to work on school projects such as performances and exhibitions, initiate activities with other subject areas and to participate in 'outside-school' subject specific and arts projects. Arts teachers have continuing and up-to-date information on the arts, including contemporary, local and cross-cultural arts. They are encouraged to participate in immersive professional development. The faculty values staff participation in and leadership of arts subject association activities and collegial multi-school arts projects. The faculty promotes the importance of outside school cultural activities for families and students. Neighbourhood cultural activities are supported and the school actively promotes a wide range of cultural practices, genres and media, not simply dominant art forms.

Middle leaders in the arts advocate for the arts within the school and beyond. They explain and evidence the learning produced through arts education. They have oversight of arts provision but also take up whole school responsibilities. They provide ongoing information about the arts to governors, teachers and parents. They support arts teachers to collaborate with teachers in other subject areas. They represent the arts in relevant management fora, arguing for parity of esteem in time, space and resources and the recognition of the necessary beyond-school activities of arts teachers through the provision of time and esteem.

Faculty leaders ensure that arts education is of high quality. As disciplinary leaders they ensure that they are well informed about curriculum and pedagogy, disciplinary debates and discussions and trends in the wider arts community. They lead by example, ensuring that they continue to develop their pedagogical and disciplinary knowledge and skills. They also demonstrate what it means to broker the arts, by bringing their own networks and practices to the faculty table. They initiate and adjudicate faculty selection of activities and materials, ensure that planning is coherent and inclusive. They welcome creative improvement and productive innovation. They take responsibility for ensuring that the arts curriculum is clearly documented and available for perusal.

Faculty leaders support teachers to mediate the impact of examinations on the curriculum, while also ensuring that students get the best possible results. Arts leads ensure that arts teachers are supported in both discipline-specific and more general professional development. They encourage the artist in each teacher and support all arts teachers to develop and maintain a programme of continued professional learning. They evaluate excursions, activities and performances to ensure that they are of high quality. They advocate for adequate budget for cultural excursions, visiting artists and performances.

Faculty leaders work to maintain the arts as central to the school's ethos and identity. They ensure that students' and teachers' work is represented in the story the school tells about itself in displays and promotional materials, etc. They have collegial relationships with senior leaders as well as with other faculty members. In relevant school fora, they advocate for arts subject choices, work on the timetable to ensure choices, support the appointment of qualified and experienced arts teachers and ensure that the budget is used in line with actual costs of arts activities. They take oversight of well-maintained and equipped arts facilities.

Arts-broker teachers

Arts-broker teachers are deeply knowledgeable about and steeped in their arts discipline. They understand its history, major trends and contemporary practices and debates. They have rich understandings of how their arts discipline has developed a distinctive school curriculum and pedagogy. They continue to develop their subject expertise at the same time as building understandings about how to adapt their subject to the interests, strengths and needs of the particular students in their particular school.

Arts teachers want all students to see themselves as artists. They are strongly inclusive, seeing every student as capable of having ideas, building technical skills and disciplinary knowledges. They make arts and cultural media, genres, events, disciplinary norms and professional practices available to all students. They are interested in students' cultural activities beyond school, and use students' funds of arts knowledge as the basis for ambitious, challenging work.

Arts teachers understand the importance of 'good results'. These are not only important for maintaining the subject in the school. They are also crucial for students and are key to life choices and opportunities. They are also aware that examinations are not all that matters in the arts, and they carefully mediate the impact of examinations on each student's progress.

The arts teachers support students to become cultural citizens, showing through their own everyday arts passions and pastimes what engaging with the arts can mean. They are arts-brokers who embody what it means to be culturally engaged.

They engage deeply with the arts themselves: they regularly attend a range of events, exhibitions and performances; some direct, act, make and show their own work; some are part of local, regional and national artistic networks. They are committed to continuing to learn about the arts. They share their knowledge and out-of-school experiences with their students, routinely talking about what they have seen and done and read, creating an ongoing classroom conversation.

Arts-broker teachers make sure students visit local and national cultural events, institutions and organisations. They see visits to cultural institutions as integral to their classroom programme, not a treat or an optional extra. They think of visits as opportunities to extend students' horizons, see and understand new places and also to see their own place afresh. They help students see arts as more than just school subjects. They seek out and use students' and communities' cultural resources. They see neighbourhood and students' own arts practices as cultural participation and as learning resources. They take a critical interest in the popular and everyday. They encourage discussion of and improvisation around community events and concerns and pressing social issues in the media.

Arts-broker teachers organise visits to their schools from creative practitioners and cultural organisations. They see the importance for students of regular contact with professional artists and their work. They find ways to connect with local artists and arts organisations that bring new practices and experiences to students. They also provide opportunities for students to exhibit and perform their work for wider audiences. They encourage students to make work not just for assessment, but for wider and public audiences. Students' families can see and understand what their children are doing; other faculties in the school see and understand what happens in the arts. Sometimes joint work with local and national arts organisations allows students to experience arts disciplinary processes and norms in semi-professional contexts.

Arts-broker teachers connect students to arts workplaces. They build new connections, through work experience and visits, to bring their students into contact with the arts and culture industry so they can find out what working in the arts is like. They also work to enhance the arts participation in their communities. They bring arts practitioners into school to create cultural experiences for the local community. They engage in local arts initiatives that benefit students out of school. They appreciate and support the ways in which the arts can help build a sense of place and community.

Partner arts and cultural organisations

Arts-rich schools have a rich and thick web of relationships with artists and arts organisations. Arts organisations do not simply focus on work with students. They understand that they have the power to inspire teachers and that arts teachers particularly value the chance to have access to new professional and disciplinary knowledge and skills.

Arts organisations and artists develop long-term relationships with schools and teachers. They promote and work to sustain partnerships that are reliable and alert to the rhythms and time constraints of school life. They understand the importance of investing in teachers as a sustainable source of development and change in schools. Arts organisations thus invest time, money and effort in developing immersive and collaborative professional development programmes where the distinctions between teachers' and creative practitioners' roles, professional knowledge and skills are acknowledged and used in complementary ways. Because they recognise the importance of building strong mutual and inclusive partnerships that recognise each other's priorities, they plan, prepare and evaluate work with teachers and students.

Arts organisations value the distinctiveness and strengths of each school's community and work to enhance teachers' arts-brokerage and students' cultural citizenship through promoting local resources and interests.

Students

Students are ambitious, creative risk takers. They are knowledgeable about their chosen art form(s), arts disciplinary knowledges and professional practices. They can research, realise and communicate their ideas and interpretations. They can work independently as well as together. They have a strong sense of self-belief and the self/selves they can develop through the arts.

They can explain what they are doing in their arts education and what they value about it.

Students can assess their own progress. They develop critical evaluative practices as well as more refined skills.

Students take their arts learnings with them into the outside world as they move on from school. The arts are part of their everyday lives.

References

Eggleston, J. (1977). *The ecology of the school*. London: Routledge.

Goodlad, J. (ed.) (1987). *The ecology of school renewal: Eighty-Sixth Yearbook of the National Society for the Study of Education, Part I*. Chicago: National Society for the Study of Education.

Harris, D., & de Bruin, L. (2018). An international study of creative pedagogies in practice in secondary schools: Toward a creative ecology. *Journal of Curriculum and Pedagogy*, 15(2), 215–235.

Matusov, E. (1999). How does a community of learners maintain itself? Ecology of an innovative schools. *Anthropology and Education Quarterly*, 30(2), 161–186.

Snyder, K. J., & Anderson, R. H. (1986). *Managing productive schools: Towards an ecology*. Orlando, FL: Academic Press College Division.

Steketee, A., Williams, M. T., Valencia, B. T., Printz, D., & Hooper, L. M. (2021). Racial and language microaggressions in the school ecology. *Perspectives on Psychological Science*, 16(5), 1075–1098.

Theron, L. C. (2016). The everyday ways that school ecologies facilitate resilience: Implications for school psychologists. *School Psychology International*, 37(2), 87–103.

INDEX

Lightning Source UK Ltd.
Milton Keynes UK
UKHW010712130223
416858UK00006B/38